Dear Harlowe -

From the first breath
you took - Gan Gan & I
were so blessed to see
your first sweet stretch
and yawn as the nurse
bundled you up for
your amazing mom -
we saw, felt, and
were awed by your
presence.

Enjoy life's journey
love,
Auntie
Anne

OTHER BOOKS BY RITA M. GROSS

Buddhism after Patriarchy:
A Feminist History, Analysis, and Reconstruction of Buddhism

Beyond Androcentrism:
New Essays on Women and Religion
Edited by Rita M. Gross

Unspoken Worlds:
Women's Religious Lives
Edited by Nancy Auer Falk and Rita M. Gross

FEMINISM
AND
RELIGION

An Introduction

RITA M. GROSS

Beacon Press

BOSTON

TO MY MANY COLLEAGUES

CONCERNED WITH FEMINISM AND RELIGION

Beacon Press
25 Beacon Street
Boston, Massachusetts 02108-2892
www.beacon.org

Beacon Press books
are published under the auspices of
the Unitarian Universalist Association of Congregations.

First digital-print edition 2005

Text design by Wesley B. Tanner/Passim Editions
Composition by Wilsted & Taylor Publishing Services

Library of Congress Cataloging-in-Publication Data can be found on page 280.

Contents

Acknowledgments

COMPLETING A BOOK is always a joyful occasion that depends on help from many quarters. First of all, I must thank the students to whom I have taught feminism and religion for more than twenty years. They have helped me enormously in my attempt to clarify complex, often emotional issues. I must also thank the many colleagues in the feminist study of religion who have encouraged me to continue my often difficult investigations of feminism and religion and who provided sorely needed companionship.

Those of us who work at public undergraduate institutions, as I do, often have heavy teaching loads that minimize the time available for research and writing. Grants from the University of Wisconsin–Eau Claire, which reduced my teaching schedule during the 1991–92 academic year, were extremely helpful. I am grateful to department chairperson Richard deGrood, who graciously dealt with my reduced teaching schedule, and to the University Research Office, which gave advice on the application process and administered the grants.

Friends with whom one can discuss one's projects and who lend their support are crucial in the process of writing a book. I want to thank the members of the Women's Research Network who cheered me on regularly. I especially want to thank Susan Moch, feminist colleague par excellence, and Patricia Ward, the best housemate ever. During the final stages of revising the book, the friendship of Dale Roble was most wonderful. I should not forget my cats and dog, and my houseplants, with whom I often communed as I thought about what to write next, and for that matter, the incense, candles, and music that were always with me as I wrote.

Finally, I thank those who carefully read the manuscript in various stages of development and made many excellent suggestions, especially Rosemary Ruether and the anonymous Beacon Press reader. I also want to thank my editor at Beacon, Susan Worst, for her expeditious handling of the manuscript and her many valuable suggestions. Any remaining mistakes and misunderstandings are, of course, my own.

Rita M. Gross
from Feminism & Religion:
An Introduction
(Beacon Press 1996)

Introduction

THIS BOOK SURVEYS the issues that have been central to feminism and religion over the past twenty-five years. In my view, two agendas are crucial to this task. First, it is important, insofar as possible, to discuss feminism and the entire scope of *religion*, not just Christian and post-Christian feminist theology, which so often happens in books on women and religion. Properly pursued, the field of religious studies involves study of all major religions found in human history, not merely the culturally familiar perspectives of Christianity and, possibly, Judaism. Presenting both the information about women's roles in all these religions as well as a feminist perspective on each of them is an immense undertaking.

Second, combining the study of feminism and religion requires making an important distinction between descriptive and normative approaches to religion. Unlike most other feminist treatments of religion, this book discusses religion both descriptively and normatively, rather than confining itself to one approach. I will also explore the feminist *study* of religion: what happens when feminist academic methods are applied to the data studied by scholars of religion. But I will also discuss what happens when feminists bring normative concerns to religion, when they critique and reconstruct their religions from the point of view of feminist values.

Because both religion and feminism are complex and emotion-

1

laden topics, this book begins with definitions. Chapter one defines and discusses feminism, religion, and religious studies, as well as the relationships between them. In this chapter, we will face several controversial and difficult issues surrounding the entanglement of academic knowledge and personal life choices, which can be especially keen in the intersection of feminism and religion. Chapter two offers a brief historical sketch of the interactions between feminism and religion, introducing some of the major players and issues. It begins with a discussion of the nineteenth-century background to the current women's movement and continues with surveys of feminist movements in various religions and the major trends and thinkers in the feminist academic study of religion.

The rest of this book addresses four central issues for feminism and religion. The first concerns the imperative to include information about women in all descriptions of religion, discussed in chapter three. The second issue is more controversial, even among feminists: Are the world's major religions inevitably sexist and disadvantageous to women, or are they inherently egalitarian and reformable, despite their patriarchal veneers? Chapter four then questions whether religions post the sign "No Girls Allowed" at the entrances to their most hallowed sanctuaries. Attempts to answer this question have led to the third major issue in feminist scholarship: Once we rid ourselves of androcentric methodologies and patriarchal assumptions, it is necessary and instructive to "reread" the past, asking "Has It Always Been That Way?"—the title of chapter five. The final major concern of feminist scholars and theologians, addressed in chapter six, is speculative and future-oriented, concerning the forms of postpatriarchal religion. Thus this book deals with what Buddhists call the "three times": past, present, and future. Throughout, I have endeavored to balance attention to feminist studies of religion and feminist transformations of religion.

I write this book as someone who has been involved in both the feminist study and the feminist transformation of religion throughout my career. I can list many "firsts" in my own record, including the fact that I was one of the first to insist on methodological self-declarations like this one. I wrote the first dissertation on feminism and religious studies, the first article on female God-language in Judaism, and the first major feminist analysis of a non-Western religion. I also coedited the first comprehensive book about women's religious lives in cross-cultural perspective.

My involvement in these ventures colors my reporting on them. Those with a different perspective might include materials I have omitted and omit perspectives I have included. Since my training is in the cross-cultural study of religion, and because I am personally involved in a major non-Western tradition, I constantly strive to redress the imbalance and Eurocentrism of current feminist and neofeminist perspectives on religion. In my view, the Western orientation of most feminist thinking about religion is a serious limitation. In this book, I omit some of the fine-tuning in Christian and Jewish feminist discussions in order to include more material on the cross-cultural study of women and religion and on non-Christian and non-Western feminism. Clearly, chief among my methodological biases is the conviction that relevant thinking can no longer afford the luxury of Eurocentrism. Therefore, the great intellectual and spiritual systems of Asia, as well as the many indigenous traditions throughout the world, play into my outlook and are represented in this book.

In keeping with the cross-cultural nature of the discipline of religious studies, I will always discuss at least one major Western religion and one other major religion in each of the four central chapters. The Western religion most frequently discussed will be Christianity, both because Christian feminist scholarship and theology are extremely well developed and because so many who will use this book come from a Christian background. The non-

Western religion most frequently discussed will be Buddhism, both because it presents significant contrasts to and similarities with Christianity and because it is Christianity's most significant partner in interreligious dialogue and interchange. Furthermore, though feminist perspectives are less developed in Buddhism than in Christianity, they are more developed in Buddhism than in other Asian or non-Western traditions.

CHAPTER ONE

Defining Feminism, Religion, and the Study of Religion

BOTH FEMINISM AND RELIGION are academic subjects taught at most colleges and universities. But they are also controversial, emotion-laden systems of belief that directly affect people's lives. Those just beginning formal study of women and religion often already have strong emotional, prereflective opinions about both religion and feminism, and many who teach about them are themselves personally involved in writing feminist theology or practicing a feminist form of religion. Because both teachers and students may come to the study of religion and feminism with strong emotional convictions and commitments, academic study of either topic can be particularly challenging.

Even without the complicating factor of feminism, the academic study of religion can often feel threatening, in part because the distinction between the study of religion as an academic discipline and the personal practice of religion is not often made in our culture. Therefore, the academic study of religion challenges one's personal beliefs more than the study of other academic subjects. Likewise the study of feminism or the use of feminist methods can be disconcerting to those new to feminism, particularly because media stereotypes about feminism seldom accurately describe feminists' concerns. To ease this transition to thinking about topics often charged with strong feelings and loyalties, this book begins

5

with definitions of religious studies, religion, feminism, and the interactions between them.

The Discipline of Religious Studies and Its Relationship with Religion

Students with strong personal religious beliefs, or students' families, are sometimes concerned about the effect that the academic study of religion will have on their beliefs. The politics of learning and teaching about religion are similar to problems encountered in learning and teaching science, especially some generations ago. The professor is explaining a worldview that competes with the worldview of the student or her family. The professor is imparting the values of neutrality and empathy central to the academic study of religion, whereas the student or her family insists that religion should be absorbed only personally and confessionally. They fear that academic knowledge about religion may blunt confessional zeal. *And they may well be correct in their fears*, despite the fact that the academic study of religion has nothing to do with religious instruction, conversion, or spiritual direction.

The Academic Study of Religion

Religion was the last of the controversial, passion-inspiring human pursuits—such as politics, economics, and ethics—to be accorded its own academic discipline in the neutral setting of research, debate, and free thinking that characterizes the university. As an undergraduate, I could not major in religious studies because the state university system in which I was educated did not believe it was possible for a public institution to teach religion without violating the separation of church and state. Eight years later, I returned to that same system to teach religious studies to undergraduates. What had changed in educational philosophy in the intervening years?

The single greatest change that enabled religious studies to emerge as an academic discipline was the recognition that one could *understand* a religious position without *adhering* to it. I believe that this recognition was made possible by the study of non-Western religions; more removed from sectarian battles within culturally familiar religious settings, scholars realized that they could understand and appreciate, with great empathy, a point of view that they did not share. Therefore, such understanding could also be taught to others, without the rancor, dogmatism, competitiveness, hostility, and suasion that typically characterize sectarian religious education. Knowing about and understanding a religion is quite different from believing in it. The academic study of religion depends on that distinction.

Another major factor in the development of religious studies was the recognition that since religion has been a major mover and motivator in human culture from time immemorial to the present, it is impossible to understand human history and culture while ignoring religion. Only an extremely artificial division of human life and culture could tolerate the teaching of history, art, or social custom without understanding their connection with religion. Those trained in these disciplines are not fully prepared to explicate the religious beliefs that inform their subject matter; scholars formally trained in religious studies could contribute greatly to the overall environment of inquiry and learning that characterize a university.

Finally, the new imperative to understand divergent cultures, worldviews, and value systems in our complex world has brought religious studies to the fore. Except for anthropology, no academic discipline is so thoroughly imbued with the mandate to study its subject matter cross-culturally as is religious studies. In fact this characteristic of religious studies was essential to its development; to justify themselves as practitioners of a genuine academic discipline rather than a sectarian recruiting exercise, professors of religious studies encouraged a cross-cultural, comparative dimension in the field from the beginning. "To know one religion is to know none" paraphrases a famous and widely circulated statement made by Max Müller (1823–1900), often credited as the founder of comparative studies in religion.[1]

What is the academic study of religion? At the most basic level it is a descriptive discipline that gathers and disseminates accurate information about the variety of religious beliefs and practices people have entertained and engaged in throughout time and space. The academic study of religion, I often say on the first day of class, takes controversial material about which people care deeply and places it in the neutral setting of the academic classroom, so that we can examine it and learn about it. Personal agreement or disagreement with the symbols, rituals, and beliefs about which we are learning is largely irrelevant at this stage. Scholars may debate alternative hypotheses about the information being studied, but debating the truth or falsity of the religious ideas is irrelevant to the academic study of religion as a descriptive discipline. If one truly understands what the academic study of religion is about, it will not be problematic or stressful to learn that Hinduism and Christianity have very different ideas about deity, and to learn both sets of ideas. And it will not be too tempting to argue that the Christian, Hindu, or some other view of deity is "correct."

How do we decide which beliefs and practices will be studied— that is, which beliefs and practices are "religious"? Everyone has an intuitive sense of what is meant by the concept of religion, but these definitions are often limited by ethnocentrism. They often assume that all religions are more or less like religion in one's own culture. For example, someone once suggested this to me concerning Native Americans: "It's as if they don't even have a religion. All they do is worship nature." Lurking in the background is the culturally familiar definition of religion as requiring a belief in a supreme being. Sadly, definitions of religion found in some dictionaries reinforce such ethnocentrism, for example, by defining religion as "recognition on the part of man [*sic*] of a controlling superhuman power entitled to obedience, reverence, and worship."[2] Although that definition describes Judaism, Christianity, and Islam, it excludes Buddhism, Confucianism, Taoism, Shinto, and the many other religions that involve no such belief. When discussing religion, one must avoid such ethnocentric and androcentric definitions of religion if one wishes to include all the relevant data.

Though professionals in the study of religion do not agree on a single definition of religion, it is clear that a nonethnocentric definition of religion would not focus on the *content* of belief systems. There are no universally held religious beliefs or symbols. But the various beliefs and symbols found in the world's religions do share a similar *function* in human life. Religious beliefs and behaviors typically answer people's questions regarding matters of significant, overriding importance to them. Thus, many widely used definitions of religion in the academic study of religion talk of religion as one's "ultimate concern" or what one regards as sacred. Central to any particular religion is its worldview, the basic, often unconscious presuppositions its followers hold about the nature of reality.

By this definition, any belief that functions as the most significant arbiter for decisions and actions and any behaviors whose value is unlimited to the actor are religious beliefs and behaviors, whatever their content. This definition is both broad enough to avoid ethnocentrism and specific enough to distinguish religious phenomena from nonreligious phenomena. Things of limited importance or significance are not religious. This definition also allows one to study the "religious" dimensions of phenomena not usually classified as religion, such as political allegiance and deeply held psychological orientations. This working definition of religion is especially helpful when considering the impact of feminism on religious studies.

Religion and Religious Studies

When discussing controversial subjects about which people already have strong opinions, employing empathy is the only pedagogically appropriate method. Without empathy, we cannot attain the accuracy that is so central to academic teaching and learning.

How does empathy work in the academic study of religion? I define empathy as a two-step process. First, it involves temporarily dropping, or "bracketing," one's own worldview, values, and preconceptions as much as possible while engaged in study. The subject matter should be approached with an open mind, which includes the possibility of leaving the learning situation changed by new knowledge. Second, empathy involves imaginatively entering into the milieu of the phenomenon being studied. One cannot *become* an insider, contrary to the expectations of some who want to appropriate completely the perceptions and views of the insider. But one can and should understand and appreciate why insiders feel compelled by their views and behaviors. Scholars of religion try to speak as if they participate in the point of view under discussion, though they well may not. For example, one of my all-time favorite teaching evaluations, meant as a criticism but taken as a compliment, read, "The problem with her is that she teaches all those religions as if they were true!"

To continue the example introduced earlier, the academic study of religion may seek to impart accurate information about Christian and Hindu concepts of deity, which are quite different from each other. Those involved in the learning enterprise should be able to explain and *understand* why a Hindu finds a plurality of divine images cogent with the same facility that they can explain and understand why a Christian finds monotheism compelling. Without such empathy, one can be neither accurate nor informed about religion, nor can one acquire what limited objectivity is possible in the study of religion. More dangerous, without such empathy, the acquisition of information may increase ethnocentrism, intolerance, and chauvinism. Someone who learns that Hinduism encourages multiple images of the divine and that such images are often venerated in their painted or sculpted forms, without learning to understand *why* such concepts and practices make sense to the Hindu, has not been helped by the academic study of religion. She may, in fact, be more dangerously ill informed than before, precisely because she has more facts at her disposal, but does not understand them accurately and empathically.

Thus, as empathic scholars, we come to the issue of the relationship between religious studies as a discipline and the personal practice of religion, an issue which should be faced head-on rather than skirted. Although religious studies is not instruction about what one should believe religiously, learning information about religious views and behaviors other than one's own can still be unnerving. Truly understanding religious data requires empathy, but empathy often changes the way we think about the world and our place in it. This is not to say that our religious affiliation will change when we study religion academically and empathically, but our *attitudes* about religion may well change. Some attitudes we had previously rejected may become more appealing, whereas others that had seemed obviously correct may become less tenable. Such changes are especially likely when studying feminism and religion together. To expect or advocate otherwise is to promote academic learning in the worst sense of the term *academic*: a collection of irrelevant information that does not affect its bearer in any way.

If the practice of empathy is so important to the academic study of religion, does that mean that one can never evaluate the religious beliefs and behaviors being studied? This question is quite important in the study of feminism and religion, since most feminists criticize religious patriarchy. The practice of empathy does not mean that one must agree with or approve of the point of view being studied; although empathy involves appreciatively entering into the spirit of that which is being studied, one could not agree with all the positions one understands empathically because many are mutually exclusive.

Some kinds of evaluation are not incompatible with empathic understanding, if a few basic ground rules are observed. First, an empathic understanding of the religion must *precede* evaluation. Before formulating suggestions or critiques, it is important to have some idea of the justifications for current beliefs and behaviors put forth by those who adhere to them. Otherwise the evaluation is likely to be extremely ethnocentric, a problem to which feminism is not immune. Second, the same evaluative standards must be applied to all traditions, whether familiar or foreign, whether one's own or that of another.

Most scholars of religious studies talk more about the importance of neutrality and objectivity than they do about empathy, and indeed certain commonsense meanings of neutrality and objectivity are appropriate for the academic study of religion. The academy is not the place for proselytizing for any specific religion or religious position. Full and fair presentation of the strengths and weaknesses of all positions studied can and should be expected. However, although students and teachers should exhibit neutrality concerning interreligious competition and rivalry, a completely value-free position is impossible. Being objective and neutral when discussing controversial issues does not mean being value-free. On closer inspection, "objectivity" often turns out to be nothing more than advocacy of the current conventions and not a neutral position at all. Some perceive feminist scholarship as adversarial because it challenges such conventions; still, feminist scholarship can claim to be more "objective" than male-centered scholarship, because it is more inclusive and therefore more accurate.

Looking more deeply into neutrality and objectivity as they pertain to the academic study of religion helps to fully clarify the relationship between religious studies and religion. Students of religion sometimes expect or even hope that academic neutrality means that what they learn about the variety of religious phenomena will not affect their beliefs in any way. But simply because the academic study of religion is neutral vis-à-vis competing religions' claims does not mean that it is value-free. The study of religion can never be value-free because the very existence of the discipline depends on this value: the development of a worldview that cherishes a neutral position vis-à-vis the various religions as well as an ability to see the internal coherence and logic that empowers each of them. This value is emphatically rejected by at least some segments of all major religions.

In other words, living with religious diversity and regarding it as an interesting resource, rather than an undesirable deviation from truth, are the values that dominate the academic study of religion. Information about unfamiliar perspectives on religion is meant to challenge monolithic or universalistic presuppositions about the world. One *should* feel that sexist, racist, ethnocentric, and religious chauvinisms, if present, are being threatened by the academic study of religion. Even neutral and objective information, if absorbed rather than merely memorized, can change the one who assimilates that information. It is rarely possible to conclude one's studies carrying the same opinions regarding religious, ethnic, class, gender, and cultural diversity with which one began.

The academic study of religion is radically deabsolutizing because accurate information about and empathy for the other is radically deabsolutizing. Once one really understands the point of view of "the other" or the foreign, claims that one's belief is the only truth are no longer as attractive or compelling. This is the most significant point of contact between the academic study of religion and the way in which religion is sometimes practiced as a personal faith perspective. If religion necessarily involves war among absolute truth claims, its subject matter would be too disruptive and counterproductive to the rational and dispassionate discourse favored in the academy. But the empathic understanding required in the academic study of religion encourages one to separate the absolutism some religions claim for themselves from information about their beliefs and practices, resulting in deabsolutized understanding of all religions and deabsolutized appreciation of religious pluralism and diversity.

For some, the appreciation of religious diversity is difficult because it contradicts religious instruction they have received. It may be helpful for people experiencing this difficulty to realize that it is quite possible to appreciate one's own perspective without believing that all people everywhere should adopt it. Such appreciation is a *different*, not a *lesser*, valuing of one's own particularity. This distinction is often difficult to appreciate at first, but I believe that no other alternative is possible in the global village in which we live. No lesson learned from the academic study of religion could be more valuable.

Like neutrality, objectivity in the study of religion is more complex than it appears. Because religion is so controversial and engenders such passion, calls for objectivity—approaching the subject without a point of view—are frequent. But all scholars speak and write from a particular point of view whether or not they claim objectivity for themselves. Once scholars agree upon methodological rules that determine what data are relevant and what techniques of interpretation are standard, scholarship can, in fact, be relatively "objective" within the limits of that system. For example, male-centered scholarship agreed upon the rule that data about women did not need to be included. Scholars abiding by that rule can do "objective" scholarship that is not gender inclusive. But when other scholars challenge that rule by demonstrating that one should also include data about women, it becomes clear that male-centered scholarship was objective only in a limited sense.

Because academic fashions can become relatively entrenched and long lasting, methodologically less reflective scholars sometimes think that their work is genuinely objective. Nevertheless, their work does not transcend the worldview and the methodology within which they record and interpret. It is not objective in the sense of having no perspective or reflecting no interests and values. Claims of objectivity from a scholar who is relatively unaware of his biases and perspectives do not obviate or negate his actual standpoint.

This issue is especially important for feminist studies in religion, since feminist scholarship is often thought to be "biased" because it self-consciously and deliberately includes information about women, whereas conventional androcentric scholarship is not similarly regarded as biased because it includes more information about men. For example, some believe courses on women and religion or gender-balanced mainstream courses on religion to be biased because they present more information about women than other courses do. But these kinds of claims only mask a desire to hear familiar perspectives and emphases, a wish that assumptions that have been taken for granted should not be challenged. This mistaken perception of bias is intensified because feminist scholars usually make their methodological values explicit, whereas conventional androcentric scholars usually do not, thereby fostering the illusion that they are without any specific agenda. But first-generation feminist scholars such as myself, who were reared to regard the generic masculine as genuinely generic and inclusive but could not find ourselves and our sisters in the data we studied, will never again be naive enough to think scholarship can be value-free.

Instead, scholars need to practice intense methodological self-awareness and introspection, combined with honest self-disclosure. Once one recognizes one's own standpoint, one can then argue on its behalf, making the case openly that this specific standpoint is more adequate than the alternatives. For example, when teaching my course on world religions, I always explain that I teach from a perspective that values diversity because only that approach promotes harmony and well-being in the global village. I also explain that the course will be gender balanced, which, to those used to androcentrism, may give the false impression that the course focuses on women. Likewise, in my course on feminist theology, I explain that, by definition, this course is quite critical of conventional religious points of view. Furthermore, in a course on feminist theology, neutrality involves presenting the various options *within* feminist theology but does not include antifeminist arguments or conventional theology in addition.

I also state openly that in my *viewpoint*, scholarship that values pluralism and diversity is more moral and humane than scholarship that longs for universal agreement and unity, and that in my *viewpoint*, gender-balanced and gender-inclusive scholarship is far more objective than androcentric scholarship, simply because it is more complete. Having stated the values that guide my scholarship and teaching, I have achieved the level of objectivity that is possible. Everyone, including me, knows *why* I include the data that I include and why I prefer the interpretations that I prefer. I can argue cogently for those preferences. Other scholars may offer other points of view, but not greater objectivity.

Feminism as Academic Method and as Social Vision

Learning feminist perspectives is more likely to change one's personal point of view than the academic study of religion. But popular perceptions of feminism, many of which are negative, have little to do with feminism as it intersects with the academic study of religion. Because such different impressions of feminism are found in our culture, it is important to clarify what is meant by feminism in this book.

The most basic definition of *feminism* is the conviction that women really do inhabit the human realm and are not "other," not a separate species. Sometimes I wear a T-shirt that proclaims: "Feminism is the radical proposition that women are human beings." This proclamation seems so simple and obvious, but its implications are profound and radical because neither conventional scholarship nor lifestyles really take the humanity of women seriously. Fully internalizing that statement involves a subtle and profound change of consciousness for both men and women. Living it out definitely involves a change in lifestyle for most people.

This definition of *feminism* has implications for both the academic study of religion and for the personal practice of religion because feminism can be understood as both an academic method and as a social vision. Although these two forms of feminism are interdependent because both grow out of the paradigm shift that occurs with the realization that women *are* human beings, they are more easily understood if they are initially separated. I prefer to call feminism as academic method *women studies*, to highlight the fact that it has no political implications or agenda (even though it arose out of one) and to differentiate women studies from *feminism*, by which I mean a critical and reconstructive stance vis-à-vis the institutions and values of one's own culture, religion, and academic environment.

Women Studies: Feminism as Academic Method

One can use feminism as an academic method without embracing feminism as a social vision. Scholars who are reluctant to change their lifestyle to transcend gender roles and stereotypes and otherwise accommodate the full humanity of women nevertheless should recognize the need to study women as thoroughly, as critically, and as empathically as men. To do less is to fail to understand the human. Women studies has irrevocably changed our information-gathering habits, so that we can never again be content to know only what men did or thought, or to have a reading list that includes only male authors (unless men are the subject of the study). Every course in the religious studies curriculum would change if those who taught it and took it understood that women are human beings whose lives are not adequately covered and included by the "generic masculine."

The first challenge of women studies is to expose and critique the androcentrism that underlies most traditional scholarship. I will offer a simple example of this androcentrism in lieu of a definition. I have often heard or read the equivalent of the following statement: "The Egyptians allow (or don't allow) women to . . ." The structure is so commonplace that even today many do not see what is wrong with it. But for both those who make such statements and for those who hear them without wincing, real Egyptians are men. Egyptian women are objects acted upon by real Egyptians, but are not themselves full Egyptians. What, in more analytical terms, is behind this long-standing habitual pattern of speech? The androcentric model of humanity has three central characteristics that, when stated bluntly, suffice to demonstrate both the nature and the inadequacy of androcentrism.

First, the male norm and the human norm are collapsed and seen as identical. Recognition that maleness is but one kind of human experience is minimal or nonexistent. As philosopher Simone de Beauvoir states:

> In the midst of an abstract discussion it is vexing to hear a man say:
> "You think thus and so because you are a woman," but I know that
> my only defense is to reply: "I think thus and so because it is true,"
> thereby removing my subjective self from the argument. It would be
> out of the question to reply: "And you think the contrary because you
> are a man," for it is understood that the fact of being a man is no pecu
> liarity. A man is in the right in being a man; it is the woman who is
> in the wrong. . . . Woman has ovaries, a uterus; these peculiarities im
> prison her in her subjectivity, circumscribe her within the limits of her
> own nature. It is often said that she thinks with her glands. Man su
> perbly ignores the fact that his anatomy also includes glands, such as
> the testicles, and that they secrete hormones. He thinks of his body as

a direct and normal connection with the world, which he believes he
apprehends objectively, whereas he regards the body of woman as a
hindrance, a prison, weighted down by everything peculiar to it.[3]

Thus in androcentric thinking, any awareness of a distinction between maleness and humanity is clouded over, and femaleness is viewed as an exception to the norm.

The second characteristic of androcentrism follows directly from the first. When I first questioned the completeness of androcentric accounts of religion, my mentors told me that the generic masculine includes the feminine, making it unnecessary to study women specifically. This is a logical implication of collapsing maleness with humanity, but the result is that research about religion actually deals mainly with the lives and thinking of males, whereas women's religious lives are treated much more peripherally, as a footnote or a short chapter toward the end of the book. The habit of thinking and doing research in the generic masculine is so ingrained that many scholars are genuinely unaware that the religious lives and thoughts of men are only part of a religious situation.

The third and most problematic aspect of androcentrism is its attempt to deal with the fact that, since men and women are taught to be different in all cultures, the generic masculine simply does not cover the feminine. The generic masculine would work only in religions or cultures that had no sex roles, but no such culture exists. Therefore, women must sometimes be mentioned in accounts of religion. At this point, adherents of the androcentric model of humanity reach a logical impasse. Their solution to this impasse is the most devastating component of the androcentric outlook. Because women inevitably deviate from male norms, androcentric thinking deals with them only as objects exterior to "mankind," needing to be explained and fitted in somewhere, having the same epistemological and ontological status as trees, unicorns, deities, and other objects that must be discussed to make experience intelligible. Therefore, in most accounts of religion, although males are presented as religious subjects and as namers of reality, females are presented only in relation to the males being studied, only as objects being named by the males being studied, only as they appear to the males being studied.

Nothing less than a paradigm shift in our model of humanity will remedy these problems. Instead of the current androcentric, "one-sexed" model of humanity, we need an androgynous, "two-sexed" or bisexual model of humanity. A more accurate model of humanity would compel recognition that humans come in two sexes and that both sexes are human. It would also recognize that in virtually every religion, culture, or society, gender roles and stereotypes intensify biological sexual differences. As a result, men's and women's lives are more separate and different from each other's than is biologically dictated. An accurate model of humanity would also forbid placing one gender in the center and the other on the periphery. Androgyny as a two-sex model of humanity, as the conviction that despite gender and sexual differences, women and men are equally human, meets those requirements; both traditional androcentrism, which objectifies women, and a sex-neutral model of humanity, which ignores the reality of culture-based gender roles, do not.

Guided by the androgynous model of humanity, let us return to the example of androcentric speech presented earlier: "The Egyptians allow women . . ." Someone who understands the inadequacies of the androcentric model of humanity and the need for a more accurate, two-sexed model of humanity would write that "in Egyptian society, men do X and women do Y," or perhaps, in some cases, she might write that "Egyptian men allow Egyptian women to . . . ," thereby recognizing that Egyptian men have patriarchal control over the society but that Egyptian women are nevertheless Egyptian human beings, not a different species.

When this model of humanity and these methodological guidelines are applied to virtually any subject in the humanities or social sciences, massive changes in scholarship result, affecting what one studies, how one studies it, what conclusions one draws from research data, the analyses one finds cogent, and the overarching theories that one accepts as good basic tools with which to understand the world. Furthermore, internalizing this model of humanity often results in a transformation of consciousness so profound that one's everyday habits of language and perception change as well. Once one makes the change from an androcentric to an androgynous model of humanity, other models seem completely inadequate.

It is important to recognize that feminist scholarship does not inherently make judgments about what women's position in society should be. It only entails a requirement to study women thoroughly and completely. To construct a feminist vision of society is a different task. Therefore, feminism, at least in the academic context, is first and foremost an academic method, not a socio-political perspective. The key issue is including information about women in *all* studies about any human phenomenon. The scholar's personal views are irrelevant to whether he has an academic obligation to teach a gender-balanced course: Even nonfeminists must include information about women in their scholarship if they want to claim that their scholarship is accurate.

Feminism as Social Vision

My claim that feminism is, *first*, an academic method is controversial because the emergence of the feminist method was inextricably linked with a movement of social protest and dissatisfaction. Indeed, the methodological demand to gather and include information about women could not have emerged and flourished apart from feminism as an alternative social vision, for it was protest against women's limited options in American society that first impelled feminist scholars to notice and name androcentrism and to create women studies methodology.

Feminism as social vision deals with views about ideal social arrangements and interactions between women and men. Therefore, almost by definition, all feminist perspectives are radically critical of current conventional norms and expectations and advocate some degree of change in social, academic, political, religious, and economic institutions to foster greater equity between men and women. Just as feminist scholarship finds androcentrism to be the basic problem with previous scholarship, so feminist social philosophy has focused on patriarchy as the fundamental obstacle to human well-being for women, as well as for men, to a lesser extent. Just as androcentrism regards men as normal and women as exceptions to the norm, so patriarchy regards men as rightful leaders and holders of all positions that society values, whereas women should be subservient and help men maintain their status. As such, the word *patriarchy* has become feminist shorthand for the anti-vision of female subservience and irrelevance that fueled much of society and religion for the past several thousand years and led to the mind-set in which the androcentric model of humanity not only found acceptance, but reigned without conceptual alternatives.

For more than twenty years, feminists have discussed the creation, outlines, and inadequacies of patriarchy and have formulated visions of a postpatriarchal world. Because women in a number of religious traditions are feminist and use feminist ideals to critique and reenvision their traditions, feminism as a social vision, although different from women studies, does in fact intersect with the academic study of religion. Feminists' use of feminism as a social vision in their reflections on their religions has become data for the academic study of religion. Therefore, the ways in which feminism as a social philosophy has affected, criticized, and changed the world's religions must be included in academic study of contemporary religion.

Feminism as social vision relies upon the results of feminist scholarship in history, sociology, and psychology, as well as religion. The most important conclusion of feminist scholarship is that patriarchy is the cultural creation of a certain epoch in human history, not an inevitable necessity of human biology.[4] The importance of this claim is that whatever is created within time is subject to decay and dissolution—a point commonplace in Buddhism among other major religions. This realization overcomes the advice given to generations of rebellious daughters: "You can't do anything about *that*." One *can* do something about patriarchy, though the task is immense.

Well before feminists felt confident of the case that patriarchy emerged relatively late in human history, they were very clear in their critique of it. The early literature of feminism was an outcry of pain; from the nineteenth century on, feminists have claimed that patriarchy is "without redeeming social value," that it is clearly linked with the most destructive forces in human history, and that it harms all people, including men, though not as obviously, directly, or extremely as it harms women.

What about patriarchy makes it such an offensive system to its critics? The literal meaning of patriarchy—"rule by fathers"—provides two clues. First, patriarchy is a system in which rulership, "power over," is quite central; second, by definition, men have power over women. The extent of men's power over women was the first element of the complex to be thoroughly recognized and described. Men monopolize or dominate all the roles and pursuits that society most values and rewards, such as religious leadership or economic power. Therefore, inequality became one of the first patriarchal demons to be named. Furthermore, men literally ruled over women, setting the rules and limits by which and within which they were expected to operate. Women who did not conform, and many who did, could be subjected to another form of male dominance—physical violence.

As the analysis of patriarchy deepened, many feminists focused not merely on the way in which men hold power over women, but also on the centrality of the concept of having power over others in patriarchal society. Many see male power over females as the basic model of all forms of social hierarchy and oppression. From this conclusion, many analysts move on to link patriarchy with militarism and with ecologically dangerous use of the environment. This conclusion is based on the fact that all these policies share an attitude of glorifying and approving the power of one group over another as inevitable and appropriate.

In my view, these typical feminist diagnoses are correct but incomplete because they do not sufficiently clarify the fundamental aspiration of modern feminism, which is far more important than equality or total lack of hierarchy: *freedom from gender roles.* I believe that gender roles are the source of the pain and suffering in current gender arrangements and that eliminating them is the most essential aspect of the program to overcome that pain. If people are forced to find their social place on the basis of their physiological sex, then there will be suffering and injustice even in a situation of "gender equality"—whatever that might mean.

The difference between freedom from gender roles and gender equality is profound. Any concept of gender equality presupposes the continued existence of gender roles and all the imprisoning implied in such conditions. Early liberal feminists usually envisioned equality as meaning that women should be able to do the things men had always done, and, sometimes, that men should be forced to do the things that women had always done. This definition depends on the fact that the male role (rather than men) is preferred to the female role. A frequently cited alternative meaning of equality is that what women do should be regarded as of *equal value* with what men do—a version of separate-but-equal thinking that is often advocated as a conservative alternative to patriarchy.

Neither of these visions of equality escapes the prison of gender roles. Claiming that the female role is distinctive, but of equal rather than of inferior value, still assumes that only women can fulfill the female role and that all women must conform to that female gender role. Giving women access to men's roles, which often requires an attempt to get men into women's roles as well, comes closer to conceptualizing the basic truth that gender roles are the problem to be overcome, but it still collapses sexual identity and social roles. Whenever sexual identity and social roles are conflated, even when the possibility of "cross-over" is acknowledged, the result is a kind of anatomy-is-destiny thinking, which allows no hope for postpatriarchal vision of life outside the prison of gender roles.

On the other hand, if we do not merely suggest or validate crossovers between sexual identity and social role but break the links between sexual identity and social roles altogether, then a social order beyond patriarchy becomes inevitable. Patriarchy depends, in the final analysis, on fixed gender roles. Without gender roles, no one will have automatic access to any role or automatic power over another because of her physiological sex.

Seeing the problem as gender roles and the vision as freedom from gender roles also puts the feminist critique of patriarchy as "power over" in another light. The abuse of power is certainly a major human problem, and patriarchy is rife with abuse of power. But one of the most abusive aspects of patriarchal power is men's automatic, rather than earned or deserved, power over women. Though we must guard against abuses of power, a totally egalitarian society in which no one has more influence, prestige, or wealth than anyone else seems quite impossible. Given that hierarchy is inevitable, therefore, the issue is establishing *proper hierarchy.* This complex and difficult topic cannot be fully explicated in this context, but I must clarify that proper hierarchy is not the same thing as what feminists mean by "domination" or "power over" in their critique of the patriarchal use of power. It connotes the proper use of power that has been properly earned, a topic not much explored in feminist thought.[5] But if postpatriarchal vision is freedom from gender roles, men would no longer automatically receive any power, prestige, influence, or position simply because of their sex. Though following this guideline would not, by itself, guarantee proper hierarchy, it would abolish the worst abuses of patriarchal power.

My claim that the problem of patriarchy is the very existence of gender roles and that postpatriarchy is freedom from gender roles is both radical and controversial. Some may well feel that a world without gender roles is even more unlikely to develop than a world without relationships of domination and submission. Some may think that feminists' goal should be finding and institutionalizing more equitable and just gender roles, rather than abolishing them. It is clear, however, that virtually every feminist critique of patriarchy and every feminist agenda for the future really derives from an unstated assumption that sex is not a relevant criterion for awarding roles or value. Furthermore, any set of gender roles whatsoever will be a prison for those who do not readily fit them. Because the prison of gender roles has been one of the greatest sources of suffering in my life, I am reluctant to make any place for them in a visionary postpatriarchal future.

What might life free from gender roles be like? In some ways, one's sex is important and in other ways not at all. In some ways, it remains necessary to rely on traditional concepts of masculinity and femininity, at least in the short run, and in other ways they are already irrelevant. I think of my own life as participating in a postpatriarchal mode of existence. I am a female; I do not fill the female gender role or the male gender role; I believe that my psychology and lifestyle are both traditionally feminine and traditionally masculine. Thus, my own experience provides me with some of the guidelines for a postpatriarchal future free of gender roles. Sexual identity remains clear. Sexual differentiation is so obvious and so basic that it seems impossible to ignore or deny one's sex. But one's sex implies nothing inevitable about one's reproductive decisions, one's economic and social roles, or even one's psychological traits and tendencies.

Would "masculinity" and "femininity" have any meaning in a world free from the prison of gender roles? On this question, there is no feminist consensus. My own views, largely derived from Tibetan Vajrayana Buddhist ideas about the masculine and the feminine, call for completely severing the idea that men should be masculine and that women should be feminine, while continuing to use the terms as symbols. Because the experience of paired entities is so common, we have inherited a whole repertoire of traits and qualities that are commonly labeled "masculine" and "feminine." That, in itself, is not problematic, so long as we remember that these labels are products of culture, not biology, and differ considerably from culture to culture. What imprisons is the expectation that women should be feminine and men should be masculine. But without the prison of gender roles, these expectations would not hold. Instead men and women would become whatever combination of "masculine" and "feminine" best suited them. In such a context, the symbols of femininity and masculinity might well become more finely tuned, not less.

However, a *society* free from gender roles will be much more "feminine" than current patriarchal society. Why? Because in patriarchy, women must be feminine, which demands that they be silent, whereas men must be masculine and therefore can be articulate. As a result, in patriarchy, most public policy and most religious thought is "masculine" and quite incomplete. Some argue cogently that such partial views, although not wrong, are dangerous so long as they remain incomplete. When women become more articulate and women's experiences of femininity and masculinity become part of public discourse and public policy, society will become both more feminine and more androgynous. At that

point individuals of both sexes will more easily become androgynous, whole persons instead of "half-humans" trapped in female
or male gender roles.

Conclusion

It is important to note what links these two arenas of feminist
thought. Feminism as scholarly method is critical of the androcentric mind-set. Feminism as social vision is critical of patriarchal
culture. Androcentrism and patriarchy share the same attitude toward women. In both cases, women are objectified as nonhuman,
are spoken about as if they were objects but not subjects, and are
manipulated by others. In both cases, the end result is silence about
women and the silencing of women. Androcentric scholarship
proceeds as if women do not exist, or as if they are objects rather
than subjects. Patriarchal culture discourages women from naming reality, and patriarchal scholarship then ignores the namings of
reality that women create nevertheless. But women studies scholarship takes seriously women's namings of reality, even in patriarchal contexts, and feminism as social philosophy encourages
women's authentic, empowered namings of reality and demands
that these namings be taken seriously by the whole society.

CHAPTER TWO

Feminism's Impact on Religion and Religious Studies: A Brief History

A GREAT VARIETY OF VOICES has spoken out on feminism and religion during the past two centuries, though the nineteenth- and twentieth-century voices are separated by a long period of silence. This chapter will name some of those voices and survey the major issues with which they were concerned. Although nineteenth-century feminism was not *primarily* concerned with religion, it did make some contributions to it. By contrast, beginning in the late 1960s, feminist scholars of religion have challenged and changed the religious landscape considerably. Beginning with Judaism and Christianity, but now extending to all religions, feminist clergy and laypeople have called on their traditions to take the religious aspirations and lives of women more seriously. Twentieth-century religious feminism also includes the voices of those who have left the established religions for feminist reasons and have gone on to advocate religious practices inspired by ancient and contemporary "pagan" traditions.

Origins and Foremothers: The Nineteenth Century

When feminists began to discuss religion in late 1960s, many of us were not aware that we had nineteenth-century foremothers. History books didn't mention them, and we found the 1950s cult of domesticity in which we had grown up so strong and the male dominance so severe that most of us didn't think other women could possibly have challenged them. We felt that we were the first generation of women to be so self-conscious about our liabilities in male-dominated culture and the first generation of women to call out so strongly for change and transformation. Little did we realize that those who had written history had no stake in preserving the stories of strong, self-defined women of high achievements; they had instead an interest in writing history as if women had always kept to their assigned place in patriarchal culture without protest or analysis. Subjugated classes and ethnic groups are routinely denied their history as part of the dominant culture's attempts to keep them subservient.

This heritage of which we were unaware began in the late eighteenth century, with the writings of Abigail Adams and Mary Wollstonecraft, and lasted into the early twentieth century. During that period, many thinkers wrote on "the woman question," presented in that androcentric fashion. Only after World War I did concern over "the woman question" die down; in many countries women had achieved the vote, superficially the goal of many advocates of women's rights. Gradually, women's levels of professional and political achievement declined, so that by the 1950s, there were many fewer female professionals than there had been several generations earlier. The current women's movement began in the 1960s, at first as if this "century of struggle"[1] had not occurred.

The lesson is grim. If feminist scholarship and thinking do not become part of the academic canon taught to each new generation of aspiring scholars, they are lost to consciousness and must be rediscovered. The mental energy lost in "reinventing the wheel" in each generation is enormous and severely slows down the process of reconceptualizing the world in nonpatriarchal terms. Furthermore, it can be depressing and enraging to discover how little we have progressed, how our ideas that seem so radical and innovative actually reduplicate ideas that forgotten generations of feminists had already articulated.

Before turning to the nineteenth-century women's movement itself, I want to explore two other nineteenth-century movements that were not overtly feminist but actually bear more resemblance to current feminist transformations of religion. One of them was a scholarly discussion, conducted largely by European men, about early societies and human origins. The other involved women's new modes of participation in religions, especially in evangelical Christian and new religious movements.

Early Matriarchal Theory

Nineteenth-century debates about early society prefigure some of the issues debated today by advocates of the prepatriarchal hypothesis, discussed at length in chapter 5. The nineteenth-century debate, part of a much larger conversation about human origins and evolution, questioned whether society and religion had always been patriarchal, or whether "matriarchy"—a mirror image of patriarchy in which women dominated men—had preceded the current patriarchies. Since nineteenth-century anthropologists argued that all societies passed through the same stages on their way from barbarism to civilization, those who advocated matriarchy believed that all societies had originally been matriarchal.

In 1861, two influential books initiated this debate. In *Das Mutterrecht* (*Matriarchy*), J. J. Bachofen sought to demonstrate that patriarchal civilization had been preceded by a matriarchal period in human society. In the same year, Henry Maine argued in *Ancient Law* that all human societies were originally patriarchal. Debate over this issue continued for over half a century; the same period saw a great deal of debate and social activism regarding women's legal and political rights in patriarchal societies. Thirty years after

the books by Bachofen and Maine, the book most relevant for today was published by Friedrich Engels. This book, *The Origins of
the Family, Private Property, and the State*, places the discussion of
prepatriarchal society in a socialist context. How did these early
advocates of the claim that patriarchy emerged relatively late in human history justify their case?

Das Mutterrecht is a less substantiated and more ideological
forerunner of current scholarship on prepatriarchal society. The
earliest stage of human society, according to Bachofen, was a
female-dominated matriarchy. More than any other scholar, Bachofen saw the prepatriarchal period as a mirror image of patriarchy: Women dominated society, inheritance flowed through the
mother rather than the father, and daughters were favored over
sons. The religion of the matriarchate involved an earth-centered
veneration of the goddess: Bachofen believed that this religious
outlook would have predisposed all people, both male and female,
to a psychological and spiritual life dominated by the so-called
"feminine" pole of cosmic duality—night, moon, earth, darkness,
death, and mourning. Additionally, he argued that the "feminine"
qualities of unity and brotherhood prevailed over the "masculine"
traits of divisiveness and strength.

This early stage of civilization, however, was destined to be overcome by its opposite and superior stage of evolution. Patriarchy
succeeded matriarchy as an "ascent from earth to heaven, from
matter to immateriality, from mother to father."[2] In patriarchal societies, which Bachofen saw as more civilized because they evolved
later, the qualities that fitted women for leadership in early society now won them only "bejeweled servitude."[3] Materiality and
immersion in maternity, qualities Bachofen saw as essential to
women, had no other utility in civilized patriarchy.

Engels's views on social evolution and matriarchy are somewhat
different. Though he also believed in unilinear human evolution,
he was less convinced that each successive stage was an improve-

ment. Specifically, Engels saw the evolution of women's position as part of the rise of private property, the monogamous family, and the state—a package that, as a socialist, he did not evaluate positively.

In the earliest human societies, Engels believed, a woman was not economically dependent on her husband, and her labor was socially necessary and useful for the entire tribal group. He thought that this early prepatriarchal period could be divided into two stages. In the first, private property did not exist in any form; the only division of labor was by sex, and every man in the group was a potential mate for every woman. Private, exclusive relations were not the norm. This was followed by a second period in which pair bonds were stronger, but the relationship could be easily ended by either partner, and women were not dependent economically on men. This period, Engels felt, was characterized by warm marital relations. But growth in clan property gradually led to the existence of private property, which, in turn, encouraged monogamy. When the property-owning family became the primary economic unit of society, women's labor, formerly useful and necessary for the whole society, became the private property of their families. Because of this transition, women became economically dependent on their husbands. Their work, according to Engels, came to be performed under conditions of virtual slavery, from that time until the present day.

Women in Nineteenth-Century Religions

Just as the speculations of nineteenth-century European men prefigured twentieth-century feminist discussions of prepatriarchal society, so some nineteenth-century women's involvement in religion provides significant parallels with twentieth-century religious feminism. As Barbara MacHaffie and other historians have shown, the nineteenth-century cult of true womanhood reversed traditional Christian stereotypes about women. Rather than viewing women as inevitably prone to lust and sin (like Eve), nineteenth-century theologians saw them as morally and spiritually superior to men, though also so weak and delicate that they must avoid the rough worlds of politics and business.[4] As a result, women became the mainstays, though not the leaders, of most religious bodies, as men occupied themselves less and less with religion. At least for middle-class women, the combination of education, free time, and a sense of their own moral superiority led many into religious organizations dedicated to charity at home and missionary activity abroad. These various societies, run by and for women, fulfilled rather than violated women's "proper place," but at the same time, they allowed women some activities outside the home, provided companionship, allowed women to develop organizational skills, and gave them activities in which they could experience a sense of accomplishment.[5] Women's missionary societies, dedicated to spreading the Christian message in places where it had been previously unheard, were especially successful and well organized, contributing greatly to the overall success of nineteenth-century missionary movements.

During the nineteenth century, the first controversies over the preaching and ordination of women also occurred. Nineteenth-century Christian evangelical groups were much more open to women preachers than are their twentieth-century counterparts. For example, Charles Finney, an important evangelical preacher, believed that women should preach if they felt deeply moved to do so. The acceptance of women preachers in evangelical circles raised the question in older, more established Protestant denominations, but in them women's preaching was not generally accepted. For those denominations that practiced formal ordination rather than a less formal call to preach, ordination of women to the ministry also first occurred in the nineteenth-century. In 1853 Antoinette Brown, a Congregationalist minister, became the first woman to be ordained. A few Congregationalist churches continued to ordain women, as did some branches of the Methodist Church, the Unitarians, and the Universalists, but women's ordination was neither common nor easy.[6] Few women were ordained, and many denominations did not begin to consider the question until the 1970s or later.

Finally, women played atypical roles in a number of the sectarian movements found in nineteenth-century America. The Shaker movement and the Oneida community both thoroughly challenged conventional notions of the family, and of men's and women's roles. Neither of them allowed traditional nuclear families; the Shakers were entirely celibate, and the Oneida community considered every man to be married to every woman and discouraged permanent alliances. Both groups also discouraged strict division of labor along sexual lines and involved women in the economic production that made the communities self-sufficient.[7] Other less radical nineteenth-century movements nevertheless deviated significantly from Catholic and mainstream Protestant gender norms. Some of these alternative movements were established by women, most notably the Christian Science movement, founded by Mary Baker Eddy, and the Theosophy movement, founded by Madame Blavatsky. Most of them also offered women greater participation and recognition than was available in mainline Protestant denominations. Many of these sectarian groups, both those that were socially radical and those that were more conventional, challenged the common theological language as well. The Shakers, the Oneida community, and Christian Scientists all assumed and insisted that God had feminine as well as masculine dimensions.[8] Generally speaking, these groups were attractive to women, who joined them in greater numbers than did men. In attempting to explain why, some have concluded, in the words of one scholar, that "by joining sectarian groups . . . women may have . . . been unconsciously rebelling against their status in Protestant churches and American culture."[9]

The Nineteenth-Century Women's Movement

For the most part, overtly religious issues were not central to the nineteenth-century women's movement. Most nineteenth-century feminists wished neither to blame religion for women's position nor to advocate a changed position for women in the church. They simply wanted to gain certain basic rights for women without taking on religion as either ally or foe. Nevertheless, it was impossible for them to ignore religion completely because religious authorities did not ignore them.

The nineteenth-century women's rights movement grew out of women's antislavery activities. Both the hostile reactions of some abolitionists to women who took a public role in the abolition movement and women's comparison of their own lack of rights and self-determination to that of slaves encouraged women to question their place in society.

We can explore the first of these motivations by looking at the issue of women's public speaking about the slavery issue. The norm for women, enforced by centuries of Christian practice, was to be silent at public gatherings, whether religious or political. Through the centuries there had been exceptions to this rule, perhaps most notably Anne Hutchinson in seventeenth-century New England, but the first women to speak in public *regularly* were the Grimké sisters, Angelina and Sarah. They knew slavery firsthand as the daughters of a Southern slave-owning family and, beginning in 1836, spoke eloquently against it. But churches reacted with furor that women would dare to address a mixed public assembly, denouncing their actions as unwomanly and unchristian. Deeply hurt by this opposition, the sisters responded with lectures and pamphlets dealing directly with women's rights. Sarah wrote "that God has made no distinction between men and women as moral beings. . . . To me it is perfectly clear *that whatsoever it is morally right for a man to do, it is morally right for a woman to do.*"[10]

When Lucretia Mott and Elizabeth Cady Stanton, American women delegates to the World Anti-Slavery Convention held in London in 1840, were denied seats on the convention floor with the male delegates, they responded by organizing the famous Seneca Falls Convention of 1848, which launched the American women's movement. The Declaration of Sentiments and Resolutions, written by Mott and Stanton and adopted by the convention, was modeled on the American Declaration of Independence, but included women where that famous document had excluded them. Thus, it begins by stating that "all men and women are created equal; that they are endowed by their Creator with certain inalienable rights."[11] The document goes on to list a history of "repeated injuries and usurpations on the part of man towards woman," including men's usurpation of the prerogative of God "himself, claiming it as his right to assign her a sphere of action, when that belongs to her conscience and to her God." To correct the situation a number of resolutions were adopted, including one that acknowledged "that woman is man's equal—was intended to be so by the Creator," and another declaring "that woman has too long rested satisfied in the circumscribed limits which corrupt customs and a perverted interpretation of the Scriptures have marked out for her."[12]

Though the women's rights movement as a whole went no further in exploring links between women's inferior position and religion, Elizabeth Cady Stanton and a committee she recruited went on to compile *The Woman's Bible*, the major nineteenth-century feminist interpretation of religion. Stanton was convinced that women working for equality would not succeed until the spell of the Bible had been broken. *The Woman's Bible*, not an alternative bible but a collection of commentaries on passages dealing with women, attempted to establish that the Bible was the creation of a certain cultural epoch containing *both* divine truth and culturally limited views. This position is very much like those taken by some contemporary feminist interpreters of the Bible, and many of the specific interpretations are likewise familiar. For example, Stanton's commentary differentiates between the two creation stories in Genesis and emphasizes the egalitarianism of the first account: "Here is the sacred historian's first account of the advent of woman; a simultaneous creation of both sexes, in the image of God. It is evident from the language that there was consultation in the Godhead, and that the masculine and feminine elements were equally represented."[13]

Stanton goes on to elaborate on the importance of the divine feminine implied in the Genesis passage:

> *The first step in the elevation of woman to her true position, as an equal factor in human progress, is the cultivation of the religious sentiment in regard to her dignity and equality, the recognition by the rising generation of an ideal Heavenly Mother, to whom their prayers should be addressed, as well as to a Father.*
>
> *If language has any meaning, we have in these texts a plain declaration of the existence of the feminine element in the Godhead, equal in power and glory with the masculine. The Heavenly Mother and Father!*[14]

These conclusions are familiar to contemporary feminist theologians and scholars. The difference is that Stanton's conclusions, which were presented late in the history of the nineteenth-century women's movement, were not only rejected by most church officials but also by women's organizations (including the one of which Stanton was president, the National American Women Suffrage Movement) almost as soon as they had been published.[15] By contrast, these same conclusions were voiced at the *beginning* of the current women's movement and have already had a great impact, both on Christianity and Judaism and on alternative religions.

Awakening Consciousness:
Religion and Feminism in the Twentieth Century

Feminist consciousness waned in the years after women won the right to vote and reached its lowest point during the 1950s. Women's involvement in religious leadership, whether as ordained or lay leaders, was lower than at any point in the previous century. Women's participation in the professions was corresponding low, and girls were largely taught to be economically and emotionally dependent wives and mothers. This was the decade that produced "the problem that has no name"—Betty Friedan's label in *The Feminine Mystique* (the book often credited with launching twentieth-century feminism) for the frustration and boredom that gripped so many "happy homemakers" in the 1950s. For a young woman like myself, who had other dreams and visions, being socialized in this era was a nightmare, and the awakening of feminist consciousness in the late 1960s and early 1970s a welcome relief.

In the euphoric beginnings of this feminist awakening, three closely related and interwoven movements dominated feminist discussions of religion. First, many Christian and Jewish women began the painful process of discovering how sexist their religions could be and the exhilarating process of finding, often in the collegial sisterhood of women, other ways of understanding and practicing their religions. Second, some found that such understandings and practices did not go far enough and began to develop a feminist spirituality movement outside the bounds of Christianity and Judaism. Finally, for the first time ever, significant numbers of feminists received doctorates in religious studies and began a systematic feminist appraisal of religion and religious studies. This movement developed two branches: scholars identified with one of the world's religions, and others who began as feminist Jews or Christians but switched allegiance to the feminist spirituality movement later.

Brave Beginnings: Early Developments
in Feminist Christianity, Judaism,
and the Feminist Spirituality Movement

At the beginning of the current women's movement in religion, in the late 1960s and early 1970s, feminists pointed out how women often were completely excluded from the full practice of Judaism and Christianity. The generic masculine language of the liturgy, the monolithically male images used of deity, and the male monopoly on all visible roles beyond singing in the choir, baking, and teaching young children were the objects of satire as well as analysis.[16] Nevertheless, even though largely barred from leadership roles, women formed the bulk of many congregations and did much of the day-to-day work required to keep a religious institution functioning.

In 1971, a major event occurred in each of the three emerging feminist religious movements. Mary Daly, one of the earliest outspoken Christian feminists, was invited to preach the first sermon ever delivered by a woman at Harvard's Memorial Church. Although this invitation signaled a certain success for Christian feminism, it was the end of her Christian feminist efforts for Daly herself: She ended her sermon, "The Women's Movement: An Exodus Community," by walking out of the church and inviting those who were so moved to accompany her.[17] On the other side of the continent, Zsuzsanna Budapest, convinced that the feminist movement needed a spiritual dimension, founded the Susan B. Anthony Coven No. 1 on the winter solstice, an event that marked the beginning of the feminist spirituality movement. Finally, the feminist academic study of religion also reached a milestone with the formation of the Women's Caucus of the American Academy of Religion, the professional society for those who teach religion at universities, colleges, and seminaries.

For feminist Jews and Christians, certain events in 1973 and 1974 are crucial watersheds. In March 1973, an emerging Jewish women's movement held its first conference in New York City, an empowering event for many who attended. For Christians, several important events involving the ordination of women took place. Though ordination of women to sacramental (as opposed to preaching) ministry is not the only important indication of whether or not women have genuine membership in their religion, it has become a symbol, almost a shorthand sign, for quickly assessing how women fare in any given denomination. Many major denominations did not ordain women until sometime during the current women's movement; some major denominations, most notably Roman Catholicism, Eastern Orthodoxy, and Orthodox Judaism still do not.

In 1973, in an emotional, hotly contested decision, the Episcopal Church voted not to ordain women. Some months later, on July 30, 1974, eleven women were ordained priests of the Episcopal Church in Philadelphia by sympathetic bishops, but without the approval or sanction of the church hierarchy. Two years later, the Episcopal Church hierarchy recognized those ordinations and sanctioned the ordination of women to the priesthood, though individual priests were allowed to refuse to regard women as priests or to participate in ordinations. The Episcopal Church has continued to be racked with dissent over the issue, though by 1989, it had already ordained its first woman bishop. Finally, in November 1992, the Church of England voted to ordain women, a move that has also been controversial.[18]

The case narrated above was only the most dramatic. Other denominations went through similar changes. In November 1970, Elizabeth A. Platz was ordained by the Lutheran Church in America, becoming the first woman Lutheran minister. Other Lutheran groups followed, but some conservative Lutheran groups still do not ordain women. Most other mainline Protestant churches now ordain women, as do Reform, Reconstructionist, and Conservative (but not Orthodox) Judaism. The first woman Jewish rabbi, Sally Preisand, was ordained in 1972 at the Reform Jewish Seminary. The Reconstructionist Jewish movement quickly followed, ordaining Sandy Eisenberg in 1974, but Conservative Judaism, a large and influential movement, ordained Amy Eilberg in 1985 only after more than a decade of difficult debate.[19]

The major but not unexpected disappointment of the mid-1970s regarding women's ordination involved the Roman Catholic Church. Though many American Catholics and some elements in the American hierarchy support women's ordination, the Vatican issued an official statement in 1976 declaring that women could not be admitted to the priesthood. The Vatican argued that the priest is a representative of Jesus before the Christian congregation; since Jesus was a male, only another male could represent him. This argument has been heavily criticized on theological grounds.[20]

In the 1970s and 1980s, the number of women training to become ministers or rabbis increased dramatically. In the 1990s women often make up more than one third of the student body at theological seminaries. However, women ministers and rabbis continue to face employment difficulties. The first appointment is often relatively easy to obtain, but the move to being head pastor or rabbi of a large, influential congregation is difficult. Often women find themselves tracked into jobs that seem to be derived from traditional ideas about woman's "proper place," such as youth minister or hospital chaplain.

In addition to the ordination of women, the other major focus of feminist Jewish and Christian groups was to rewrite traditional liturgies that used masculine language both to describe worshippers and to describe the deity. (This issue will be dealt with more fully in chapters 4 and 6.) Very early in the women's movement, the extent to which such language excluded women was pointed out, and various solutions were proposed. Already in 1979, the anthology *Womanspirit Rising* contained a theological justification for the use of female imagery to name deity, some concrete examples of liturgies transformed to take those arguments into account, and discussions of how ritual might take better account of women's experiences. For Christianity, such early reforms culminated in *An Inclusive-Language Lectionary*, the first volume of which was published in 1983. This book carefully suggests ways to include women in the people of God and femininity in the Godhead. Theologically conservative, in that it does not challenge the attributes and nature of either God or the people of God, the lectionary has nevertheless drawn a good deal of hostility.

In Judaism, similar experiments have resulted in new translations of the Jewish prayer book issued both by large Jewish denominations and by smaller congregations and communities. Though some translations go further, in most cases the language is made inclusive by naming the foremothers of the faith—Sarah, Rebecca, Rachel, and Leah—along with the forefathers, Abraham, Isaac, and Jacob, and by referring to the daughters as well as the sons of Israel. However, most translations stop short of referring to deity as feminine. Like the inclusive Christian lectionary, the new prayerbooks do not change traditional theology in any way.

Not unsurprisingly, both because these reforms are relatively conservative and because they still are resisted by segments of the Jewish and Christian worlds, others have moved in more radical directions, away from the authorized versions of Judaism and Christianity. These movements can be divided into two groups, depending on the degree of perceived relationship to the Jewish or Christian tradition. The first group encompasses individuals who consider themselves Jews or Christians but who draw on resources outside the Jewish or Christian Bibles, liturgies, and generally recognized theological authorities for their spiritual lives. The second group includes people who have rejected biblical religions altogether in favor of new, explicitly feminist forms of religious expression.

Among many Christian experiments in the first group, the Women-Church movement is most prominent. Growing directly out of Catholic women's frustrations with the Vatican's intransigence on the issue of women's ordination, the movement was launched with a major conference held in Chicago in 1983. Unwilling to suffer exclusion while waiting for the conventional churches to exorcise their sexist forms, Women-Church practices a distinctly and explicitly feminist form of Christianity. According to one of its major spokespersons, Rosemary Ruether, it reflects "the perspective of religious feminists who seek to reclaim aspects of the biblical tradition, Jewish and Christian, but who also recognize the need both to go back behind biblical religion and to transcend it."[21] Her book *Women-Church: Theology and Practice of Feminist Liturgical Communities*, published in 1985, provides a convenient single resource for learning about this movement and the rituals and liturgies it has developed.

Religious feminists in the second group came to the conclusion that not only were the institutional churches and synagogues too entrenched and too sexist to be tolerable, but also that biblical religions themselves were inherently sexist in their symbolism and theology. Their solution was to abandon biblically based religion entirely, often in favor of spirituality inspired by paganism, an umbrella term for a wide variety of pre- and nonbiblical religions that often include female images of the divine. Collectively, these numerous and various groups are known as the feminist spirituality movement, or as feminist Wicca. Reclaiming the word *witch* to mean "wise woman," the Wiccan movement began almost as soon as the current feminist movement fully emerged into consciousness. By the early and middle 1970s, some of its best-known advocates were already publishing ritual manuals and theology, and its impact was being felt in the circles of feminist scholarship on religion and feminist theology. The landmark anthology *Womanspirit Rising*, published in 1979, includes essays by Starhawk and by Zsuzsanna Budapest, two of the most widely read practitioners of feminist spirituality, as well as Carol P. Christ's concluding essay, which reflects her growing immersion in the goddess movement. The first feminist spirituality conference, held in Boston in 1975, was attended by eighteen hundred women. In 1974 appeared the first issue of *WomanSpirit*, a widely read feminist magazine, which was published quarterly for ten years by a women's collective in Oregon. By 1979, Starhawk had already published *The Spiral Dance: A Rebirth of the Ancient Religion of the Goddess*, a widely used guide to one version of feminist Wicca. Starhawk and many other authors have continued to generate a great volume of literature, so that today, a women's bookstore may well stock more books representing goddess spirituality than any other point of view in its section on religion.

Feminism and Religious Studies

Just as the practice of religion has been transformed by feminists, so has the academic study of religion. All areas within the discipline, from biblical studies to the comparative study of religion, have been affected by feminist methods. Feminist scholars have been quite successful in establishing a well-respected, influential presence in their discipline, despite the fact that it was one of the most male dominated of all academic fields just thirty years ago. When I began graduate studies in 1965, there were just twelve women among the more than four hundred graduate students at the University of Chicago Divinity School. Six of us had entered that year, prompting comments that an "unusually large number" of women were now enrolled in the divinity school. When I returned to address the students and faculty just twelve years later, more than one quarter of the graduate students were women.

The groundwork for this transition was laid in the late 1960s. During those years, a few pioneering publications appeared, including Mary Daly's *The Church and the Second Sex* and some of Rosemary Ruether's early articles, but knowledge of them was not yet widespread. A number of female graduate students, myself included, were struggling to develop feminist questions and methods of study. However, our mentors and graduate institutions were usually uninterested in, unsupportive of, or even opposed to our efforts, for feminist scholarship threatened not only the male monopoly of the field, but also its androcentric methodologies, which were even more sacrosanct to the establishment.

Partly because we were few in number, partly because we had no network, and partly because our mentors did not regard feminist issues as relevant to scholarship, we did not know of each other's efforts or of previous feminist writings relevant to our work. For example, even though I was writing a dissertation that critiqued scholarship on women's roles in religion, no one suggested that I read *The Second Sex*, which would have been the single most relevant source for me to have read while I struggled to figure out what was wrong with the scholarly interpretations of women's roles in aboriginal Australian religion. It was one of the first books I read after I completed my dissertation—and I was very frustrated to realize that I had been forced to discover on my own that the problem lay with objectification of women, not so much by aboriginal culture as in the Western mind-set.

In June 1971, Alverno College hosted the first gathering of women theologians and scholars of religion ever held. Out of that conference came plans to meet the following fall during the joint national meetings of our major professional societies, the American Academy of Religion (AAR) and the Society for Biblical Literature (SBL). The agenda was to establish a women's caucus in the field and to demand that program time be allotted to papers and panels on women and religion.

That meeting, which occurred in November in Atlanta, was probably the single most generative event for the feminist transformation of religious studies. Before the meeting, isolated, relatively young and unestablished scholars struggled to define what it meant to study women and religion and to demonstrate why it was so important to do so. After the meeting, a strong network of like-minded individuals had been established, and we had begun to make our presence and our agenda known to the AAR and the SBL. Through an unorthodox parliamentary tactic, we even elected Christine Downing as the first woman president of the AAR that year. A women's caucus, which has met every year since then, was formed. This caucus later convinced the entire AAR/SBL not to meet in states that had not ratified the Equal Rights Amendment while that piece of legislation was still before the state legislatures. It now sponsors a task force on the status of women in the profession. We also took the initial steps that led to the formation of the Women and Religion Section of the AAR, which provides a venue for feminist scholars to talk about their work in a supportive atmosphere. Many feminist scholars, including myself, presented their first academic papers for the Women and Religion Section at these meetings. Especially in the early years, these papers were eagerly collected and published, becoming the nucleus of the courses on women and religion that we were beginning to teach. Readings for such courses were then very scarce,[22] a problem we certainly no longer face.

From that time onward, an extremely mutually beneficial relationship developed between the more established women scholars, who began to do feminist theology later in their careers—such as Beverly Harrison, Nelle Morton, and Letty Russell[23]—and the more numerous and younger women just entering the field, who entered as feminists. Christine Downing, the first woman president of the AAR, has written of her own experience of that relationship with "the younger women . . . who were just entering my field, women who looked to the women of my generation as role models but who really initiated *us* into the challenges of creating a genuinely feminist theology."[24] An essay by Valerie Saiving,[25] written in 1960, was much reprinted and studied as a model of what it means to study religion from a woman's point of view. Saiving suggested that theology is not abstract, but is grounded in the particularities of human experience, which are different for women than for men. Therefore, she argued, that without women's contributions, theology will be incomplete. The work of Mary Daly and Rosemary Ruether was also attracting the attention of the field as a whole. Ruether's early studies in patristics (the thought of the early Christian theologians) led her to formulate her influential theory that the dualistic and otherworldly outlook of early Christianity had fostered negative attitudes toward women.[26] When Daly published *Beyond God the Father*, with its radical and thorough critique of conventional Christianity in 1973, the young feminist theology movement was well launched.

Two important anthologies published at the end of the decade brought to fruition this first developmental phase in feminist scholarship in the academic study of religion. *Womanspirit Rising: A Feminist Reader in Religion*, published in 1979 by Carol P. Christ and Judith Plaskow, became probably the single most influential and widely used book in the field of feminist studies in religion. A veritable "Who's Who" of many of the leaders in feminist theology, it has not gone out of date, though much more recent work supplements it. In 1980, Nancy Auer Falk and I published the first edition of *Unspoken Worlds: Women's Religious Lives*, the first book to discuss women's religious lives in a wide variety of cultural contexts in some depth and detail. This book has been influential for many graduate students in the cross-cultural comparative study of religion who wanted to do women studies in their area of specialization.

Several academic journals are critical tools for the feminist study of religion. In 1985, the major journal *The Journal of Feminist Studies in Religion*, edited by Judith Plaskow and Elisabeth Schüssler Fiorenza, published its first issue. Published by the Scholars' Press, the publishing agency of the American Academy of Religion, this journal gives prestige and visibility to the new work in feminist studies in religion. It is highly recommended as a resource for anyone seeking the cutting edge of the field. Between 1974 and 1994, *Anima: An Experiential Journal*, first edited by Harry Buck, published many innovative articles of interest to students of women and religion. The latest entry into this field is *The Annual Review of Women in World Religions*, published by SUNY Press and edited by Katherine K. Young and Arvind Sharma. This annual allows "the comparative dimension to appear in bolder relief" and also fosters more dialogue between the humanistic and the social scientific approaches to the study of women and religion.[27]

Maturing into Diversity

In retrospect, it is clear that diversity—of aims, concerns, and perspectives—was always present within feminist ranks, even when feminist gatherings felt unified, exuberant, and triumphant in its stand against patriarchal religions and androcentric scholarship. It has also become clear that some of the earlier feeling of exuberant unity was based on limited representation *within* the feminist movement in religion, that many constituencies had not yet been heard. In the early 1980s, significant differences in approach and agenda began to surface among religious feminists. These disagreements were disorienting and painful as feminists discovered that they disagreed deeply over things about which they cared intensely. The fact that affirming diversity had been part of the feminist vision from the beginning made these disagreements even more painful. Carol P. Christ and Judith Plaskow had written in their introduction to *Womanspirit Rising* that "the diversity within feminist theology and spirituality is its strength."[28] Nevertheless, ten years later, in the introduction to its sequel, *Weaving the Visions*, Plaskow and Christ discussed at length the anger, pain, and frustration that had erupted over disagreements among those who worked in feminist theology and scholarship.

For the feminist movement, actually *manifesting* diversity, rather than simply applauding it, turned out to be quite difficult. Although all women share the experience of being female, differences of class, race, culture, religion, and sexual orientation separate them. Just as early feminists complained that women's experience had been omitted by androcentric theology and scholarship, feminists who were not white, middle-class, heterosexual Christians pointed out that the phrase "women's experience" often excluded them and that their experiences were taken no more seriously by the dominant white, middle-class, heterosexual, Christian feminist perspective than androcentric theology and scholarship had taken women in general. Furthermore, not only had the experiences of such women been overlooked; to many, it seemed that white, middle-class, heterosexual, Christian feminists had assumed that they could speak for all women. During the 1980s, many diverse voices spoke much more loudly and clearly, sometimes with frank frustration, so that today feminist theology more accurately reflects the diversity of women.

In addition to difficulties caused by different social locations, feminists have also found ideological differences difficult to handle. In particular, disagreements between feminists who choose to retain ties with a traditional religion and those who join post-Christian or post-Jewish feminist spirituality movements have sometimes become acrimonious. Some feminists began to fight with each other, not only critiquing each other's work, but attacking each other, which is quite different. In one way or another, some began to say, "Unless you're my kind of feminist, you've been co-opted by patriarchy," a claim that obviously does not promote a diverse sisterhood. In my view, such conflict is an inappropriate throwback to patriarchal monotheism—a perhaps unconscious or unstated feeling that ultimately, there is one best way to do things. Another factor has been the emotional difficulty, perhaps born of female socialization and women's tendency to prefer harmony to conflict, in dealing with the disagreements and criticisms that push forward the thinking of any mature religious or spiritual position. Disagreement over basic issues has always occurred in all movements for social change, but it has been very hard for feminist theologians of different opinions and commitments to debate without fighting, without hurt feelings and a sense of betrayal.

All of these factors are intertwined with the deeply entrenched tendency in Western thinking to turn differences into a hierarchy. We were ill prepared to deal with genuine diversity because of cultural values in which we had all been trained. If we are different, then one of us must be better—the classic scripts of patriarchy, monotheism, and Western thought in general assume this. No wonder real, as opposed to theoretically affirmed diversity, is difficult to handle.

I believe that some simple guidelines may help us deal better with the difficulties brought up by diversity. The first is to realize that no one person can speak for all genders, races, classes, or sexual orientations, and no one should try to do so. Therefore, since no one can speak for all perspectives, many voices are required to articulate feminist theology and scholarship about religion. Second, since no one can speak for all perspectives, every position, every scholar, will overlook or underemphasize something vital. That is not a failing, since it is inevitable. The more diversity is affirmed, the more difficult inclusivity becomes, simply because human diversity is almost infinite. How can anyone include or understand infinite diversity? The question is not whether a scholar has included every possible perspective, but whether she speaks authentically and nonimperialistically from her own standpoint. That we all take responsibility for articulating our own voices is

the only way we can both appreciate diversity and affirm inclu-
siveness—two tasks fundamental to feminism that often seem to be
on a collision course with each other.

"Breaking Up Is Hard to Do": The Great Divide in Feminist Theology

Almost from the time that feminist theologians began to critique
patriarchal religions, it was clear that two major positions were developing. On the one hand, some argued that the most effective
feminist strategy was to maintain some links with traditional religions, such as Judaism, Christianity, Buddhism, or Islam, while
also engaging in radical transformations of those religions. Other
feminists saw current world religions as hopelessly patriarchal and
well beyond the scope of any feminist repair; therefore, the best
feminist strategy would be to abandon traditional religions for new
religious forms. Clearly, there is much room here for argument
about who is the "one true feminist," and about the grave dangers
inherent in the other position. In fact, acrimony and divisiveness
between these two positions have been severe and painful, and
communication between those in each position has often been
broken. In particular, Rosemary Ruether and Carol P. Christ have
exchanged sharp words about the merits and problems of post-
Christian feminist spirituality and radical Christian feminism.[29]

During the 1970s and into the 1980s, this division became ever
more pronounced. On the one hand, Elisabeth Schüssler Fiorenza,
Elaine Pagels, and Phyllis Trible wrote radically innovative feminist interpretations of scripture, which could be used by those attempting to reconstruct Christianity or Judaism from a feminist
point of view. Rosemary Ruether and others continued to write
ever more radical feminist critiques and reconstructions of Christianity, while Judith Plaskow did the same for Judaism with *Standing Again at Sinai: Judaism from a Feminist Perspective* (1990).

On the other hand, several important early works clearly delineated non-Christian and post-Christian or Jewish stances. Naomi Goldenberg's *Changing of the Gods: Feminism and the End of Traditional Religions* (1979) was adamant in its assessment that feminism and the traditional religions are incompatible. In 1981 Christine Downing published *The Goddess: Mythological Images of the Feminine*, an intensely introspective book that explored ancient Greek goddesses as myth-models for contemporary women. Carol P. Christ found it increasingly impossible to remain within the monotheistic framework, chronicling her journey in *Laughter of Aphrodite: Reflections on a Journey to the Goddess*, published in 1987. As is clear in her title, the issue of feminine imagery of deity, already raised by Elizabeth Cady Stanton, became an increasingly important concern during the 1980s, though two major essays in *Womanspirit Rising* had already raised the issue. Though she did not take up the cause of feminine imagery of the divine, Mary Daly continued to publish increasingly radical and anti-Christian feminist theology throughout the decade, at times making it quite clear that, in her view, no self-respecting feminist could maintain connections with any of the traditional religions.

Expanding the Circle: Diversity of Race, Class, Sexual Orientation, and Culture

Through the 1980s and into the 1990s, scholars writing from a tremendous variety of Christian perspectives have enhanced the meaning of the term "Christian feminist." Womanist, *mujerista*, Latin American, Asian, and lesbian voices have all articulated visions and versions of Christian feminism. They have shown that factors beyond sexism must be taken into account to explain and understand their situations because not only male dominance but also classism, racism, and homophobia affect the religious lives of women in these groups. In all of these movements, understanding of patriarchy and male dominance is nuanced by dynamics of class, race, culture, and sexual orientation that white, middle-class, heterosexual women have often not taken into account. Class and race analyses are especially important to womanist, *mujerista*, and Latin American perspectives. Asian Christians practice Christianity in cultures that are vastly different from the Christian West, and sometimes they must deal with a heritage of colonial domination. Lesbians identify heterosexism as a major defect of conventional religions. A convenient and helpful anthology that brings together all these perspectives except for lesbian Christianity is Ursula King's *Feminist Theology from the Third World: A Reader*, published in 1994. These discussions also continue in several newer program units of the American Academy of Religion: the Womanist Theology Section, which sometimes holds joint sessions with the Women and Religion Section and the Lesbian Issues Section. Several issues of the *Journal of Feminist Studies in Religion* have also dealt with these topics. (Interestingly, the AAR has recently also included the Gay Men's Issues group.)

The womanist perspective developed in the 1980s as black feminists sought to articulate their own experience and the ways it differs from that of other feminists. The term "womanist" itself was coined by novelist Alice Walker, who writes that "womanist is to feminist as purple is to lavender." Womanist theologian Toinette Eugene explains that "womanist theology agrees with black theology in its critique of white racism and the need for black unity, and it agrees with feminist theology in its criticism of sexism and the need for the unity of women."[30] Among the most frequently read books in this growing body of literature are Katie Cannon's *Black Womanist Ethics*, Delores Williams's *Sisters in the Wilderness*, Jacquelyn Grant's *White Women's Christ and Black Women's Jesus*, and Emilie Townes's *Womanist Justice, Womanist Hope*. In addition, a white feminist, Susan Thistlethwaite, has surveyed this literature and sought to address the issue of how racism and sexism intertwine in *Sex, Race, and God* (1989).

Feminist theology has also grown to include women of Latin

American heritage, both those living in the United States and those living in Latin America. *Mujerista* is the word Hispanic religious feminists living the United States have coined for themselves as theologians. Ada María Isasi-Díaz and Yolanda Tarango explain: "A *mujerista* is a Hispanic woman who struggles to liberate herself not as an individual but as a member of a community."[31] Their book *Hispanic Women: Prophetic Voice in the Church* is perhaps the best-known work in this field. Because theology in Latin America so often consists of liberation theology written by men, who may not especially take sexism into account, Elsa Tamez and other Latin American feminists have tried to correct this one-sided view, starting with *Through Her Eyes: Women's Theology from Latin America*.

Asian Christian feminists have also added their voices to the chorus of feminist Christianity. The first Asian feminist theology was Marianne Katoppo's *Compassionate and Free: An Asian Woman's Theology*, published in 1979. The anthologies *We Dare to Dream: Doing Theology as Asian Women* (1989) and *With Passion and Compassion: Third World Women Doing Theology* (1988) draw together much of the discussion by Asian Christian feminists, who also have maintained a lively feminist theological journal, *In God's Image*.[32] A particularly complete Asian feminist theology is Chung Hyun Kyung's *Struggle to Be the Sun Again* (1990). Its Korean author is also famous for her 1991 plenary address to the World Council of Churches, in which she invoked the Holy Spirit through the ancestral spirits of her people and stated that, for her, the image of the Holy Spirit in part comes from the image of the Buddhist figure Kwan-Yin, venerated as goddess of compassion and wisdom in East Asian women's popular religion. She adds, "Perhaps this might also be a feminine image of the Christ . . . who goes before and brings others with her."[33]

During the 1980s a number of religious feminists, both Christian and non-Christian, began to write explicitly of the issues most relevant to them as lesbians. They coined the term *heterosexism* to

connote compulsory heterosexuality, the fears directed by a homo-
phobic society toward lesbians and gay men, and the belief that
men must, at all costs, control female sexuality. Books such as Carter Heyward's *Touching Our Strength* (1989) also speak passionately
of the connections between unalienated erotic experience and spiritual growth. Christine Downing's *Myths and Mysteries of Same-
Sex Love* (1989) and Virginia Ramey Mollenkott's *Sensuous Spirituality: Out from Fundamentalism* (1992) are also important contributions to this voice.

Feminism and Religious Diversity

Today diversities of race, class, culture, and sexual orientation are
being taken seriously by feminist scholars of religion. Nevertheless,
one fundamental element of diversity has not been taken into account by most feminist scholars and theologians—religious diversity itself! Feminist theology and religious studies scholarship remains a profoundly *Western* movement, both conceptually and in
terms of its subject matter. Nothing illustrates this limitation better than Plaskow and Christ's *Weaving the Visions.* The book struggles with and includes all the other diversities that surfaced in the
1980s, but remains completely within a Western context, despite
the fact that serious feminist movements had developed in non-
Western religions by then. In my view, the single greatest weakness
of feminist thinking about religion at the beginning of its third decade is that so much of it is primarily Western, and even primarily
Christian.

I believe that feminist scholarship and theology should be genuinely cross-cultural, not limited to familiar Western religions and
their precursors in the Ancient Near East or pre-Christian Europe.
Understanding diversity *among* religions is at least as important as
understanding diversity *within* religions. Nor is such knowledge
always only knowledge of another. Images and symbols from other
cultures can be taken seriously by feminist theologians trying to re-

flect upon and reenvision their own religious and spiritual positions, whether as Christians, Jews, or spiritual feminists. Of all the calls to affirm and appreciate diversity, the call for genuine, serious cross-cultural interreligious study and thinking in feminist theology and scholarship has been the least heeded.

In the late 1980s, however, several anthologies were published that presented information about women and religion globally and in cross-cultural perspective. Of particular note are four volumes edited by Arvind Sharma: *Women in World Religions* (1987), which describes the roles of women in each of the major world religions; *Today's Woman in World Religions* (1994), which presents information about the current situation in each of the religions discussed in the earlier book; *Religion and Women* (1994), which presents information about the smaller religions not included in the first volume; and a forthcoming volume on feminist transformations of those religions. Another helpful resource is Serinity Young's painstaking collection of primary texts, *An Anthology of Sacred Texts by and about Women* (1993).

In addition to such women studies scholarship, feminist analyses and reconstructions of the world's religions are also beginning to appear. More recent anthologies on women and world religions are more likely to be feminist analyses than to be information-gathering exercises. Leonard Grob, Riffat Hassan, and Haim Gordon's *Women's and Men's Liberation* (1991) and Paula Cooey, William Eakin, and Jay McDaniel's *After Patriarchy: Feminist Transformations of the World Religions* (1991) were the first such feminist anthologies. More important, feminist analysts from major religions, such as Buddhism, Islam, and Hinduism, are beginning to publish and become better known. Fatima Mernissi's *The Veil and the Male Elite: A Feminist Interpretation of Women's Rights in Islam*, published in 1987 and translated into English in 1991, discusses how to argue for women's rights in a Muslim context. Another Muslim feminist is Riffat Hassan, who has taken up the topic of reinterpreting the Qur'an from a feminist point of view.[34] Lina Gupta and Vasuda Narayan have emerged as feminist interpreters of Hinduism.[35] In the case of Buddhism, my book *Buddhism after Patriarchy* (1993) is the first book-length feminist discussion of the religion as a whole, and Anne Klein's *Meeting the Great Bliss Queen* (1994) brings Buddhism and poststructuralist feminist theory into conversation with one another. Little feminist analysis of the East Asian religions—Confucianism, Taoism, or Shinto—has been done in English to date.

This literature is framed somewhat by Western definitions of feminist concerns and orientations. However, women's movements, which are far less well known and much more difficult to document, are found in other major world religions. They are smaller and less well defined than those found in Christianity and Judaism. Though they are quite varied, they tend to differ from the Western women's movements in some significant ways.

First, most want to create their own feminism rather than simply imitate the Western varieties, which many feel are inappropriate for their specific situations. For example, Muslim and many other Asian feminists do not see the Western tendency toward separatism—some women's desire to separate themselves from men as much as possible—as at all desirable and want to promote a kind of feminism that will not be detrimental to their relationships with men or encourage what they see as the destructive breakdown of family life in the Western world. Instead, they tend to emphasize education and the ability to work outside the home. But many Western scholars who have studied the effects of these changes note a problem familiar to Western women: As women move into the workforce, they still are expected to do all the tasks of housekeeping and child rearing that constituted their traditional work.

A second difference from Western feminism is that in some countries, especially India, men were early leaders in a movement to improve the lives of women.[36] Finally, women's movements in other major religions are closely intertwined with secular women's movements, and often the women's movement appears superficially to have more to do with secular than with religious issues. Therefore, one does not usually find the same kind of religious work, such as feminist reenvisioning of the major religious doctrines, in Asian traditions.

Because Buddhism has become a religion of choice for many Westerners, its women's movement has developed differently from those in many other non-Western religions. Beginning with the conference on women and Buddhism held at Naropa Institute in Boulder, Colorado, in 1981, Buddhist women have gathered regularly both in North America and in Asia. A historic gathering of Buddhist nuns from all over the world was held in 1987 in Bodh Gaya, India, the site of the Buddha's enlightenment; it was followed by an equally historic worldwide gathering of Buddhist women, both monastic and lay, in Bangkok, Thailand, in 1991. Since then such international Buddhist women's conferences have been held every two years.

Out of these conferences has come an international organization for Buddhist women, Sakyadhita, which publishes a quarterly newsletter. Two other important newsletters of the Buddhist women's movement have emerged: *Kahawaii: A Journal of Women and Zen* was published in Hawaii from 1979 through 1988, and the *Newsletter on International Buddhist Women's Activities* has been edited by Chatsumarn Kabilsingh in Bangkok since 1984. In the Buddhist women's movement, restoring ordination of nuns in those segments of Buddhism in which it has been lost as well as upgrading the status and treatment of nuns have been important issues; Buddhist women, especially in the Western world, are also concerned with the full range of feminist issues.

In India, as in almost every other part of the world, the nineteenth century saw the beginnings of a women's movement. During the colonial era, the British often justified their rule of India by claiming that Indian men oppressed Indian women. A vigorous Hindu reform movement, led by men, responded by improving the status of women; child marriage and suttee (a widow's suicide on her husband's funeral pyre) were abolished, and women were educated in basic literacy.[37] During the Indian independence movement of the 1930s and 1940s, women were quite visible, and the Indian constitution and laws are quite liberal (though they are not always enforced today). Women's issues receive significant attention in some circles in India today. The magazine *Manushi: A Journal about Women and Society*, which has been published since 1978, is especially important. Its editor rejects the label "feminist," but that label is still often applied to the magazine. Currently, Hindu society is in upheaval, and the growing Hindu fundamentalist movement could have negative implications for women.

In the more specifically religious sphere in India, women's roles have been changing dramatically in some ways. For the first time, women are functioning as religious gurus and initiating disciples. Although Hinduism has not traditionally encouraged women to become world renouncers, today, according to some analysts, women ascetics are seen as the bearers and proclaimers of Hindu spirituality.[38] A significant number of male gurus and teachers have passed their spiritual lineage and authority on to women, something which would not have occurred in the past. Katherine K. Young also points out that the key to religious expertise has traditionally resided in knowledge of Sanskrit, which was once guarded as a male (and upper-caste) privilege. But today many women study Sanskrit in universities as men abandon it for more lucrative fields. "When the current generation of Sanskrit male priests and ritual experts dies, the next generation may have to be women if they alone possess the expertise."[39]

Islamic societies have likewise known women's movements for some decades, beginning with strong secular feminist movements in the 1920s. Today, however, as fundamentalism becomes an ever-

stronger force in Islamic societies, there is mounting pressure to retain or return to traditional gender relationships. Islamic critics of
feminism see women's rights movements as inappropriate incur-
sions of Western influence, even when such movements seek only
to restore rights that women have under Islamic law, but which
they have not been exercising. In Islamic societies, religious law derived from the Qur'an (the Muslim sacred revealed text) is the basis
for treatment of women and for relationships between men and
women. Those who defend Islamic feminism generally agree that
the problem is not with Islam as a religion or with Qur'anic teachings, but with "a patriarchy that is reinforced and perpetuated
through the fundamentalist brand of Islam."[40]

In Jane Smith's survey of the Muslim world today, she finds that
dress codes for women are important feminist issues almost everywhere, though whether women are pressured to wear traditional
modest Muslim dress or forbidden to do so differs from country to
country.[41] Education for women is also a major feminist concern.
But since traditional Muslim cultures segregate men and women,
there is no consensus over what kinds of jobs women can have, or
even whether they can be educated with men. (Saudi Arabia has
separate university systems for women and men.) Regarding specifically religious issues, it does not appear that there is any great
move for women to seek traditional religious educations, or for
women to take the public religious roles usually filled by men.

The strongest cultural force in East Asia, Confucianism is generally thought to be quite patriarchal. But today Confucianism has
been challenged on many fronts, not the least of which is the Communist movement of modern China. One of the stated goals of the
Communist Party in China was to end "the oppression and suffering which economic and social systems sustained by the traditional
'Confucian' ideology caused women."[42] The title of Margery Wolf's
book *Revolution Postponed: Women in Contemporary China* ex-
presses well the conclusions of most analyses as to how well the

Communist Party succeeded in these goals.[43] Add to this the fact that from 1949 to 1980, religious groups were "simply unable to foster the religious lives of their members,"[44] and it will come as no surprise that there is not a large women's movement in religion in contemporary China. However, two of China's classic religions, Buddhism and Taoism, included monastic orders for women that gave women significant autonomy and respect. Elderly monastics of both groups did manage to survive and today are allowed to initiate some novices and pay more attention to their spiritual practices than formerly. Today, many more young women are asking to become monastics than the institutions can accommodate.[45]

Taiwan has changed in very different ways during this same period, since traditional religion, especially Confucianism, has been encouraged at the same time that rapid economic growth has fostered the kinds of changes in women's lives that are often brought about by modernization—education, wage labor, and fewer children. Some Taiwanese feminist intellectuals have written vigorous critiques of Confucianism.[46] Buddhist temples and monasteries are flourishing, and large numbers of well-educated young women are becoming nuns. In addition, Chinese folk religion or popular religion is flourishing in Taiwan; these folk religions have always offered women some leadership roles and continue to do so.[47]

In Japan, the Confucian value system is much less overt, though no less pervasive. The traditional religions, Buddhism and Shinto, have not offered women roles of religious leadership for centuries, though some scholars think that in prehistoric Japan, women held positions of authority. Japanese Buddhism did not develop the strong nuns' orders that were found in China and Korea, and both Shinto and Buddhist priesthoods were largely closed to women. The twentieth century has seen some changes in all these areas. During World War II, while many Shinto and Buddhist priests were in the army, their wives took over most or all of their duties at their family-owned temples. After the war ended, some wives continued these duties, so that quietly and somewhat informally, women became priests in both religions. On the other hand, the more formally trained nuns of the Soto Zen sect of Japanese Buddhism waged a long and difficult battle with the Soto Zen hierarchy for the right to study and teach in the traditional Soto Zen style. It took them many years of struggle to achieve their aims—and when they did, ironically, they found that the priests' wives now could also carry on many of the same leadership roles with far less training.[48] A final avenue for women's religious leadership is in the new religions that have been so successful in Japan, particularly since the end of World War II. In fact, many of these movements, such as Tenri-Kyo, the oldest and most successful, were founded by women. Though they usually teach a somewhat traditional message concerning women's status and roles, many women derive a great deal of satisfaction from their participation and leadership in these movements.

I will conclude this survey of the impact of feminism on religion with the immense topic of the various indigenous traditions around the world. Since they are not patriarchal, at least not in the same way that the major world religions are, the question of a women's movement is complex. The complexity is increased by the fact that many native traditions are in a fragile state of recovery after centuries of colonialist persecution and missionary activities. It is very difficult to recover and to reform a tradition at the same time; many of those most involved in recovery of these traditions do not feel at liberty to advocate changes to include women if they were formerly excluded. Nevertheless, changes do occur. For example, among a Lakota group with which I am familiar, women now routinely participate in the sweat ceremony and in the Sun Dance, though their participation in the past was rare. However, the menstrual taboos are also stringently enforced, so that, although women may participate in the Sun Dance, and even pierce their skin as men do (though in the upper arms, not the chest),[49] a menstruating woman cannot even camp in the Sun Dance grounds.

Other women in indigenous traditions, such as Native American feminist Paula Gunn Allen, claim that the native traditions were and are matrifocal, and that women's leadership was one of the aspects of native culture that European colonizers most abhorred and sought to exterminate. She describes "woman-centered tribal societies in which matrilocality, matrifocality, matrilinearity, maternal control of household goods and resources, and female deities of the magnitude of the Christian God were and are present and active features of traditional tribal life."[50] For native societies in which such conditions prevail, a women's movement would obviously be more involved in recovering the tradition than reforming it.

In any case, the lives of indigenous peoples are often made more complex by a strained relationship between the native religions and the dominant cultures. For example, in the United States, native traditions have been immensely inspiring both to some feminist spirituality groups and to the New Age movement. But many native peoples regard this appropriation as theft or misrepresentation of their spiritual traditions. Other teachers disagree, feeling a responsibility to share their wisdom with all seekers and even to encourage sincere non-native people to adopt tribal ways. Some native women have particularly encouraged women of European ancestry to take seriously the ways and the wisdom of aboriginal American traditions regarding women's unique physiology and lifeways.[51]

CHAPTER THREE

Where Have All the Women Been ?
The Challenge of
Feminist Study of Religion

RELIGION IS NOT ONLY an abstract set of ideas but also something *practiced* by people, half of whom are women. But, given that all cultures have gender roles, religion affects women differently than men. What have women's religious lives, roles, and images been like? Until recently, that subject matter was *terra incognita* in textbooks and was rarely discussed even in academic settings. But, as we have seen, if scholarship is to be accurate, such practices are clearly unacceptable. The remedy seems obvious—add information about women to the already existing information about men. But the solution is not really that simple. What information about women should be added? Is it really possible to treat knowledge about women as a simple add-on? When we say we want to know about women and religion, what are we seeking to know? What else changes when we know about women and religion?

This chapter will explore some of the barriers, challenges, and conclusions that arise when one attempts to study women and religion in global perspective. In most discussions of feminism and religion, such topics are relatively underdeveloped because, on the one hand, few feminists study religion globally in cross-cultural perspective, and, on the other hand, few scholars of comparative religion use feminist methods.

Barriers to the Feminist Study of Religion

Two obstacles may appear to stand in the way of those who want to study religion from an androgynous perspective. First, many believe that the necessary data about women's lives and roles are not available. As we have seen in the last chapter, although much feminist work has been accomplished in the last three decades, much more needs to be done. But in fact, in many cases, as I know from my own research, the scholar working with an androgynous model of humanity will find much information about women *in already existing androcentric scholarship*, even without new translations or fieldwork. That information has been either largely overlooked or interpreted as evidence that women are unimportant, minor participants in a male-dominant society. This belief is the second obstacle to feminist religious scholarship.

My own work, especially on aboriginal Australia, convinces me that these barriers simply do not hold up. There had been almost no systematic study of women in aboriginal Australian religion when I did my research in the 1960s, but when I studied the existing androcentric scholarship, I found enormous amounts of information about women. I also found endless repetitions of the thesis that women are regarded as profane and have no religious lives worth mentioning. However, reading the same sources with an androgynous model of humanity guiding my selection and evaluation of data, I found no actual support for that thesis despite its reiteration. Instead, I found that, although women are prohibited from participation in men's religious ceremonies, this prohibition stems not from an evaluation that they are profane rather than sacred, but from a belief that their mode of sacred being and that of the men cannot be mixed indiscriminately. Women function as mythic and symbolic models for the men's sacred ceremonies; they also have an extensive religious life of their own, from which men are rigidly excluded.[1] A later field-based anthropological discussion of aboriginal women verifies many of the reconstructions I had suggested and contradicts none.[2] However, its author, who was obviously using androgynous methods, reports that some of her mentors were incredulous about her findings.

What Is Important?—An Androgynous Perspective

Scholars doing feminist religious scholarship often encounter some version of the "great works" thesis: that women cannot be included in scholarship about religion because they do not participate in the society's most important religious events, ideas, and practices. The flaw in this position is best seen by hearing what it sounds like when said in the context of a foreign society. One commonly reads descriptions of religious events that affirm that a certain ceremony is so important that it must be attended by all—"except women and children." I didn't question these kinds of statements for years, but now I wonder how important the ceremony can be if only significantly less than half the society is involved. One must also ask *who* interpreted this ceremony as important despite its exclusion of women and children. Perhaps the society itself operates with androcentric consciousness, declaring this to be an important ceremony *because* of the fact that women and children are not involved. Or the interpretation may reflect the scholar's own androcentric values instead.

When the subject of study is the world's major religions, it is easy to make similar arguments: that since all the important and influential religious thinkers and leaders were men, the study of women is of lesser importance. For generations, such reasoning prevailed in academia. But feminist historians have begun to make a very strong case that the *choice* of what is interesting or important may already be influenced by androcentric and elitist values. *Why* are kings, wars, popes, and parliaments more interesting or important than ordinary people, peace, mystics, and domestic technology? For example, Eleanor McLaughlin suggests that historians of

Christianity might well temper their interest in the history of theology and of church institutions, which is all I remember learning about in my graduate church history courses, with study of the world of spirituality. "In this world of spirituality . . . *women* are found who speak and write, who made history and shaped a tradition."[3] Men do dominate the history of theology and of church institutions. But it is a *judgment* and a *choice,* rather than an objective datum, to conclude that these subjects are what one should study in the history of Christianity.

Or, to move to the world of Hindu observance, why are women's private vows and fasts less interesting and important than temple rituals conducted by men or Hindu men's philosophies? Certainly in terms of formal authority, Hinduism is a male-dominated religion. Nevertheless, Hindu women practice complex and fascinating rituals apart from the men, completely undercutting the stereotype of Hindu women as powerless adjuncts of men with almost no religious role. Yet these women's rituals were completely unreported in scholarship about Hinduism until recently.[4]

The perception that women are not interesting or important stems from the value androcentric scholarship places on formal hierarchical authority. By focusing heavily on those who wield such power, a good deal is missed. Specifically androcentric scholarship misses the *power* women may have in situations in which they have little *authority,* as in the Hindu case just discussed. The anthropological distinction between authority (which is public and formal) and power (which is informal and often not publicly acknowledged) is necessary to avoid seeing women in patriarchal religion only as powerless.

Another way in which traditional scholarship obscures the importance of women is that it is ill equipped to understand religions that display neither egalitarianism, in the sense that all aspects of religion are available to both men and women, nor male dominance, in the sense that men control all or most aspects of religion.

As is the case for much of aboriginal Australia, separate realms of power and concern more accurately describe power relationships between women and men in many religions. Traditional scholarship has often responded by recording the men's religion but not the women's, making women's separate and different religious lives seem invisible or unimportant.

Some of the most famous examples of religious complementarity involve West African societies in which women and men honored two parallel sets of royalty, surrounded by elaborate ritual in each case. These women had real power and authority in their societies.[5] On a less grandiose scale, the example of a Bolivian indigenous group is instructive. These people live at the various levels of Mount Kaata, growing crops suitable to the various elevations and herding animals at the top level. Men, who always remain in the locations in which they were born, symbolize the stable mountain. Therefore, male ritual leaders specialize in establishing and stabilizing good fortune. Women, on the other hand, flow up and down the mountain, marrying away from their communities of origin. They are associated symbolically with the rivers, which also flow. Furthermore, Kaatans are also keenly aware of menstrual flow from women's bodies, which is said to cleanse women from misfortune. Therefore, female ritual leaders specialize in rituals of removing bad luck and restoring wholeness.[6] Many other societies in Africa and North America also display such complementarity, which is almost always misinterpreted as male dominance in androcentric scholarship.

Even for the more numerous male-dominated societies, androgynous study of religion is no less necessary. No matter how male dominated a society may be, it also includes female members. How women react to such male dominance is an important and interesting issue. Often conventional interpretations find male dominance to be more complete than is the case. If the researcher talks only with men, he may indeed gain the impression that men are in complete control, but a more balanced set of informants usually provides a different picture. The case is nowhere clearer than for traditional Hinduism, a religion whose texts affirm male dominance very strongly and in which most public aspects of religion are in male control. Nevertheless, women have a rich, well-developed, and largely female set of religious practices that involve no male participation or control. In Islam, a religion that appears to be even more male dominated from its texts and its public face, similar practices are found in some areas.[7]

Studying a male-dominated religion through an androgynous lens gives insight into another limit to formal male dominance. Women do not necessarily believe the males' stereotypes about them or fulfill male expectations for their behavior. In one humorous example from Iranian Islam, it is reported that on one occasion a female preacher at an all-female ceremony had told her audience that "any woman who did not make love with her husband when he wanted to would be hung by her breasts in hell." One of the women to whom this was reported replied, "If a man doesn't make love with his wife when she wants to, what do they hang him by?" Others were worried that the foreign anthropologist among them would get the wrong impression of Islam from such comments.[8] Equally instructive is the comment of an illiterate, poor Muslim Iranian village woman in a cultural context of extreme male dominance. "She thought that religion, as preached and practiced, was not made by God but by men in order to suppress women! God himself had meant men and women to be equal."[9]

At stake is the sometimes unrecognized assumption that what women do is intrinsically less interesting and less important than what men do. The androgynous paradigm demands that scholars be interested in women and what they do in the same way that we have always been interested in what men have done and thought.[10] Fortunately, once we concede that androgynous scholarship is necessary, most scholars discover that women are actually much more interesting to study and much more important in the society than was imagined by scholars working under androcentric models. This is the case even for the societies that seem most male dominated and patriarchal, such as those of the Middle East, about which a great number of androgynous analyses have been written.[11] Perhaps this judgment is also part of the inevitably value-laden character of scholarship. After all, at present, most scholars using androgynous methods and models are also feminists, and many are women. And most of the scholars who find studying women uninteresting or unimportant are not feminists, and many are men. The standpoint of the scholar does affect the scholarship and does influence what is seen as interesting and important.

An Accurate and Usable Past

Feminist scholars of religious history face an even greater challenge than feminist scholars of contemporary religion. New fieldwork will not answer their questions; they must rely on the historical record. Sometimes information about women's experiences and roles simply can't be found for a particular historical context. At other times, the problems of recovering women's voices are immense, as I discovered in doing historical research on women in Buddhism. Often only androcentrically colored information about women's roles and images, as viewed by men, can be recovered. If information about women is almost totally absent, the historian has another obligation. The omissions in the historical record can and should be pointed out and explained. This information would allow the reader at least to know what isn't known, as well as what would need to be known to give a reasonably accurate portrait of the historical materials being studied. It would also remind the reader that women need to be included in any adequate study.

Because what is recorded as history is always a *selection* from the myriad events that occurred in the past, the discipline of history is not purely objective. Every historian makes choices about who and what should be remembered for what reasons. As in the study of contemporary religions, many conventional historians are most interested in those who wielded power, which means that not only women, but other disempowered groups have been left out of many historical records. Thus the attempt to create androgynous history is only part of a much larger project to write the poor and ethnic or racial minorities back into history.

As I have analyzed in another context,[12] a quadruple androcentrism colors and limits much historical scholarship. First, in most religious traditions, those who kept that tradition's records chose to record men's experiences and thinking much more frequently than women's. Second, even when information about women was recorded, later commentators often neglected to keep those records alive in communal consciousness and memory. Third, when contemporary academic scholars study the history of a religious tradition, they usually focus on what the tradition itself has emphasized—the records of its male heroes. Finally, many, if not most, contemporary practitioners within that tradition are ignorant of the history of women in their tradition and, perhaps relatedly, are hostile to feminist scholarship about the tradition.

Despite these obstacles, scholars attempting to record and interpret androgynous history can do a great deal. Feminist historians of religion face the same basic methodological issues that all historians should deal with self-consciously: Whom are we remembering, and for what purposes? As an overarching guideline, one could say that feminist history is about finding a record of the past that is both *accurate* and *usable*. Though these essential goals are interdependent, they are distinct, especially within the discipline of religion. Discovering the "accurate" past is part of the agenda of the descriptive scholar, whereas determining the "usability" of that past has more to do with the work of the constructive commentator who wants to transform her tradition in accord with feminist values.

The subtle balance attained in a historical record that is both accurate and usable has been clearly delineated by Eleanor McLaughlin, writing about medieval Christian history. She claims that we need to write history that is

> *at once* responsible—*that is, grounded in the historicist rubric of dealing with the past on its own terms—and* usable. *I mean by the search for a usable past . . . an . . . examination of history with a new set of questions that arise out of commitments to wholeness for women and for all humanity. Following from new questions, this is a history that redresses omissions and recasts interpretations.*[13]

The concept of a "usable past" would not be admitted as legitimate by many conventional historians, who believe that historical accounts can be objective and neutral and that the scholar's standpoint does not affect scholarship. But since objectivity and neutrality prove to be impossible ideals, as we saw in chapter one, historical accounts are always put to some use. Feminist historians are not the only scholars who study history with specific objectives in mind. Peace advocates, environmentalists, economic historians, and others all probe the past, hoping to discover the causes and conditions that lead to more or less destructive policies. Androcentric histories, whether their authors intend them to or not, foster the impression that male dominance is normal, appropriate, omnipresent, and unalterable, and they discourage questions about or challenges to contemporary gender norms.

Questions about a usable past are especially critical in religious studies because of the ways in which history is typically used by religious communities. Religious communities constitute themselves in the present at least in part through their collective memory, the past that is ritually recalled, celebrated, and emulated. The religious significance of its remembered past to a religious community cannot be overestimated, especially for Western religions.

Therefore, it makes a great deal of difference whether a religious community remembers and celebrates its patriarchal past or its androgynous past.

Androgynous history can empower previously disempowered segments of the community. However, most scholars would argue that this usable past must, at the same time, be accurate. That is to say, one cannot, in the interests of empowering disempowered segments of the human community, construct a *desirable*, rather than an *accurate*, past. That some feminists construct such a desirable past for which they cannot provide convincing historical evidence is a charge leveled against some feminists who reconstruct early religion, as we shall see in chapter five.

A commitment to surveying the past with concern for women's history could be fulfilled by studying a number of subjects. Does one study history to document misogyny and patriarchy as the history of women? Or does one study history to find the many great women who have simply been buried by androcentric traditions of memory? Or are both these questions still androcentric in their form?

When studying the history of the world's religions, it is not difficult to find a history of misogyny and patriarchy. In fact, that is perhaps the easiest history to find because cultural beliefs about women were widely recorded in religious literature written by men, as we shall see later in this chapter. Therefore, some of the earliest histories of women in religion were collections of misogynist writings, such as Julia O'Faolain and Lauro Martines's *Not in God's Image: Women in History from the Greeks to the Victorians* (1973) or Vern L. Bullough's *The Subordinate Sex: A History of Attitudes toward Women* (1974). It is important to retain knowledge of that history and to remind people that such history happened. On the other hand, the study of women cannot end there, for misogyny is not the whole story of any religion. As Eleanor McLaughlin puts it:

My historical judgement and theological understanding tell me it is unlikely that the Christian tradition has been unrelievedly destructive of only one half of humanity. Accordingly, I ask whether, in addition to the negative image of woman and the male image of God, the tradition holds ideals or moments of realization of human wholeness.[14]

After acknowledging the depths of misogyny and patriarchy found in religious history and coming to terms with the resulting shock and anger, most feminist historians seek the rest of the picture, the "ideals or moments of realization of human wholeness." An accurate past certainly includes such moments, and only the most thoroughgoing skeptic would say that every moment of the past is utterly useless because those moments coexist with patriarchy and misogyny.

A second frequently used approach to women's history is to look for great women in history who have been overlooked. Certainly one can find them, as many publications in the last fifteen years attest.[15] But though no feminist historian wants to deny or downgrade their achievements, a cautionary note is also important. As I wrote when dealing with such figures in Buddhist history:

These stories, neglected by androcentrists, are inspiring and should be brought into the record. However, though these stories are highly useful, their utility is also limited. These women are heroines, but they are also tokens in an androcentric and patriarchal past. We need to know about and celebrate our heroines and role models, but on the other hand it is important not to overcompensate by making more of them than is justified. They can also be used against us. . . . I often encounter the statement that, since some women have been acknowledged as enlightened beings by Buddhist tradition, Buddhism is not sexist or patriarchal and feminism is irrelevant to Buddhism.[16]

In addition to discovering these heroines, it is important, whenever possible, to recover ordinary women's religious lives throughout history. Such history is difficult to reconstruct, but reading between the lines of the historical record to discover the religious lives of both extraordinary and ordinary women is a discipline that is alive and well.

Finally, it is also necessary to rewrite the history of *thought* to include forgotten contributions by women and forgotten female imagery. Many now-forgotten writers in many traditions used images and concepts that may well prove useful to a feminist trying to reconstruct her tradition. For example, the existence of biblical imagery of deity as feminine, noted by Elizabeth Cady Stanton among others, is a well-kept secret, unnoticed and left out of dozens of conventional discussions of the Bible.[17] Medieval mystics routinely envisioned both God and Christ as female and mother.[18] Many more examples exist. Could these images and concepts have been forgotten or suppressed for the very reason that they are too profeminist? One of the best examples of writing that uses these intellectual resources is Rosemary Ruether's *Sexism and God-Talk: Toward a Feminist Theology* (1983). This book is particularly exemplary because it uses both nontraditional resources and more mainstream understandings of basic Christian doctrines to construct a feminist theology.

What Difference Does It Make?

Feminist scholars often discover that information about women cannot simply be added to the picture they already have. *In almost all cases, they discover that they have to repaint the whole picture,* which may be why many scholars resist the paradigm shift from androcentrism to androgyny. It is much more troublesome to repaint the picture than merely to fill in some details in a blank corner of the canvas.

To detail only one example, I am convinced that the standard model for organizing the Hindu pantheon reflects an androcentric outlook on the part of both Hindus and scholars of Hinduism. Many Hindus tell scholars that their religious mythology revolves around a trinity composed of god the creator, god the preserver, and god the destroyer—all male deities. But the creator god Brahma has not been widely worshipped for centuries, and today most of his functions are associated with Vishnu, god the preserver. Because this Hindu model of the pantheon does not describe contemporary practice, most scholars of Hinduism and some Hindus suggest a different trinity—Vishnu, who is god the preserver, Shiva who is god the destroyer, and the goddess, whose title covers a multitude of female deities lumped together. The deities are always presented in this order, and in almost all cases, the number of pages or lines devoted to each decreases with each deity. Thus, all the goddesses together come in as a poor third, seemingly a minor phenomenon that can be quickly discussed. This model of the pantheon is repeated in virtually every introductory account of Hinduism.

But this model of the pantheon simply does not describe Hindu theism as one would encounter it in most contexts. The goddesses are not faceless duplicates interchangeable with one another but highly distinctive individuals, just like the male deities. Each of the major goddesses needs to be named and described, and her distinctive attributes and stories should be detailed. In addition, it is misleading to present the goddesses in a few pages at the end of a discussion of Hindu deities. Goddesses are extremely popular and omnipresent; if anything, in practice one encounters them more frequently than male deities, which would suggest that they should be discussed first and in greater detail. Perhaps one of the best-kept secrets in comparative religion is that Hinduism, the only major polytheistic world religion, is also the only one that worships female deities as a central aspect of its expression.

Finally, rather than a trinity of deities, the more frequent Hindu image presents a divine couple, female and male (though each deity in the couple also functions independently in Hindu myth and ritual, and not all goddesses are paired with male deities). Many such divine couples, endowed with many different symbolisms and specializations, are commonplace. In fact, each of the three male deities in the trinity referred to above also has a consort who is an important goddess in her own right. It might be more accurate to refer to the three *couples* basic to the Hindu pantheon, rather than to the Hindu trinity, if the trinitarian model is retained.[19]

Many other examples show the way in which androgynous scholarship can foster an entirely different picture of a given subject. As discussed at the beginning of this chapter, I found in my own work on aboriginal Australian religions that many common generalizations simply did not stand up under androgynous analysis of the materials. Feminist biblical scholars have convincingly shown that many standard, longstanding interpretations of key biblical passages are the result of an androcentric reading of the text.[20] I have already mentioned Eleanor McLaughlin's challenge to redefine the relevant subject matter of church history. Within the closely allied discipline of anthropology, the shift from androcentrism to androgyny has demolished the hypothesis that "man the hunter" was solely responsible for human evolution, as was widely taught in the 1950s and 1960s.[21] This development brought significant changes in how primate behavior is used to hypothesize human evolution and early human behavior.[22] Recently, Nancy Jay, using feminist methods to study the extremely male-dominated phenomenon of ritual sacrifice, has suggested a new theory of sacrifice.[23] This list of examples could be extended easily.

In sum, probably every aspect of religious studies *is thoroughly recast*, not just supplemented, by feminist scholarship. Thus, scholarship using the androgynous model of humanity is critical not only for *completeness* but also for *accuracy* of scholarship. Without this paradigm shift, not only will we not have all the relevant data—we will not have accurate methods for organizing, understanding, and interpreting the data that we do have. Therefore, we will arrive at false or partial hypotheses regarding these phenomena. So major issues are at stake in the call to study what women have done and thought.

Finding the Subject Matter and Defining the Issues

In the early days of androgynous scholarship on women and religion, one of the most difficult questions was what subject matter we wanted to study. In the early days, we were often expected to look into androcentric cultural stereotypes *about* women, investigating textual statements about women, for example, or determining why women's involvement in religion was so limited. We were expected to continue the prevailing androcentric methods of scholarship and understandings of women.

Among these, the most common was the thesis that women's low status, passivity, and lack of involvement in religion were due to the fact that "male is to female as culture is to nature."[24] Advocates of this thesis claimed that men need to create meaning culturally through religious symbol, myth, and ritual, whereas women, identified with their biology, find it sufficient to live out a natural, biologically dictated life plan. Thus, for example, it was commonly claimed that male initiation ceremonies are more elaborate than female initiations because the onset of menstruation makes female maturity obvious, whereas male maturity is less obvious; what is not clearly given in nature must be created by culture. Furthermore, all goddesses were assumed to be mother goddesses, since femaleness was understood as a biological, natural category rather than a culturally created symbol, and maternity was taken to be a female's distinctive biological function and destiny.

These prevailing assumptions were never convincing to many of us, but stating why and coming up with alternatives was not easy. Unfortunately, we had been so thoroughly socialized into the androcentric outlook by our previous academic and cultural training that it was difficult to articulate what we wanted to study, despite our frustration with the models and norms presented to us.

As women seeking graduate degrees in a highly male-dominated field, the process of survival had made us so male-identified that we had become largely inarticulate as women.

Twenty-five years later, it seems unbelievable that it was so hard to articulate that we wanted to study *women*, not just cultural norms and expectations *about* women. We wanted to study women as *subjects*, not merely as objects in an androcentric world construction. We wanted to evaluate critically, from an female-identified, androgynous point of view, the many cultural norms and stereotypes about women that are so widely reported in cross-cultural and historical studies. Equally, we wanted scholars to understand that questions about women are not adequately answered with data detailing cultural stereotypes, roles, and images of women, even though that material is an important part of the information being sought. Finally, if and when we studied goddesses, we did not want to perpetuate the impression that questions about women could be answered with information about goddesses. Equally, we wanted goddesses to be investigated as distinct entities, and we wanted them to be studied as seriously as were their male counterparts, rather than being regarded as exotic and primitive.

Today it is clear that an androgynous account of religion must include information about all three areas we struggled to define. Such accounts must include descriptions of women's lives and consciousness, of their own experience of the religious context in which they live. Such accounts must also include the cultural stereotypes and norms made about women or femininity in any religious context, especially investigating the consonance or discontinuity between those norms and people's actual lives. Finally, such accounts must describe the female personalities populating the mythological universe fully and accurately, without androcentric projections, expectations, or stereotypes. These three subject areas within the broad topic of women and religion are, of course, intertwined, mutually affecting one another. Nevertheless, I will deal with each area separately here. Androcentric scholarship often seriously blurs the boundaries between these three topics and has overlooked the most important questions.

Women's Religious Lives

Feminist scholarship stresses and requires, first and foremost, the study of the *actual* lives and thoughts of women. Cultural stereotypes and normative laws *about* women are no substitute for information about what women actually do and think. We need to know what religious practices women engage in, whether with men or apart from them. We need to know, whenever possible, what these activities mean to women, how women explain and understand what they are doing. We need to know how women perceive and cope with the inferior status to which they are often assigned. We need to know how they are socialized into their roles and the extent to which they accept those roles or silently protest them. We need to know how women leaders are chosen, how their perceptions differ from or agree with those of other women, and how they interact with men. We need to know how women's experience and understanding of a religious tradition may deviate from or be consonant with men's understanding of that same tradition. In short, we need to study women as religious subjects in their own right, not merely as objects in the religious universes of men.

When one takes this task as one's primary goal, as Nancy Auer Falk and I did when editing *Unspoken Worlds*, some patterns in women's religious lives become apparent. The most obvious generalization that leaps from the materials, which partially explains why this material has been so overlooked in androcentric scholarship, is the silence, the often nonverbal and almost always nontextual context of women's spirituality. (The word *unspoken* in the title derives from that fact.) For the most part, women have had little to do with the textual traditions of the great world religions, the aspect of religion in which Western academic scholars have been most interested. If a scholar does not look at nontextual dimensions of a religious tradition, he will see little evidence of women's religious lives.

A related observation is that in many cases, women's religious lives seem to emphasize performance more than theory. Women act religiously to take charge of certain situations; they do not always explain, even to themselves, what they are doing or why they do it. Even if they do, often men, both the men of their own culture and scholarly researchers, do not accept what they say, fueling the impression that women have insignificant religious lives. Learning to ask the right questions and to listen carefully for the often unexpected answers have been critical to feminist methodology.

Several other generalizations about women's religious lives are notable. First, religious experience appears to have two widely contrasting effects on women's lives. On the one hand, religion can validate women's ordinary domestic roles, sometimes powerfully comforting them even in highly patriarchal contexts. This possibility has often been overlooked by feminists. On the other hand, religious experiences, often compelling and disruptive, can pull women away from their usual activities into more unusual roles as nuns, leaders, healers, shamans, and founders of new movements. Although the priesthood and textual studies are often reserved for men, charismatic and spiritual movements *within* traditions have rarely been successfully closed off to women.

Second, whether religious experience encourages women to follow ordinary domestic roles or calls women into extraordinary roles of leadership, women experience vastly different levels of support and approval from their traditions. Sometimes ordinary women following domestic pursuits experience a great deal of religious support and approval, but sometimes established religion provides little more than negative stereotypes and criticism.[25] When religious experience calls women into extraordinary roles, their tradition is often ambivalent about their new status. Sometimes, as in the case of contemporary Hindu women gurus, they are widely accepted once they make the transition from ordinary member to unusual leader. In other cases, such as the ancient Indian order of Buddhist nuns, their initial success was followed by decline, as Buddhists supported monks more readily than nuns. Nor do we always find the same attitudes everywhere within a religious tradition; some Islamic, Hindu, and Christian contexts strongly support women, whereas others manifest overwhelming misogyny. Clearly, generalizations about entire religious traditions are inadequate when investigating women's religious lives.

Because it is relatively difficult to do, investigation of women's religious lives lags behind other aspects of androgynous scholarship in religion. However, many brilliant and provocative monographs on the religious lives of individual women or of women in very specific situations have been published in the past two decades. The work of Karen McCarthy Brown on a Haitian Vodou priestess in Brooklyn, of Diane Bell on aboriginal Australian women, of Erika Friedl on Iranian tribal Muslim women, and Kathleen M. Erndl on women and goddess worship in northwest India, are only a few of the most notable examples of such work.[26]

Cultural Norms about Women

Despite the importance of studying the religious lives of actual women in androgynous scholarship, the temptation to slip from discussing women's lives to discussing views and opinions about women is almost irresistible. In fact, in my own work on Buddhism,[27] despite my desire to study women's experience, I was able, for the most part, to study only roles and images of women throughout Buddhist history. Occasional autobiographical literature allowed glimpses into women's lives, but, for the most part, I could investigate only what Buddhist men had said about women historically, not what Buddhist women had said or experienced.

Fortunately, one can learn much from studying cultural norms about women as long as they are not confused with women's subjectivity and self-consciousness.

To examine a culture's beliefs about women, one must cast a wide net. Women's prescribed roles, expectations of them, stereotypes about them, limitations placed upon them, their status relative to men, how they should behave, how they should feel, and symbols and concepts of femininity and their effect on male and female behavior are all legitimate and interesting concerns. In fact, one could rightly contend that it is impossible to study women's religious lives without also studying cultural norms about women and femininity, since women's lives will be deeply affected by those norms.

The critical task for androgynous scholarship is not collecting the data about cultural norms of women, which are plentiful and relatively accessible, but reconstructing the interpretations. Quite often, androcentric and feminist analyses of these materials will be at odds. For example, a widely known and commonly quoted assertion about proper female behavior in the traditional Hindu law code, *The Laws of Manu*, reads:

> *In childhood a female must be subject to her father, in youth to her husband, when her lord is dead to her sons: a woman must never be independent.*
>
> *Though destitute of virtue or seeking pleasure [elsewhere] or devoid of good qualities, [yet] a husband must be constantly worshipped as a god by a faithful wife.*[28]

Though often quoted in androcentric contexts as *the* Hindu view of a woman's obligations, anyone familiar with androgynous scholarship would be suspicious and would wonder whether this obviously patriarchal text gives us the entire picture. More recent fieldwork by women studying Hindu women indicates that women try to control the quality of their lives despite their culturally prescribed passivity. An Indian woman's calendar is filled with holidays and ritual observances through which she actively seeks a good, kind husband, a prosperous household, healthy offspring, and a long-lived husband.[29] She does not merely accept her passivity meekly, as *The Laws of Manu* might lead one to expect, but that was the impression many androcentric scholars were content to convey.

Systematic cross-cultural research into and reflections upon such cultural stereotypes of women and symbols of femininity utilizing androgynous methods is relatively underdeveloped. One anthology, Caroline Walker Bynum, Steven Harrell, and Paula Richman's *Gender and Religion: On the Complexity of Symbols* (1986), explores how gender-based religious symbols reflect or fail to reflect a culture's assumptions about being male or female, but much more work needs to be done before generalizations can be made.

Goddesses and Other Mythological Females

A final area for which feminist scholarship is badly needed encompasses the various mythological and theological constructs of "the feminine," popularly known as "the goddess," which are present in almost every religion in one form or another. As in the study of cultural stereotypes of women, it is often relatively easy to do research on goddesses. Many myths and texts include goddesses as central figures, and they are abundantly present in religious art. Rituals for and devotions to goddesses and other female personifications of sacred power are often extremely popular, especially with ordinary believers, both male and female.

Probably no topic of study has been more profoundly shaped and changed by feminist scholarship than goddesses and estimates of their prevalence and importance. Before the feminist paradigm shift, theologians never discussed the possibility of feminine symbols of the divine, and comparative and historical scholars of religions generally regarded goddesses as exotic, primitive, and unim-

portant. Goddesses in all religions were portrayed much as were
the Hindu goddesses already discussed; all goddesses were lumped
together as "the mother goddess." Furthermore, the individuality
of the goddesses was often not recognized or conceded.

These errors probably stemmed from a number of factors, including androcentrism. If males are considered to be the human
norm, it is not surprising that they were also the expected divine
norm. The absence of feminine divine imagery in Western culture,
home base for most comparative scholars, made goddesses seem
exotic and foreign in a way that non-Western male deities did not.
And, for the most part, goddesses are more evident in popular religion than in the classic textual traditions that had been more preferred by most Western scholars.

A generation of feminist scholarship has now erased the possibility of seeing goddesses as an aberration from the norm. More
and more people are beginning to realize that if anything needs to
be explained, it is not the presence of goddesses in almost all religious traditions, but their relative absence in the Western monotheistic traditions. On further scrutiny, it is also becoming clear
that even in monotheism, there is an undercurrent of female imagery of the divine from biblical times to the present.[30]

Yet goddess scholarship is by no means complete. At present,
the most common approach taken in published scholarship is to
make a collection of goddesses. Chapter by chapter, we hear about
different goddesses, their stories, their symbolism, sometimes the
rituals performed on their behalf. Although this approach fills
in missing information, it does little to clarify the meaning and
significance of goddesses in their specific cultural context or in
general.

India and Western antiquity offer the two richest mines for examples of goddesses, but few scholars or popular authors are conversant with both areas, which means two separate collections of
books—one on ancient Western goddesses and one on Indian god-

desses—are required to study the scope of the subject.[31] Sometimes an attempt is also made to acknowledge many feminine sacred beings in contemporary indigenous traditions, such as African or Native American traditions. East Asian goddesses are also sometimes mentioned, but scholarship on both East Asian and indigenous goddesses lags behind.

Frequently books on Western goddesses are meant to support the prepatriarchal hypothesis (to be discussed in chapter five). Because of their interest in supporting this thesis, these authors present the material in historical sequence, beginning with Paleolithic evidence and ending with the goddesses popular in the Greco-Roman religions that coexisted with early Christianity. Scholarship on Indian goddesses is less involved in political argument about the rise of patriarchy and the political consequences of the presence or absence of goddesses. Because much of it is based on contemporary fieldwork, it is also less speculative.

In addition to scholarly discussions about the history and meaning of goddesses in their ancient or foreign contexts, some feminists have begun genuine theological inquiry into the meaning goddesses might have for contemporary people. Christine Downing's courageous and provocative reflections on the Greek goddesses as myth mirrors for modern women set the standard for such thinking.[32] The entire Wiccan movement is based on goddess worship, and Wiccans engage in mythic and theological portraits of her that are not dependent on historical precedent or the results of scholarly research. And the very widespread contemporary movement to bring feminine imagery into Jewish and Christian namings of the divine (to be discussed at length in chapter four) certainly should be seen as one dimension of theological speculation on the goddess.

At this point, therefore, we have a great deal of information about many important goddesses and many books, of uneven quality, on goddesses. However, a great deal of work still needs to be done on this topic. Even though it presents a great deal of information, conceptually much of the scholarship on goddesses is very weak. Almost no genuinely cross-cultural comparative reflection on goddesses has been done. Two books, David Kinsley's *The Goddesses' Mirror* (1989) and Carl Olson's anthology *The Book of the Goddess* (1983), seek to survey goddesses in a genuinely cross-cultural manner, but they lack significant analysis of the information they have successfully gathered. We still have little real knowledge of what kinds of goddesses tend to flourish under what circumstances. The even more central question of the impact of goddess mythology and symbolism on both women and men has barely been asked in any systematic, disciplined manner, even though many writers have expressed themselves strongly on the issue. Stereotypes and easy assumptions, such as a claim that the presence of goddesses always helps women or that goddesses are always loving, motherly, and nurturing, still abound, especially in popular feminist writings. Such oversimplifications cast a pall on those who wish to engage in serious scholarly research or theological reflections on goddesses. Despite many books on goddesses, this topic is a veritable gold mine awaiting androgynous scholarship.

Putting It All Together

Once we understand how and where religious studies must include information about women, we can begin to reflect on other issues. How can we best understand both the variety and the common themes of women's involvement with the world's religions? What would a picture of the world's religions that took women seriously as human beings look like? Would we classify religions differently? Would the familiar stories of historical development change? Such reflections are in their infancy in the feminist study of religion and will undoubtedly become more sophisticated in the future. To date, three approaches have been suggested. One could simply consider each major religion, including women's options within that religion, as a relatively independent and isolated entity. That approach would allow us to compare religions using options for women, rather than the currently common concepts of deity or geographic locations, as the primary category for comparison. A second approach would seek a wider explanatory framework, such as an evolutionary model of religious history, to explain women's varied levels of involvement in religions and the variety of images of the feminine, from exalted, powerful images to images of women as weak and evil. A third alternative would seek new comparative categories arising out of previously neglected and unknown materials concerning women and the feminine. Each method has certain advantages and disadvantages.

Women in the World's Religions

Since the usual approach to the study of world religions has been to present separate religions as distinct and self-contained entities, rather than to explore themes and phenomena that are found in many traditions and that cut across boundaries separating one religion from another, many authors and editors also take the traditional approach when creating books on the world's religions that include women. A common approach is to commission a feminist expert on each of the different religious traditions to write a chapter on the religion that has been her specialty. (The major offerings to date in this genre were listed in chapter two.)

Though this approach is necessary, it also has major limitations. The most frequent achievement of such scholarship in regard to women is to fill in some of the blanks left by androcentric study. Unfortunately, the newly supplied information is also often androcentric, consisting of more detailed studies of a male-dominant religion's prescriptions and views regarding women. Attempts to describe women in the Jewish or the Confucian traditions often merely explain what Jewish or Confucian men have said about women, rather than advancing our knowledge of Jewish or Confucian women as subjects.

Another problem with such an approach is that there can be significant internal, contextual variation *within* a religious tradition, as, for example, in the significant differences between urban and rural Shi'ite Muslim women in Iran.[33] Broad generalizations about any religious tradition often miss such internal variations. It is extremely difficult to make any reliable comparisons between whole traditions precisely because they are not monolithic, seamless entities.

Nevertheless, this approach does suggest that the map of the world's religions looks different when women's religious experiences are factored into our understanding. The first major distinction that emerges when one takes women's participation—and many other aspects—into account occurs between the major world religions and the indigenous traditions of both the ancient and the contemporary world. All of the major contemporary world religions are patriarchal to some extent. Often they teach that male dominance is necessary and proper, and they frequently contain misogynist tendencies in addition. Even those whose teachings about women are most positive have male-dominated religious institutions and limit women's participation in the most valued religious activities.

Such is not the case with many indigenous traditions. Few tribal traditions are egalitarian in the modern sense of the term, meaning that all aspects of religious life are equally available to all. But strong female mythological figures, who often are important in the creation story, are common. In many cases, ritualizations of the female life cycle, such as puberty rituals for girls, are well developed. And women often have significant ongoing religious lives, whether in conjunction with men or in their own separate realm. Few of these traditions are misogynist, include doctrines of male superiority, or advocate total male dominance of social and religious life.

Complementarity, rather then either equality or male dominance, is common. These traditions are important for feminist analysis of religion because they are the major evidence for the thesis that religious patriarchy is not an eternal, time-honored norm.

Within the major world religions, considerable variation in women's participation exists. In her introduction to Arvind Sharma's *Women in World Religions*, Katherine K. Young organized the world's religions along a continuum moving from the greatest formal or proclaimed male dominance to the greatest acceptance or inclusion of genuine female power. She suggested the following order: Judaism, Hinduism, Confucianism, Islam, Christianity, Buddhism, Tantra, and Taoism.[34] I would modify her continuum to read: Judaism, Confucianism, Islam, Hinduism, Christianity, Buddhism, and Taoism. I suggest these changes because Tantra is not an independent religion but a reform movement within Hinduism and Buddhism, and because Hinduism is so multifarious, and sometimes so supportive of women, that it should be higher on the scale. (It should also be noted that one could easily dispute whether Judaism, Confucianism, or Islam should have the lowest scores for accepting and including genuine female power.)

Measured by other criteria, the religions might occupy different positions on the continuum. For example, interesting results occur when one divides religions into those that are primarily oriented toward family and social units, and those that are primarily oriented toward individuals. Confucianism, Judaism, Islam, and some versions of Hinduism are primarily oriented to family and society, rather than toward individuals. Religions that are oriented toward the family usually have very strong sex-specific codes of conduct and expectations, and are usually publicly male dominated. These religions also tend to have very precise and detailed codes of conduct; complying with these codes of conduct can be seen as the central spiritual discipline of these religions. Frequently women are limited to their family roles and do not participate significantly in religious activities that occur outside the home, which is why these religions appear to be so male dominated. Therefore, until recently, formal religious education for women was rare, and women almost never exercised public religious or political leadership. Usually there is a cultural preference for maleness, and male offspring are regarded as essential to family well-being; therefore, males are often better cared for that females, both physically and psychologically. In some cases, women do have significant separate religious lives and ceremonies, which means that these religions can tend toward the complementarity so characteristic of indigenous religions. However, there is little place or purpose for women who are not wives and mothers in these religions. Practitioners and advocates of these religions would also claim that the family is so central to human well-being that women's family roles are of overwhelming significance. They thus claim that women are honored and valued, precisely in their family roles, and have a hard time understanding feminists' claims that these religions' prescriptions for women's lives are sexist.

Christianity, Buddhism, Taoism, and some segments of Hinduism are less centered in the family and more concerned with the individual's spiritual well-being. (Islam also is concerned with the afterlife, which depends on individual merit.) These religions, especially the first three, also have monastic institutions in which women have participated, sometimes in great numbers. Thus, women do have an alternative to their family roles in these religions. In some form or another, all these religions also contain teachings about sexual equality and the ultimate irrelevance of gender. Nevertheless, for the most part they are institutionally male dominated, and women's access to the most treasured and important dimensions of spiritual life is often limited. Interestingly, despite their emphasis on the irrelevance of gender, these religions (except for Taoism) also have the most misogynistic tendencies, in part because of their asceticism and the value placed on celibacy in some versions of these religions. These religions, especially Christianity and Buddhism, justly deserve their reputations for having negative views of women, because in them women are widely regarded as less spiritual and more material than are men.

Considering world religions based on this distinction between family and individual orientations would prove to be unsettlingly interesting for several reasons. First, it genuinely takes women's religious lives seriously. Second, it thoroughly undoes the usual classifications of Eastern versus Western religions and of monotheism versus nonmonotheism. In so doing, it shows that geographic origins and theological concepts of deity may not be so basic to religious difference as we have taken for granted. All geographic locations and both monotheism and nonmonotheism have produced religions of social orientation and religions of individual spiritual well-being. But women's lives and options can be vastly different in these two types of religion.

If we classify the world's religions on yet another scale, the presence or absence of female divine beings, a different continuum emerges. The monotheistic religions are ambivalent about female deities; officially, there are no goddesses, though the monotheisms never quite succeeded in ridding themselves of female aspects of divinity. Goddesses are commonplace in the rest of the world's religions. Thus, we might derive a continuum of Islam, Judaism, Christianity, Taoism, Buddhism, Shinto, Hinduism, moving from the absence of divine females to their presence. (Confucianism is not on the scale because deities are irrelevant to it. Shinto is included, even though it is not usually regarded as a major world religion, because of its important sun goddess Amataresu.) To compare these continua is interesting, since there are significant differences between them. The fact that some male-dominated religions have goddesses undercuts the thesis that there is a direct correlation between the presence of goddesses and high status for women. Since this thesis is commonplace in feminist theories of religion, this information from the feminist study of religion is important.

Developmental Patterns in Women's Participation in Religion

Another intriguing option is to discuss religion developmentally, beginning with presumably older, more basic types of religion and moving on to more recently developed types of religion. Such an option would definitely give more emphasis to indigenous traditions than is typical in religious studies.

One version of a developmental organization of religions is fairly common in the anthropology of religion. Anthropology commonly classifies societies as foraging, horticultural, agricultural, and industrial. Certain types of society seem to correlate with certain levels of women's involvement in religion. For example, it is fairly easy to demonstrate that in foraging and horticultural societies, women and men have more egalitarian and complementary roles, and that women often play significant roles in religion. Furthermore, it is also easy to demonstrate that agricultural societies are generally patriarchal, that women play a diminished role in public religion, and that misogyny often further limits women. Because agriculture, rather than foraging or horticulture, has dominated European and Asian cultures for so long, patriarchal religion has come to seem normal and inevitable, but the full panoply of the world's cultures presents plenty of alternatives.

In some feminist studies of religion, a more political version of a developmental classification of religions has become popular. Many advocate some variant of the hypothesis that contemporary patriarchal religions represent a late development, something of a "fall" regarding women's participation in religions. The most popular version of this thesis asserts the existence of prepatriarchal societies found particularly in parts of Europe and the Middle East during Paleolithic and Neolithic times. (Thus, as in the anthropological classification just discussed, foraging and horticulture seem to promote higher status for women, whereas male dominance is part of the agricultural revolution.) These scholars emphasize that during this period, goddesses were the dominant deities and women had much higher positions in society than in later patriarchal religions and societies. The fall into patriarchal religion is then presented in great detail, but after that fall, religion is portrayed as uniformly, unrelievedly, unchangingly patriarchal all over the world. Because this theory of history is an important thesis for feminist studies in religion, I will examine it in depth in chapter 5.

Another way of studying the development of religion would focus on the development of specific religious movements. Some scholars use this method to demonstrate that a specific religion was more egalitarian in its earlier forms than in its later forms or that it represented an improved status for women from that offered by its predecessor. The former argument is often made on behalf of Christianity. In some ways, the work of the foremost feminist New Testament scholar, Elisabeth Schüssler Fiorenza (to be discussed in chapter five), could be considered an example of this developmental thesis. The latter thesis, that the new religion improved women's lot, is a commonplace of Islamic apologetics, but it has not, to my knowledge, yet been subjected to a feminist critique. Some would also argue that Buddhism offered women better options than did the surrounding Hindu culture. It can also be argued that new situations in general, such as reform movements within an established tradition or times when a religion is crossing cultural frontiers, are times when women take on roles and responsibilities that they later relinquish or are forced to concede. One can find countless examples of this pattern in all major religions. Finally, in "marginal," nonmainstream religions, women often have more power and autonomy than in the major religion found in their society,[35] a pattern we have noted concerning the nineteenth-century United States.

Such developmental theses are helpful in that they break down

assumptions that male dominance has always prevailed everywhere. They also are a viable alternative to simply discussing individual religions as discrete entities, since they draw attention to
patterns that prevail across denominational lines. The greatest
difficulty with such developmental theses is the sheer quantity of
data with which the scholar must be familiar in order to develop
such theses with creditability. It is easy to move from empirically
based demonstrations of historical change to sweeping generalizations and speculations that sometimes have more to do with a desirable past than with an accurate past.

Patterns in Women's Religious Lives

The most difficult alternative to simply studying women and religion, tradition by tradition, is to attempt to do genuinely comparative work, seeking patterns in the data regarding women and religion beyond the developmental hypotheses outlined above. In
such scholarship, the patterns emerge from the materials being
studied, rather than being imposed on them. Nancy Falk and I
used this method in editing *Unspoken Worlds: Women's Religious
Lives.* We collected and commissioned what we thought would be
a good representative sampling of the possible variations regarding
women's religious lives, but we imposed no standard order upon
them, grouping them neither by tradition, by region, nor by historical period, because "such an approach would blur and scatter patterns, rather than drawing them out and emphasizing them."[36]
Eventually some patterns emerged, and we used them to organize
the book.

The virtue of this kind of comparison is that it breaks down
superficial expectations. Sometimes a movement within a great
world religion presents a pattern of balance or equality more typical of the indigenous traditions. In some patriarchal contexts,
women have very active complementary religious lives. The pattern of women's experiencing a call out of their ordinary roles into

extraordinary responsibilities cuts across a wide spectrum of the more standard religious typologies. Such unexpected correlations help us look at women's religious lives in fresh and vivid ways. I believe that this method yields the most innovative understandings, but it is also the most difficult to do because many hours of patient reflection and intuition are required before any patterns emerge. In my view, such an approach needs to be taken much more frequently as we move toward genuinely androgynous accounts of religion.

Another book that seeks unconventional patterns in human diversity is Peggy Reeves Sanday's *Female Power and Male Dominance: On the Origins of Sexual Inequality* (1981), which is based on a sample of 156 societies listed in the Standard Cross-Cultural Sample.[37] Though she was not working directly on women's participation in religion, her conclusions are important for religious studies scholars. Perhaps her most important conclusion is that not all societies are male dominated. Defining the relationship between the sexes as unequal if men display aggression to women and women have no political or economic authority, she found unequal gender relations in only 28 percent of societies, whereas women and men held equal status in another 32 percent. The remaining 40 percent evidence mythical male dominance (which means that although men may display aggression toward women, women nevertheless have economic and political power) or present situations in which women have economic, but not political, power.[38]

Her conclusions regarding patterns that lead to sexual equality or inequality are extremely important for those involved in the feminist transformation of religion, since she finds religious factors to be important in the presence or absence of male dominance. She finds that "almost always in male-dominated societies, the godhead is defined in exclusively masculine terms,"[39] which provides anthropological evidence for a claim that is often made by feminist scholars of religion. Her list of factors that are correlated with male dominance is extremely interesting and instructive: "increasing technological complexity, an animal economy, sexual segregation at work, a symbolic orientation to a male creative principle, and stress."[40] She further explores the relationships between these factors, claiming that work segregation or a male creative principle often causes male dominance to occur when a society experiences stress.[41] And once stress leads to violent conflict, which seems more likely in male-dominant societies, tendencies that are very difficult to reverse are set in motion. The concluding sentence of her book is enlightening.

> If there is a basic difference between sexes, other than differences associated with human reproduction, it is that women as a group have not willingly faced death in violent conflict. The fact, perhaps more than any other, explains why men have sometimes become the dominating sex.[42]

Values in the Feminist Study of Religion

Despite my emphasis on the need for descriptive and analytic feminist religious studies in which judgments play no role, values and the evaluation of religions phenomena are important at many levels in the feminist study of religions. At one level, we might consider the value of androgynous and androcentric scholarship. Can one even claim that androgynous scholarship is *better* than androcentric scholarship, or is one left merely stating that one *prefers* androgynous scholarship, perhaps because of one's own values? Recognizing the inevitably political content and implications of scholarship does not, in my view, make it impossible to distinguish better from worse scholarship. Less complete, less accurate scholarship is not as good as more accurate, more complete scholarship. Furthermore, I see no grounds on which one could reasonably argue that the androcentric model of humanity yields more complete and more accurate scholarship than the androgynous model.

What could and should be argued is that *some* androgynous reconstructions of materials previously analyzed by androcentric scholars are wrong, inappropriate, ill conceived, illogical, or not based on a reasonable reading of the data. But one cannot argue that the *intention* to do androgynous scholarship is wrong or misguided. In other words, in terms of my own work, some or conceivably all of my androgynous reconstruction of aboriginal Australian religion could be wrong, but the fundamental project is nevertheless on target because the androgynous model of humanity is superior to the androcentric model.

Androgynous cross-cultural and historical studies often raise much more serious and subtle questions about the interpenetration of values and scholarship. For example, what is the role of judgment? Once we believe deeply that androgynous scholarship is superior to androcentric scholarship, can we study male-dominant cultures and religions without passing judgment on them? In fact, our very organization and selection of data will serve either to highlight or diminish the level of male dominance, thus portraying the religion either more "negatively" or "positively" than "the facts" may warrant. (This is not to suggest that androcentric scholarship is any less prone to such problems of interpretation and emphasis. But since we are more used to its slant, we are less likely to notice it.)

The general guidelines for scholars are easy to ascertain. Clearly, the first and most basic critique in which feminist scholars should be engaged is a critique of *androcentric scholarship* and the reporting, organization, and interpretation of data engaged in by androcentric scholars. When we criticize androcentrism, we are criticizing *methods of scholarship*, not the historical epoch or the culture being studied. We are claiming that this religion has been poorly reported on and misunderstood because scholars did not include women in their study and therefore gave us incomplete and inaccurate accounts of the religions. For example, we might conclude that a scholar of Hinduism has used androcentric methods to report on a religion that may or may not be patriarchal. The androcentric methods deserve to be criticized. The patriarchy of the religion should merely be reported. This subtle but extremely important distinction is easily missed: Many will write of androcentric Hinduism, for example, when they mean patriarchal or male-dominated Hinduism.

A second level of analysis involves making the judgment, not that a society is *too patriarchal,* but that a phenomenon *is,* indeed, *evidence of patriarchy.* Once we agree on definitions of patriarchy, misogyny, sexism, and egalitarianism, we can claim that a religion is patriarchal in its forms without thereby passing judgment on it, just as an economic historian could claim that a society was feudal in its socioeconomic organization without necessarily condemning that society. That judgment should be made only on the basis of truly androgynous scholarship, because androcentric scholarship will not provide enough information about women to make that judgment. Androcentric scholarship often finds a religion to be more male dominant than a more complete description might warrant. But when that judgement can be made, it is not a value judgment but a descriptive statement, though it may inspire defensiveness and anger nevertheless.

A problem still remains. As feminists we dislike patriarchy. It is very easy to conclude with a shudder that one is glad one does not live as a woman in certain other times or places. Yet such judgments deal harshly with other peoples' religions and lives and usually elicit hostile and defensive reactions from them. At no point in the study of women and religion is empathy more appropriate and more needed. We truly must bracket our own ideas about what we want for our lives and try to enter the spirit of another viewpoint. Otherwise we will learn nothing.

Western feminism has often, and justly, been criticized for its cultural imperialism in judging and condemning other women's lives when, in fact, we do not understand them on their own terms.

Empathic understanding of some religious practices may indeed be difficult. But in many years of studying and teaching about these materials, I have found that a useful thought exercise consists of exploring unexpected "positive" results for women ensuing from practices that Western feminists may find objectionable, such as arranged marriage or polygyny. For example, arranged marriages free one from the dating scene and from being evaluated solely on the basis of appearance, since parents looking for a bride for their son are often more interested in a young woman's intelligence and industriousness. Polygyny brings built-in help with child care and the company of other women. In polygynous societies, very few women find it impossible to marry if they want to. And in most patrilineal households, women gain power rather than lose power as they age.

However, I am not suggesting complete relativism on the part of the scholar, for I believe that stance to be both impossible and unwise. I have dealt with this issue at some length in another context.[43] Briefly, I suggest that the "engaged scholar" must *first* develop what objectivity is possible and must treat all religions evenhandedly and with empathy. But I believe a well-trained student of comparative religion also has some ethical responsibilities regarding her knowledge. She needs to use knowledge to promote genuine pluralism in our conflicted world.

> An advanced task of the fully engaged historian of religions involves taking a critical stance against some of the values espoused in some of the symbol systems one studies. Some traditional values studied by the comparative scholar may well undermine the dignity of some members of that religion, as do the patriarchal values common to many religions. . . . Obviously it is important to avoid ethnocentrism and colonialism when one takes up this difficult critical task of making such evaluations.[44]

Currently, one of the most heavily contested such questions concerns widespread African practices of female genital opera-

tions. The operations are dangerous, painful, and destroy or severely limit a woman's sexual sensations. Nevertheless, they are
viewed as necessary to adult womanhood by many African cultures. It is difficult for a feminist from outside the culture not to be
repulsed. But we should also recognize that criticism from without,
especially in a postcolonial era, may have the effect of entrenching
the custom further.

For another example, the Hindu practice of suttee (a wife's self-
immolation on her husband's funeral pyre) was the object of much
British criticism. As a result, Hindu reformers vigorously combat-
ted the practice, and it was thought to have been eliminated. But in
a highly publicized case in 1987, a young Hindu widow, encouraged
by her in-laws and an enthusiastic crowd, joined her husband on
his funeral pyre. Hindus who defended this act claimed that the
practice of suttee, an old Indian custom, was part of the meaning
of "freedom of religion" for them. Many religions, they point out,
honor religious martyrdom and suicide, and Westerners or feminists do not condemn them. Furthermore, the right to euthanasia
is sought in many Western societies, they point out.[45]

Feminist scholarship invites value judgments, but the practice
of empathy tempers those judgments, or at least makes us question
how best to express them. When we do move, finally, from description to evaluation, I suggest that it is most appropriate to begin
with evaluating one's own contemporary culture and religion. It is
slightly more difficult to evaluate the history of the religious or cultural situation with which one identifies, but also inevitable and
appropriate. The most difficult cases involve studies of "the other,"
of a culture and religion with which one is not involved, but which
one studies. These situations should not quickly or easily be taken
as models or antimodels. Great care, based on deep knowledge of
the cultural context, is necessary if one wishes to praise or blame
such a context for its values and mores. Otherwise the all-

important guideline of empathy for the foreign cultural system will be violated.

Reasonable guidelines for dealing with this difficult interface between descriptive scholarship and normative judgment can be made by comparing two instances of such scholarship. In *Gyn/ Ecology*, Mary Daly includes long chapters on Hindu suttee, Chinese foot binding, African genital operations, and American medical practices, all of which she presents as evidence for "global patriarchy and gynecide."[46] In *Unspoken Worlds*, Erika Friedl's chapter on tribal women in Iranian Islam leaves most readers depressed, whereas Diana Paul's chapter on Empress Wu reconstructs this usually maligned leader sympathetically.[47] All of these writings work with materials from "other" cultures, and all of them give the reader a distinct impression as to the *value* or desirability of the phenomena being discussed. Yet I find Mary Daly's treatment of cross-cultural materials problematic, which is not the case with the studies of Iranian tribal women or Empress Wu. What is the difference? Friedl and Paul's works show the presence of serious training in the cross-cultural study of religion or culture, combined with an intent to understand otherness accurately and empathetically. On the other hand, Daly appears to use materials from another culture or historical epoch selectively, only to strengthen an already formulated feminist hypothesis about gender, which is no more acceptable than using cross-cultural data to strengthen a favorite androcentric hypothesis.

The final question of values in the feminist study of religion concerns the passage from the feminist study of religion to the feminist transformation of religion. In this effort, one might wish to use certain religious phenomena about which one has studied as symbols "to think with," to use Claude Lévi-Strauss's felicitous phrase. This activity presents few problems for the scholar working within the religion that is traditional to her culture. In other words, a feminist Christian theologian could readily use little-known Western female imagery of the divine as a theological resource. But the matter becomes much more complicated if she wants to use Native American or Tibetan Buddhist images in her feminist theology. To put it bluntly, there is no easy passage from studying another culture to utilizing those materials in one's own world construction because undisciplined appropriation and mindless borrowing are disrespectful. I make this statement very strongly, despite my own consistent plea to Western feminist theologians to widen their canon to include the serious study of the non-Western world.

On the other hand, despite the care and respect required in using cross-cultural resources to think with, the serious thinker should not confine herself to the cultural resources of Western thought when engaged in feminist transformations of religion, but should do the apprenticeship required for using cross-cultural resources appropriately. Mature feminist thought needs to be informed by the resource of all human creativity from all cultures and historical epochs. My major criticism of both Christian feminist theology and the post-Christian theologians is their failure to take non-Western and non-Christian religions serious as symbols that are "good to think with." I continue to be amazed at the extent to which they privilege Western materials in their feminist world constructions.

CHAPTER FOUR

No Girls Allowed ? Are the World's Religions Inevitably Sexist ?

MANY PEOPLE ARE DRAWN to the study of women and religion to examine their own religious tradition with a feminist eye. This chapter will examine sexism in the world's religions and how feminists have chosen to respond to it.

There is no religion that labels itself as "patriarchal" or "sexist." Instead, religions generally teach their members that they treat women properly—indeed, in the only possible manner—though they may criticize the treatment of women in *other* religions. This kind of critique reveals an interesting value judgment. All religions agree that women should be treated properly, not abused or mistreated. Some religions, in fact, argue that their norms represent an improvement in the treatment of women over what their predecessors did. Mistreatment of women is found only in other traditions. Therefore, most people grow up believing that women are well treated in their religion, if they consider the status of women at all. Even when taught that women are inferior to men or that women must submit themselves to men, religious men and women alike are encouraged to see these teachings as valuable and useful, rather than problematic, aspects of their tradition. Many religious organizations actively promote the view that feminism is an antireligious movement and a great danger to the faithful.

Nevertheless, no scholar or theologian who uses feminist definitions of humanity would pronounce a clean bill of health on any of the world's major religious traditions. As has already been shown, none of the major world religions—Judaism, Christianity, Islam, Buddhism, Hinduism, and the East Asian philosophical traditions of Confucianism and Taoism—treat women and men equally, though they fail to a greater or lesser extent. As already noted, whether such evaluations apply to small-scale tribal and ethnic traditions, such as Native American or African traditional religions, is a much more complex question, and therefore I will not discuss these traditions here.

Applying standard definitions of patriarchy or sexism to any of the great world religions quickly reveals sexist teachings and institutions. In many cases, men are thought to be spiritually superior to women, more likely to meet the tradition's definition of the ideal believer or practitioner. The birth of males is often preferred to the birth of females; women who give birth to males are rewarded, whereas those who do not suffer. In most cases, men hold most or all of the roles of authority and prestige in religious organizations. From these positions, they control and dictate the norms of the tradition for all women. Women are often not invited or allowed to participate in the interpretation or construction of tradition. Often women's ability to participate in key rituals is severely limited, and they are almost never allowed to be the leaders or officiants of such rituals. In the private sphere, men are given authority over females in their households, and women are taught to submit to that authority. Some religious teachings blame women for the limitations and painfulness of human existence. Images of ultimate reality or the divine are frequently male in gender, whereas female images are forbidden and called idolatry. By feminist standards of evaluation, all these extremely common religious practices and judgments are patriarchal and sexist, hence degrading to women and inappropriate.

Discovery of sexist beliefs and practices like these was the first achievement of feminist theological discussion. By the mid-1970s, feminist scholars and theologians were routinely claiming that this phase of our work, the discovery and demonstration of the sexism present in many common religious practices and beliefs, was over. We were eager to take up the more exciting and rewarding task of charting our course, whether into reconstructions of existing religions or into exploring nontraditional and postpatriarchal forms of religion.

Basic Issues in Feminist Theology

In my view, the most difficult question facing a feminist who discovers her traditional religion to be patriarchal and sexist is what to do next. Some of the bitterest disagreements within feminist theology concern this question. Will one continue to identify in some way with one of the major religions, despite its sexism? Or will one abandon that tradition as unworkable, but, still wanting a spiritual practice, take up a new, postpatriarchal religion? This question has divided feminists almost from the beginning.

Very early in the feminist theology movement, Carol P. Christ proposed names for these two points of view. In a 1977 article, she suggested that those feminists who sought to transform religion from within could be called "reformists," whereas those who sought to develop a new, nontraditional feminist form of religion could be called "revolutionaries."[1] This distinction is also central to the 1979 collection *Womanspirit Rising*. In their introduction to the book, Christ and coeditor Judith Plaskow wrote:

While feminists agree on the general outlines of the critique of Jewish and Christian theology, . . . they very much disagree on the reformability of the tradition. For some, the vision of transcendence within the tradition is seen as an authentic core of revelation, pointing toward freedom from oppression, a freedom they believe is articulated

more clearly and consistently within tradition than without. Others
believe that the prebiblical past or modern experience provide more
authentic sources for feminist vision.[2]

Almost immediately, many rejected these labels as hierarchical.
"Revolutionaries, the word seemed to imply, are more radical and,
therefore, 'better' than reformists,"[3] though Christ and Plaskow repeatedly insisted that no ranking of the positions was intended or
implied. When they again addressed the issue, in the introduction
to *Weaving the Visions: Patterns in Feminist Spirituality,* they partially retracted their famous terminology, though they insisted,
rightly, "that the distinction names a real division between and
within women."[4]

In my view, whether or not their terminology is unwise, the distinction named by that terminology is real and basic, and the critical difference between the two positions is disagreement over how
feminist vision is best served. The degree to which feminists retain
personal links and loyalties with traditional religions, rather than
how "radical" they are, is the dividing factor. In fact, some reformists are exceedingly radical in the changes they want to make in
their traditions, but they maintain dialogue with their tradition
and recognize kinship with it. Revolutionaries, though they sever
links with the conventional religions, can be quite conservative in
the way in which they identify with the rejected ancient traditions.

In choosing between these alternatives, two questions are up-
permost. Each religious feminist must decide where her efforts at
feminist transformation of religion will be most effective. Most reformists believe that a feminist transformation of a patriarchal religion has more hope of widespread acceptance than replacing current major religions with new religions created by women. But
each feminist must also decide what she needs for her own spiritual
survival. Most revolutionaries find that the frustration involved in
trying to transform a patriarchal religion into a postpatriarchal religion is simply too agonizing to bear.

Before recounting the achievement of religious feminists who established these two positions, it is important to highlight their common ground. Most important, both positions seek a common goal: feminist *transformation* of religion beyond patriarchy. Both schools also consider the experience of women to be the starting point of all feminist theology. Feminist theologians affirm that women's experience possesses a religious authority of utmost importance, never to be overlooked or denied, never to be sacrificed in order to conform to external or traditional sources of authority, such as scripture, theology, or religious institutions. In valuing women's experience as the primary religious authority, feminist theology makes three central claims.

First, *all* theological or world-constructive thinking is actually grounded in and derives from human experience, even in traditions that call the source of their authority "revelation." This conclusion is inevitable and unavoidable to anyone trained in the cross-cultural comparative study of religion. The uniqueness of feminist theology is that it is based on human experience, but that it recognizes and admits this foundation. As Rosemary Ruether has written:

> There has been a tendency to treat this principle of "experience" as unique to feminist theology . . . and to see it as distant from "objective" sources of truth of classical theologies. This seems to be a misunderstanding of the experimental base of all theological reflection. What have been called the objective sources of theology, Scripture and tradition, are themselves codified collective human experience.[5]

The question is not whether theology is grounded in human experience; the question is *whose* experience is taken into account. The second major claim of feminist theology is that *women's* experience must be taken into account to create a viable religious tradition. Theological traditions that are based on male experience alone cannot speak to the full human experience. To quote Rosemary Ruether again:

The critical principle of feminist theology is the promotion of the full humanity of women. Whatever denies, diminishes, or distorts the full humanity of women is, therefore, appraised as not redemptive. Theologically speaking, whatever diminishes the full humanity of women must be presumed not to reflect the divine or an authentic relation to the divine, or to reflect the authentic nature of things, or to be the message or work of an authentic redeemer or a community of redemption.[6]

As discussed in chapter two, one development of feminist theology in the 1980s was the criticism that the phrase "women's experience" was too often taken to refer only to the experience of the feminist majority—white, middle-class, heterosexual women. Christ and Plaskow wrote in the introduction to *Weaving the Visions*, "Ten years later, we recognize that the term 'women's experience' too often means 'white middle-class women's experience,' in just the way that 'human' too often means 'male.' . . . We can no longer speak of women's experience as if it were a 'Platonic form.' "[7]

Despite Christ and Plaskow's retraction, I find this criticism unpersuasive. As a student of comparative religion, it has always been exceedingly clear to me that the phrase "women's experience" cannot name a universal experience that all women share despite their differing cultures. Rather, the emphasis is that women's experiences, whatever their cultures, must be taken seriously in the same way that men's experiences have always been taken seriously. Therefore, feminists should not abandon the phrase "women's experience," but always understand it to be in the plural: "women's experiences."

Furthermore, in my view, feminist scholarship offers a significant advance over androcentric scholarship on this point. Androcentric scholarship *does* seek universal definitions, norms, and conclusions, whereas the founding insight of feminist scholarship is the discovery of human diversity. The experience of conversion from androcentrism to feminism often involves simply realizing that to be different is not to be wrong. That experience is radically relativizing, *especially* if it is accompanied by cross-cultural knowledge that women's experiences are also diverse. In this situation, it seems to me, each feminist can do no more than write what she knows best, her own experience and understanding, as example and offering. It is inappropriate to criticize other feminists for not writing from other viewpoints, because they could not possibly do so.

The third claim of feminist theology is that all feminist theologians, whether reformist or revolutionary, take as our birthright the ability to "name reality." This famous phrase originated with Mary Daly, who wrote that under patriarchy, "women have had the power of naming stolen from us." She points out that in the second creation story in Genesis, the man names all the animals as well as the woman, who names nothing herself. Daly goes on to write, "Women are now realizing that the universal imposing of names by men has been false or partial." Since, in her words, "to exist humanly is to name the self, the world, and God,"[8] the work of feminist theologians, of whatever school, is critical to being human— not only to the humanity of women, but, in my view, to the humanity of men as well.

Feminist Transformations of Judaism, Christianity, and Islam

Feminists seeking to transform major religions face remarkably similar problems.[9] Therefore, one could expect them to use similar strategies to identify and counter practices and beliefs that harm women. For example, the strategies I employed to argue for a Buddhist feminism in *Buddhism after Patriarchy* are quite similar to those used by many feminists in monotheistic traditions. The starting point for these strategies is often a text or teaching from their religion that supports a gender-neutral and gender-free vision.

Having identified such texts or teachings, feminists in many traditions have typically proceeded to make a distinction that both revolutionaries and antifeminist traditionalists would reject: a distinction between aspects of the tradition that support women's empowerment and those that do not. The feminist takes the former to be what is inspiring, of lasting value and relevance, while understanding the latter to represent the vagaries of history and culture more than they represent the religion. This is not to say that empowering aspects of the religion can be separated from others in time; feminists in all traditions recognize that such a perfect moment or time never existed, that practices supporting gender equity have always coexisted with practices supporting patriarchy.

Reformists from a variety of perspectives would also probably agree that freedom and spiritual liberation are central to their traditions' visions, though in different ways. They generally argue that in a patriarchal culture, a religion's liberating messages are inevitably mixed up with patriarchal forms, imprisoned within them, and even identified with them. Since all of the world's major religions emerged and evolved in patriarchal cultures, it is not surprising that their teachings have been tainted by patriarchal institutions and ways of thinking. But, since patriarchy and freedom are mutually exclusive, those male-dominated beliefs and institutions are, by definition, part of the culturally conditioned medium in which the religious tradition has taken form, not part of the more basic message of liberation. Reformers therefore propose that religion will be truer to its most valuable insights once it is stripped of its patriarchal forms. In fact, the religion itself, properly understood, calls people away from sexism and patriarchy toward equality and freedom—the goals of feminism. Thus, reformers argue that feminist reforms are not merely a side issue or a modern demand based on secular ideologies, but something deeply true to the religion's heart and core.

In making and supporting such claims, feminist interpreters

encounter similar problems. Two basic ones concern working with traditional sources of religious authority, usually texts, that are patriarchal and sexist, and interpreting major teachings of the religion from a feminist perspective. We will examine how Jewish, Christian, Muslim, Hindu, and Buddhist reformers have dealt with each of these issues.

Feminists Searching the Scriptures

The three monotheistic religions—Judaism, Christianity, and Islam—rely heavily on scriptures that are believed to be revealed and to provide an unalterable and supremely valuable charter for the faith. Feminist exegesis of the sacred text is especially important for these faiths because scripture is often used to support traditional notions of women's nature and roles. Study of classic texts is important, but much less crucial, for reformers of other traditions including Hinduism, Buddhism, and the East Asian perspectives.

At one level, analysis of sacred texts is an extremely complex scholarly enterprise, involving recognition that scriptures are variegated, sometimes self-contradictory documents whose pronouncements derive from the cultural experiences of their human authors. Detailed archeological, historical, and linguistic study is required to become proficient in the field of historical critical biblical scholarship, for example. This field daunts even many scholars of religion because its literature is so vast, complex, and specialized. (This method of scriptural study has rarely been applied to the Qur'an, the sacred text of Islam.)

However, most adherents of religious traditions do not read their scriptures in this way. Instead, most members of religious communities are taught to regard their scriptures as the doctrinal charter of their faith, emphasizing their timeless and contemporary relevance. Historical critical questions about who wrote which sacred texts when and for what purposes are less significant to most religious readers of sacred texts outside the academy. Since the latter reading style is so prevalent, it is important to look at its possibilities for feminist commentators. There is no doubt that the scriptures have traditionally been *interpreted* as favoring male dominance because they contain many explicitly patriarchal statements. But is also possible to make a case that the scriptures do not *require* patriarchal interpretation.

Feminist commentators support this claim in several ways. First, they make a distinction between *text* and *interpretation*, while asserting that there is no text apart from interpretation. All readings of a text, from the most patriarchal to the most egalitarian, are *interpretations* of that text, not an unmediated understanding of what the text "really means." This distinction is crucial, for those who have traditionally been entrusted with the authority to interpret texts frequently claim that their readings are more than interpretations. They may claim that the text *requires* certain male dominant practices, or that it forbids practices such as the ordination of women. But in fact what is happening is that such interpreters *favor* interpreting the text to require or forbid such practices. By insisting on the distinction between text and interpretation, feminist exegetes can return the debate to its real arena—present values—and ask why more conservative exegetes *prefer* male-dominant interpretations of scripture to egalitarian ones.

Another distinction important to feminist exegesis is that between more and less basic narratives and statements found in scriptures. There is no question that, taken in isolation and interpreted literally, statements that subjugate women to men can be found in the scriptures of all three monotheistic religions. It is also clear that these scriptures came out of decidedly male-dominated cultures. But no tradition takes literally all of the passages found in its voluminous scriptures. For example, the social milieu in which the scriptures of the three monotheistic religions were written presupposes not only male dominance, but also slavery and other social institutions no longer deemed appropriate by most people. Because social institutions such as slavery and male dominance were so common in the cultures in which the scriptures originated, the scriptures accommodated them. But accommodating them is not the same as requiring them. This distinction becomes clear when we notice that those who argue that male dominance is required by scripture do not generally argue that slavery is also required, even though scripture not only allows and condones it, but even legislates its forms and conditions. It is clear that their preference for male dominance grows out of their present value systems, rather than out of their commitment to scripture. They are not alone; every religious person chooses which passages of scripture to highlight and which to deemphasize or even ignore.

Feminist interpretations of scripture frequently claim that certain messages, themes, or passages are more central or more authoritative than those that are interpreted as male dominant. For biblical traditions, feminist visions often emphasize the prophetic tradition of protest, based on religious values, against injustice, as in this excerpt from Rosemary Ruether:

> Feminism, in claiming the prophetic-liberating tradition of Biblical faith as a norm through which to criticize the Bible, does not choose an arbitrary or a marginal idea in the Bible. It chooses a tradition that can be fairly claimed, on the basis of generally accepted Biblical scholarship, to be the central tradition, the tradition through which Biblical faith constantly renews itself and its own vision. Again, what is innovative in feminist hermeneutics is not the prophetic norm but rather feminism's appropriation of the norm for women. . . . By including women in the prophetic norm, feminism sees what male prophetic thought generally had not seen: that once the prophetic norm is asserted to be central to Biblical faith, then patriarchy can no longer be maintained as authoritative.[10]

Another important component of feminist textual study is translations. Many times over, translations themselves have proved to be subtly influenced by traditional male-dominant interpretations; thus, the very *text* itself may be less patriarchal in the original language than in familiar translations.

One of the most influential demonstrations of this thesis is Phyllis Trible's work on the creation stories at the beginning of the Jewish and Christian scriptures. Though these narratives are not vital parts of most formal Jewish or Christian theology, they have been extremely influential in popular religion for centuries. Many popular Western perceptions of women as morally weak or evil can be traced to interpretations of these narratives; therefore, they are well worth close, word-by-word study. Trible demonstrates, for example, that the familiar "Adam" of most translations is not referred to as a male until the female human being is also present. *Adham*, the Hebrew term translated as "Adam," is a generic term for humanity, and literally means "the earth creature." Furthermore, in the first creation story, found in the first chapter of Genesis, this earth creature is *initially* created "in the image of God . . . male and female" (Gen. 1:27, Revised Standard Version). Thus, the wording of the first creation story indicates that the original "male and female" state of the earth creature mirrors the divine image, which is, therefore, also "male and female." If this is the case, the "creation" of woman is actually the creation of the first couple out of the original earth creature. Finally, Trible shows that the so-called curses proclaimed after the Fall, especially the curse put on Eve that her husband would rule over her, are *descriptions* of cultural conditions that limit both women and men, not statements regarding an ideal social arrangement that is *prescriptive* for humanity.[11]

For Christians, New Testament interpretation is even more important than interpretations of the Hebrew Bible. The most famous feminist New Testament claim is well communicated by the title of Leonard Swidler's 1971 article "Jesus Was a Feminist."[12] Though this article, like some other Christian feminists' work, is marred by anti-Jewish rhetoric, its general thesis has been widely accepted in Christian feminist circles. For example, Ruether writes that "the Jesus of the synoptic Gospels can be recognized as a figure remarkably compatible with feminism. This is not to say, in an anachronistic sense, that 'Jesus was a feminist,' but rather that the criticism of religious and social hierarchy characteristic of the early portrait of Jesus is remarkably parallel to feminist criticism."[13]

The Gospels do not indicate that Jesus criticized women or acted in ways that would hurt them. They do show that Jesus' words and actions favored women and accepted them as equal partners in ways that contradicted the norms of his time and culture. For example, in the story of Mary and Martha, he encourages the sister who wished to sit with him learning rather than the sister who complains about not being helped in the kitchen. As Swidler pointed out, he thus encourages women's intellectual pursuits in a time and place when that was not the norm. Significantly, the resurrected Jesus first appears to *women*, whom he commissions to report his resurrection to male followers. The irony that Christianity has nevertheless prohibited women from preaching and sacramental ministries for centuries is often pointed out.

Most Christian justifications of male dominance do not rely on the Gospels, but on the Epistles of Paul (Romans, 1 and 2 Corinthians, Galatians, Philippians, Philemon, and 1 Thessalonians) and even more strongly on later literature whose attribution to Paul is now considered erroneous (1 and 2 Timothy, Titus). The most unambiguously antifeminist passages in the New Testament, including the passage in 1 Timothy 2:11–12 exhorting women to learn in silence and submission and forbidding them to teach or exercise authority, occur in pseudo-Pauline passages, rather than in the writings of Paul himself.[14] Most modern commentators consider them to be rather different from the earliest teachings of Christianity and less authoritative.

The writings of Paul himself are conceded by all commentators to be self-contradictory and therefore difficult to interpret. For example, many authors point out that passages such as 1 Corinthians

11:3–15 seem to subjugate women to men, whereas Galatians 3:28 asserts that in Christ there is neither male nor female, as there is neither Jew nor Greek, slave nor free. Any reading of Paul's writings must concede the difficulty of finding a consistent interpretation in them. Many commentators claim that the Galatians passage is more authoritative for many reasons.[15]

Feminist interpretations of the Qur'an are more rare than feminist interpretations of the Bible, but they almost always include a discussion of a passage that has frequently been interpreted as a warrant for thoroughgoing male domination in Islam. The text in question, Surah 4: *An-Nisa'*:34, reads as follows: "Men are the managers of the affairs of women because Allah had made the one superior to the other and because men spend their wealth on women. Virtuous women are, therefore, obedient; . . . As for those women whose defiance you have cause to fear, admonish them and keep them apart from your beds and beat them." One of the few Muslim feminist scholars of Islam, Riffat Hassan, has argued that the passage should not be interpreted to mean that men must have complete power over women, but that men in general are responsible for providing for women when those women are involved in childbearing and child rearing. She finds that the word usually translated as "managers" actually means "breadwinners" and that the passage is addressed to all men and all women, not specifically husbands and wives. "In simple words what this passage is saying is that since only women can bear children . . . they should not have the additional obligation of being breadwinners while they perform this function. Thus during the period of a woman's childbearing, the function of breadwinning must be performed by men (not just husbands)."[16]

Regarding the defiant women who can be admonished, isolated, or beaten, according to this same Qur'anic passage, Hassan suggests that these punishments are permissible only in the case of a full-scale revolt by Muslim women against their childbearing role.

Hassan has also shown that the popular Muslim views justifying male dominance are not found in the Qur'an at all, but came into Islam through androcentric interpretations of the biblical creation stories, already well known in Arabia when Islam began. According to her, the Qur'an does not make a distinction between the creation of woman and the creation of man. The original creature was undifferentiated humanity, neither man nor woman, as in Trible's reading of the biblical creation stories. Most Muslims nevertheless believe that woman was made from man, specifically from a crooked rib, which also explains women's inferior nature.

Hassan's findings also dispute the notion, common to Islam as well as to Christianity, that Eve caused the fall of humanity. Hassan reads the Qur'an to say that human disobedience is a collective rather than an individual act and was in no way initiated by Eve. Furthermore, according to Hassan: "There is, strictly speaking, no Fall in the Qur'an. What the Qur'anic narrative focuses upon is the moral choice humanity is required to make when confronted by the alternatives by the alternative presented by God and the Shaitan [Satan]."[17] She seems to imply that this moral choice is ongoing, rather than once for all and that making such choices is part of being human rather than an evil deed. Finally, she claims that the popular Muslim view that woman was created not only from man, but also *for* man, is equally non-Qur'anic. According to her, "Not only does the Qur'an make it clear that man and woman stand absolutely equal in the sight of God, but also that they are 'members' and 'protectors' of each other."[18]

Clearly, these few examples of feminist scriptural interpretation show that much of a text's meaning is in the eye of the beholder, and whether the viewer is wearing androcentric lenses or androgynous lenses matters enormously. As more and more feminist scholars gain the technical skills required, they will undoubtedly reveal more and more ways in which the texts have been interpreted in a more patriarchal fashion than is required.

The examples of feminist scriptural interpretation cited thus far are somewhat traditional in that they regard the scripture as *ultimately* authoritative, which is why interpreting it matters so much. Some feminists, more influenced by modern historical and critical biblical scholarship, probably would regard these strategies as somewhat naive, since they still rely heavily on the words found in the text and ignore the cultural context in which they were written. Feminists who pay more attention to the *history* of the text often readily concede that the Bible *is* a thoroughly patriarchal and androcentric document; therefore they construe its authority differently. Often they do not regard scriptures as ultimate authorities but significant resources for religious reflection.

One such scholar is Elisabeth Schüssler Fiorenza, well known for her work on reconstructing Christian origins, to be discussed in the next chapter. She has also written several major books on feminist biblical exegesis, including *Bread Not Stone: The Challenge of Feminist Biblical Interpretation* and *But She Said: Feminist Practices of Biblical Interpretation*. Schüssler Fiorenza argues that locating authority formally in the Bible obscures what really happens in the process of deriving norms from scriptures. For her, authority truly lies in the exegete's "own processes of finding and selecting theological norms and visions either from the Bible, tradition, doctrine, or contemporary life."[19] She argues repeatedly that the Bible is best understood as "a historical prototype rather than as a mythic archetype," which is to say, "as a formative root-model of biblical life and faith." A root-model, unlike a mythic prototype, is not an absolute authority, but is "under the authority of feminist experience," which itself is an ongoing source of revelation.[20] Ongoing revelation is manifested in "a systematic analysis of reality and confrontation with contemporary struggles to end patriarchal oppression."[21] The Bible then becomes one resource among many for struggles for liberation from patriarchy.

Given this assessment of the Bible, she goes on to suggest a fourfold strategy for feminist biblical interpretation. First she begins with a "hermeneutics of suspicion," which "does not presuppose the feminist authority and truth of the Bible, but takes as its starting point the assumption that biblical texts . . . are androcentric and serve patriarchal functions." As part of her "hermeneutic of suspicion," she claims that "all androcentric language must be understood as generic language until proven otherwise." Given that modern English clearly differentiates androcentric from gender-inclusive language, this principle requires translating parts of the Bible into gender-inclusive language. Second, using a "hermeneutics of remembrance," the feminist reader seeks "to move against the grain of the androcentric text to the life and struggles of women." Such interpretation reconstructs women's lives and struggles and places them at center stage. Third, one must employ a "hermeneutics of evaluation and proclamation" to assess the "theological significance and power for the contemporary community of faith" of the biblical text. Finally, using a "hermeneutics of creative actualization," the reader can "retell biblical stories from a feminist perspective" to "reformulate patriarchal prayers and create feminist rituals celebrating our ancestors."[22]

Beyond Male Monotheism:
God-Talk in Christianity and Judaism

As the work of Schüssler Fiorenza and others shows, questions of textual authority and interpretation cannot be separated from questions of theology. Specifically, does the tradition promote an egalitarian or a sexist society? Do the religion's central symbols and doctrines, properly understood, promote gender equity and egalitarianism or male dominance? In asking these questions, a fundamental and intolerable contradiction between the tradition's vision and its patriarchal or misogynist interpretations and institutions may come to light.

For Judaism and Christianity, no issue is more central to feminism reconstruction than the male imagery consistently used for the deity. Therefore, I will focus on this issue when examining feminist claims that Christianity or Judaism can be liberating religions for women. As I indicated in chapter three, to envision deity in predominantly male terms is quite unusual in religion; only the three monotheistic religions do so. Few symbols are more entrenched in the Western religious imagination, and few are more disempowering for women. Therefore, the ways in which various feminist theologians critique and reconstruct traditional male imagery of deity is one of the most interesting and important topics in the feminist theology of the Western religions.

At its core, the issue is very simple. The masculine pronouns and images traditionally used of the deity do not and never have meant that the deity of Western monotheism is male. The vast majority of believers would agree that God is beyond sexuality, but they nevertheless continue, often insistently, to use male pronouns about that deity, not noticing the self-contradiction contained in a statement like "that God is exalted above all sexuality is part of *his* transcendence."[23] As I wrote in my 1974 essay "Female God Language in a Jewish Context," "*If we do not mean that God is male when we use masculine pronouns and imagery, then why should there be any objection to using female imagery and pronouns as well?*"[24] In my own later work on that issue, I suggested learning from the rich Indian repertoire of divine feminine imagery and proposed ways that such images could be utilized in monotheistic discourse.[25] That suggestion has as yet not been followed up by other feminist theologians, who have taken other routes around the problem.

Rosemary Ruether deals with the issue of God-language in her book *Sexism and God-Talk*, published in 1983. Like other postpatriarchal Christian feminists, she claims that, although some nonsexist God-talk can be found in biblical tradition, it is also necessary to go beyond the images found there. She considers divine metaphors grounded in images of authority and hierarchy, such as *king* or *queen*, to be inappropriate for feminist Christianity, which should try to foster egalitarian rather than hierarchical human relationships. Furthermore, she cautions against investing too heavily in parental metaphors, though, of course, the mother image should be included when parental metaphors are used. Most important, she argues that uncritical, unreflective, literalistic insistence upon the traditional male images for deity is actually idolatry, not faithfulness.[26]

Ruether proposes "God/ess" as a word for the divine, explaining it as follows: "I use the term God/ess, a written symbol intended to combine both the masculine and feminine forms of the word for the divine while preserving the Judeo-Christian affirmation that divinity is one. This term is unpronounceable and inadequate. It is not intended as language for worship, where one might prefer a more evocative term."[27] This God/ess is not so much parent as liberator, not only creator but source of being. Although the metaphor of deity as liberator stems from traditional biblical narratives, such as the Exodus story, Ruether criticizes patriarchal theologies of hope or liberation for their "negation of God/ess as Matrix, as source and ground of our being." She argues that such theologies then posit a false dualism of matter against spirit, seeing nature as source of bondage and spirit as source of liberation. Rather than affirming spirit and transcendence against matter and immanence, "feminist theology needs to affirm the God of Exodus, of liberation and new being, but as rooted in the foundations of being rather than as its antithesis." This God/ess is both "the material substratum of our existence" as well as "endlessly new creative potential (spirit)."[28] Ruether continues to insist that the deity envisioned by feminist theology does not prefer spirit to nature and that such dualistic thinking has been responsible for much Christian misogyny.

Anne Carr offers a different Christian feminist perspective on deity in 1989 book *Transforming Grace: Christian Tradition and Women's Experience.* Carr predicts that feminist theology will suggest new images of God "as mother, sister, and friend," but her main search is for language that can "freshly evoke, for our time . . . the inclusive, passionate, and compassionate love of God for all creation that is proclaimed in the message and the life, death, and resurrection of Jesus."[29]

Carr proposes six ways of understanding the deity, employing both traditional Christian concepts (incarnation, resurrection, trinity) and feminist reconsiderations of them. Like Ruether, she first evokes deity as "the *liberating* God," a concept particularly important "for all who search for new freedom today, including Christian women."[30] Second, she emphasizes that the deity is *incarnational*. By incarnational, Carr means not merely that God takes on human form in Jesus, the traditional meaning of incarnation, but also that because deity has made itself incarnate, there is no fundamental dualism between matter and spirit. Although it stops short of Ruether's suggestion that deity be seen as the material foundation of our existence, this interpretation of incarnation nevertheless points in that direction.

Carr's third suggestion is that deity is *relational*. This insight leads Carr to a feminist "resymbolization of the concept of power." Feminism understands power in the context of relationship, as the empowerment of others, rather than as coercive power over others. Seen in this light, "God's power is in *humans* as embodied human agents." Since the experience of a compassionate God is central to women's experience, Carr's fourth image of God is also drawn from feminist theology; she presents a *suffering* deity who shares in the pain of the world. This dimension of the divine "is revealed in the cross, a central Christian symbol and an important one for women who experience the pain of exclusion and denigration in their own religious heritage."[31]

Carr's fifth contemporary reformulation is "*the God who is future . . . the God of resurrection faith.*" Rather than being seen as wholly other, as completely distinct from what is found on earth, a more familiar concept, she suggests that God should be seen as wholly new. "To envision God as future, as ahead, rather than above and over against the human and natural world, is a reorientation that helps women to see the feminist dilemma in the church as a temporary one."[32]

Finally, the deity of Carr's feminist theology is the *unknown, hidden* God "who is always more than human images and concepts can suggest." This characteristic "reaches its epitome in the blinding mystery that is named by the tradition as Trinity." Following liberation theologians, Carr interprets the trinity as "a community or society of persons" and claims that such an understanding of the trinity promotes an understanding of human beings as interdependent beings who need society, rather than isolated individuals. This emphasis on human interdependence is important in many streams of feminist thinking. Carr connects this emphasis with a specifically trinitarian understanding of deity:

> The mystery of God as Trinity, as final and perfect sociality, embodies those qualities of mutuality that are feminist ideals and goals derived from the inclusivity of the gospel message. The final symbol of God as Trinity thus provides women with an image and concept of God that entails qualities that make God truly worthy of imitation. [33]

Though she is less specifically identified with feminism, the work of Sallie McFague on divine imagery is also important to any survey of feminist images of God. McFague's 1982 book, *Metaphorical Theology: Models of God in Religious Language*,[34] deals mainly with questions about metaphors and models in theological language, but her final chapter is titled "God the Father: Model or Idol?" For McFague, as for most other Christian feminists, the root metaphor of Christianity is a liberating relationship between God and humans. McFague is particularly interesting in the *relationality* implicit in all metaphors and argues that such metaphors for deity are not descriptions of God, but suggestions about the quality and type of *relationship* with deity that is being experienced. She regards the metaphor of God the Father as "*one* good model of relating to God,"[35] but decries the patriarchalism that has developed from that metaphor as "an example of a good model gone astray." She claims that, given Jesus' use of the metaphor of God the Father, it is bound to be central in Christianity, but that its growth into rigid male dominance "is a serious perversion of Jesus' understanding of the father-model and utterly opposed to the root metaphor of Christianity." She equally criticizes the way this model has crowded out other models, since in her view, many complementary models of deity are required to express the richness and complexity of the divine-human relationship.[36]

McFague's 1987 book, *Models of God: Theology for an Ecological, Nuclear Age*, takes up the problem of appropriate imagery for the divine with even more urgency. She writes that after finishing *Metaphorical Theology*, she came to see traditional imagery for deity in a grimmer light, coming to believe that patriarchal, triumphalist imagery "is opposed to life, its continuation and fulfillment."[37] Recognizing that deconstructing negative traditional images and concepts of deity is not sufficient, she begins to *remythologize* the relationship between God and the world, experimenting "with the models of God as mother, lover, and friend of the world and with the image of the world as God's body." (McFague develops the image of the world as God's body in her 1993 book, *The Body of God: An Ecological Theology*, to be discussed in chapter six.) She finds these imaginative pictures of the relationship between God and the world to be preferable to traditional pictures in a number of ways.[38]

In her discussion of God as mother, McFague first explains that it is important to use female images of God to undercut the idolatry that has developed because of the use of exclusively male images of God. Furthermore, she explains that since humans are both male and female, it makes sense that the deity in whose image we are made would also be male and female. Then she outlines two other important points: God as mother is not limited to stereotypically feminine traits, and female metaphors must include but not be limited to maternal images.

In fleshing out the model of God as mother, McFague focuses on three particular divine attributes: God's love, God's activity, and God's justice. The love of God as mother is bound up with the mystery of giving and sustaining life, both biologically and culturally. The love of God in birthing and nurturing the universe is closely bound up with McFague's second concern—the *activity* of God as mother, which is creating. In this image, the visible creation comes from God's reality and is an expression of God. She talks of "God giving birth to her 'body,' that is, to life, even as we give birth to children." Like so many other feminist theologians, McFague points out this picture's ability to undercut dualisms, whether of God and the world, or of matter and spirit. Finally, McFague discusses the *ethic* of God as mother, which is justice. An ethic of justice in the nuclear and ecological age can only be an ethic of care, in which all people see themselves as universal parents. We all must recognize that extinction, whether through nuclear or environmental disaster, would be far more devastating than our individual deaths, and we must ensure that life itself is passed along. Therefore, our circle of concern must include not just ourselves, our families, our society, even our species, but also life itself, the entire biosphere. In being universal parents, she writes, we have the responsibility "to join God the creator-mother in so arranging the cosmic household that the birth and growth of other species will take place in an ecologically balanced way."[39]

Another more recent Christian feminist account of God builds on the foundation of the justifications for and examples of female God-talk already discussed. In some ways it is the most radical of these accounts, and in some ways the most conservative. In *She*

Who Is: The Mystery of God in Feminist Theological Discourse, one of Elizabeth Johnson's explicit aims is to write about "the mystery of God recognizable within the contours of the Christian faith," utilizing both new feminist theology and "the traditional language of Scripture and classical theology."[40] The result is a book that talks about trinity and unity in deity, and about deity's relationship with the world in ways that are relatively traditional—except that feminine terms and pronouns for deity are used consistently and exclusively throughout the book.

In the beginning of her theology, Johnson appeals to the classical doctrine of *imago Dei, imago Christi* (image of God, image of Christ), interpreting it to mean that women are created in the image of God and are "christomorphic" (having Christlike form) in the same way that men are. According to Johnson, this implication of the classic doctrine was never fully articulated in Christian theology. Therefore, it is appropriate to take "female reality in all its concreteness as a legitimate finite starting point for speaking about the mystery of God."[41] After an extended and complex discussion of the female metaphors for all three persons of the trinity, as well as discussion of the trinitarian character of God in terms of "the experience of mutual love so prized in feminist reflection,"[42] the culmination of her book is a discussion of "One Living God: SHE WHO IS." Referring to the biblical story of the burning bush, during which the enigmatic name "I am who I am" is self-disclosed by God, and drawing upon Aquinas's commentary on the story, Johnson concludes that this name can be rendered "SHE WHO IS."

> *The one who speaks there is mystery in a personal key, pouring out compassion, promising deliverance, galvanizing a human sense of mission toward that end. Symbolized by a fire that does not destroy, this one will be known by the words and deeds of liberation and covenant that follow. SHE WHO IS, the one whose very nature is sheer aliveness, is the profoundly relational source of being of the whole uni-*

verse. . . . She is the freely overflowing wellspring of energy of all crea-
tures who flourish, and the energy of all those who resist the absence
of flourishing.[43]

Johnson's book supports the claim I made in my 1974 article
"Female God Language in a Jewish Context," a claim with which
many feminist theologians have disagreed. " 'God-She' is not some
new construct added onto the present resource of Jewish God language and separate from it. In other words, the familiar 'Holy One,
Blessed be He' is also 'Holy One, Blessed be She' and *always has
been*."[44] Unlike so many feminist theologians, Johnson does not focus on widening the canon to include previously excluded resources or seeking new images and metaphors for deity. Rather,
utilizing both feminist thought and classical Christian theology,
she presents the same deity, previously envisioned in traditional
classical theology, as SHE WHO IS.

Turning finally from the work of North American Christian
feminists to a Korean Christian feminist, the issue of female God-
language takes on a very different dimension. In her 1990 book
Struggle to Be the Sun Again: Introducing Asian Women's Theology,
Chung Hyun Kyung claims that "it is natural for Asian women to
think of the Godhead as male and female because there are many
male gods and female goddesses in Asian religious cultures."[45] It is
refreshing for Christian female God-talk to be so matter-of-fact, so
natural, so grounded in experience, so devoid of argumentation
and justification, so devoid of *problem*. Her writing on God as both
female and male, and on God as mother reminds me of the sponta-
neous veneration of God as female in Hinduism and Buddhism, an
aspect of those traditions that I have long admired.

Chung suggests that "an inclusive image of God who has both
male and female sides promotes equality and harmony between
men and women: 'a partnership of equals.' " Thus she uses traditional Asian images of divine complementarity to promote the

modern idea of gender equality. Chung also posits that "God as a life-giving power can be naturally personified as mother and woman because woman gives birth to her children and her family members by nurturing them."[46] This too is an image thoroughly familiar to Asians. However, in Asia such images have been used to glorify the traditional female gender role and limit women to it. Chung warns against this misuse of complementarity, noting that the values of complementarity and harmony can and are being used against women in Asia "for men's convenience in order to perpetuate stereotypical roles for women."[47] For her, complementarity must include equality.

Unlike other feminist theologians, Chung's naming of deity as female does not stop at an androgynous Godhead; she claims that many Asian women also see Jesus as woman and mother, despite his male physiology. Part of that naming stems from Jesus' compassion and the traditional Asian view of women as the "compassionate mother who really feels the hurt and pain of her child." Other points of identification between women and Jesus will be more surprising to Westerners. Quoting another Korean woman theologian, Park Soon Kyung, Chung claims that the patriarchy of our present historical situation calls for Jesus to be named as *woman Messiah*. The justification is Jesus' "identification with the one who hurts the most"—at present, women in patriarchal situations. Finally, Chung finds the Jesus who casts out demons easy to image as a woman because Korean shamans, most of whom are women, perform the same task in contemporary Korea.[48]

Concluding this survey of feminist understandings of monotheism's core symbol—deity—is Judith Plaskow's discussion of these issues in Jewish feminism. Like Judaism in general, Jewish feminism has focused less on theological issues and on God-language than has Christian feminism. Because Judaism is a religion that emphasizes behavior over belief, many Jewish feminists have been more concerned with women's rituals and with obtaining classical Jewish educations. But Plaskow feels that theology is important for Jewish feminism, and in her 1990 book *Standing Again at Sinai*, she addresses what she perceives to be several obstacles to the development of female God-talk in Judaism. First, female God-language is sometimes equated with worshipping the goddesses rejected by biblical Judaism. As Plaskow explains,

> the equation of female God-language with Goddess worship either presupposes that the God of Judaism is so irrevocably male that any broadening of anthropomorphic language must refer to a different deity, or it simply makes no sense at all. The overwhelming majority of Jewish feminists who have experimented with religious language in no way see themselves as imaging or worshipping a Goddess; they are trying to enrich the range of metaphors Jews use in talking about God.[49]

A related concern about female God-language is its implications for monotheism, especially the fear that an androgynous deity would be multiple. Plaskow agrees that it is important to protect and preserve monotheism, but argues that female God-language does not interfere with this goal. Like some Christian feminist theologians, she claims that individual images of deity need to be seen as part of a divine totality, rather than as representing different gods. Monotheism has always included many images and has never consisted of only a single image or picture of God.

Finally, Plaskow finds that female God-language arouses anxiety for the many Jews who associate it with nature and with sexuality in ways that seem "pagan." Plaskow believes that Jewish feminists must be willing to confront and defuse these fears. In classical Jewish thought, women alone were identified with nature and sexuality, and nature and sexuality have been inappropriately disparaged as a result. Both need to be reclaimed, and the most effective way to do so is by recognizing the female aspects of the divine.[50]

In her own suggestions for feminist Jewish God-language, Plaskow affirms the need to appreciate many images of deity, both traditional concepts and new ones deriving from the experiences of those heretofore excluded from the process of naming deity. Both images for deity taken from nature (God as rock, tree of life, light, darkness) and images of the presence of God in empowered, egalitarian community (God as friend, companion, lover) are needed.[51] In her view, feminist God-language has been more successful in the former than the latter task, in part because so many traditional images of the relationship between God and community are hierarchical rather than egalitarian.

When discussing images of God that reflect the experience of egalitarian community, Plaskow makes a particularly strong case for the continued use of anthropomorphic God-language, despite its limitations and dangers. She argues that impersonal language can easily mask the continued presence of old male metaphors of the divine, and that only the introduction of female images can ensure that their hold is broken. These personal, anthropomorphic images should range from "purposely disquieting female images to female and nongendered images that express intimacy, partnership, and mutuality between humans and God."[52] The use of images like "Queen of the Universe" and "Woman of War," female counterparts to familiar male images for God, would be beneficially jarring. Plaskow also states that anthropomorphic images need to be supplemented with natural and impersonal metaphors, as well as with conceptual terms that express God's relationship with all being and becoming. Thus she suggests the Eternal, cocreator, wellspring, or ground of life.[53] But in every case, it is important to avoid "the dualistic, hierarchical misnaming of God and reality that grows out of and supports a patriarchal worldview." Furthermore, that naming should cherish diversity in community, "even as that diversity has its warrant in the God of myriad names."[54]

Feminist Theological Transformations in Hinduism and Buddhism: Some Perspectives

Because Buddhism is the religion of choice for many Western converts already familiar with feminism, Buddhist feminist analysis is more developed than Hindu feminist analysis. But Hinduism, with its rich repertoire of women's religious practices and its immense heritage of female images of the divine, must have much potential for feminist analysis, in my view. In this context, I will summarize a Hindu feminist essay whose subject matter coincides nicely with one major focus of this chapter.

The Hindu goddess Kali, with her fierce facial expression, necklace of severed human heads, and skirt of arms, also holds a hooked knife and severed head in two of her four arms, while the other two sign "peace" and "blessings." She is perhaps the most horrifying and puzzling, yet attractive, of the Hindu goddesses,[55] not only for outsiders, but also for many Hindus. Lina Gupta suggests that when freed of her patriarchal overlay, Kali is "a model and image that could be used to fit the needs of today's women."[56] As a child Gupta worshipped Kali daily and remembers her "as something to fear but also something inspiring and empowering." She goes on to say:

> Soon my daily experiences made me aware of discrepancies between a religious view of the goddess and the everyday lives of women. The scriptures and religious tradition proclaim that the beloved Devi [Goddess] resides in women. But these same women are not simply revered and protected; they are also dominated and excluded from the decision-making process that gives male members of Hindu society significant power and authority.[57]

Gupta shows that Hindu scriptures and tradition contain many elements that do not support this discrepancy between image and reality. Her essay analyzes four central Hindu cosmological and epistemological terms that have traditionally been applied to Kali, showing how they reveal "the power of the goddess to be that of a liberating image." Each of the four terms—*Sakti* (energy), *Prakrti* (matter), *Avidya* (ignorance), and *Maya* (illusion)—has been interpreted negatively and associated with the feminine in some streams of Hindu theology. But other readings are possible: "From the scriptural point of view the female principle understood in terms of Sakti, Prakrti, Avidya, and Maya reveals Reality (Brahman, Devi, Kali) in all its facets: the creator, the creativity, and the created world."[58]

Gupta also presents an intriguing feminist interpretation of Kali's appearance, which is so frightening to many encountering her for the first time. She discusses Kali's nudity, her fierce demeanor, and her horrific jewelry consisting of skull garlands and skirts of severed hands as "a subtle critique of the limitations of patriarchal consciousness." Gupta suggests that Kali's terrifying jewelry, which contrasts with the usual feminine jewelry intended to please the male gaze, connotes "a hidden hostility or rage at this need to adorn and 'objectify' oneself."[59] And she suggests that Kali's grim demeanor represents "the personified wrath of all women in all cultures." Likewise, "her 'terrifying howls' are . . . a demand for equality where femininity is equated with meekness and subservience, since such anger is the only language that can be heard."[60]

Buddhist feminists face a rather different situation than monotheist feminists do because the most problematic manifestations of patriarchy in Buddhism are its institutional forms, such as monastic rules that favor men over women and a preference for male teachers, rather than its symbols and doctrines. No Buddhism symbol is as integral to its worldview and as inherently patriarchal as the monotheistic God understood only in male terms.

Mahayana (the large vehicle) and Vajrayana (the indestructible vehicle) Buddhism (forms of Buddhism that developed in India later in Buddhist history) differ from male monotheism in that they include a fully developed feminine principle of great dignity and importance. Because the absence of a creative or redemptive deity (non-theism) is so central to Buddhist doctrine, the presence of female (and male) sacred beings in Mahayana and Vajrayana Buddhism is a surprise to many, especially since earlier forms of Indian Buddhism did not include any sacred beings of either gender. In historical developments too complex to be summarized here,[61] a mythological pantheon of sacred beings of both genders arose in Indian Mahayana Buddhism and became commonplace in all forms of Mahayana Buddhism wherever found, including India, Tibet, China, and Japan.

The problem that many people experience when trying to understand these sacred beings is how a religion that does not involve a deity could also have a pantheon of sacred beings. But these beings are not deities in the monotheistic meaning of that term. These beings exist mythologically or symbolically, not metaphysically. That is to say, they do not exist as external objective realities but only as symbols useful in religious practice. Therefore, they do not violate the fundamental Buddhist principle of non-theism, the Buddhist insistence that there is no external deity responsible for us or the world.

When these sacred beings are called "deities," as they are in some literature, it is with the understanding that they are "meditation deities," widely used in meditation practices (also known as "deity-yoga") typical of Vajrayana Buddhism. In these forms of meditation, one uses the form of the "deity," either visualized or painted, or both, as the reference point of one's meditation. In some of the more advanced forms of deity yoga, one actually visualizes oneself as the deity; he or she then becomes a symbolic representation of oneself as an enlightened being, one's true form beyond confusion and mistaken identity. Identifying in this manner with the "deity" is said to speed up one's spiritual progress considerably. Because female, as well as male, meditation deities are given to both female and male meditators, it is easy to see how these mythological beings can both affirm and be affirming for women.[62] These deities can also be very comforting for women,[63] though how much they actually affirm and comfort women in traditional Asian Buddhism is questionable.

Interestingly, Tantric or Vajrayana forms of Buddhism (the two terms can be used almost interchangeably) have long been derided by both from Western scholars and other Buddhists, in part because of the presence of strong, sexually active female sacred beings. They confuse those who do not expect to find deities in Buddhism at all, they scandalize people who assume that sexuality and the sacred can have nothing to do with each other, and they mystify people who assume that the divine and the feminine should be remote from each other. Though not without problems, as feminist evaluations have noted,[64] the positive feminine symbolism integral to some versions of Buddhism demonstrates just how much the Buddhist symbol system differs from that of monotheism, even though the level of male dominance in their monastic and educational institutions is similar.

The deconstructive theological task for a Buddhist feminist is not primarily to reconstruct basic symbols but to demonstrate that the core teachings of Buddhism cannot be used to justify Buddhism's male-dominant forms. In fact, traditional Buddhism rarely, if ever, justifies male dominance by calling upon Buddhist teachings, but instead relies on popular, often non-Buddhist beliefs lifted from the surrounding culture, such as the belief, found in both Confucianism and Hinduism, that a woman should always be under the control of a male relative, whether father, husband, or son.

One major task of the Buddhist feminist interpreter is to demonstrate the feminist implications of major Buddhist concepts. For despite the fact that they have not and cannot be used to justify male dominance, neither, in most cases, have they been used to promote the well-being of women. In *Buddhism after Patriarchy*, I undertook that task, discussing all the core concepts of Buddhism in its Indo-Tibetan form. This form of Buddhism encompasses the full array of Buddhist doctrines, from the teachings of early Indian Buddhism through Indian Mahayana Buddhism and into Vajrayana or Tantric forms of Buddhism. Though I cannot present my analysis adequately here, I want to summarize my discussion of two key Mahayana concepts, emptiness (in Sanskrit, *shunyata*) and Buddha-nature (in Sanskrit, *tathagatagarbha*). These two summaries will give some indication of the methods and strategies used in Buddhist feminist analysis.

The Mahayana concept of emptiness often baffles newcomers to Buddhist thought, especially when presented in overly nihilistic colors by unskilled interpreters. The concept of emptiness is said to imply that nothing really exists, which seems counterintuitive or even ridiculous when not explained. To say that everything is empty or nonexistent is to realize that nothing has *inherent* existence or exists independent of and apart from the matrix of all existence. As the most famous text on this matter states, interdependence is emptiness.[65] The interdependence of all phenomena had long been a basic Buddhism teaching. The doctrine of emptiness simply takes this simple assertion to another level by pointing out that if everything is interdependent, then nothing has any essential, unchanging, independently existing essence or nature.

The implications of this doctrine for feminist discourse were pointed out long ago in a series of famous and influential Buddhist texts.[66] If nothing possesses inherent existence and exists independently and immutably, then certainly femininity, which had been used to disqualify women from Buddhist achievement, does not exist and cannot justifiably be used to limit or disqualify women in any way. My favorite quotation from a classic text on this topic puts it thus:

> You have said, "One cannot attain Buddhahood within a woman's body." Then one cannot attain it within a man's body either. What is the reason? Because the thought of enlightenment is neither male nor female. . . .
>
> Just as the stillness of space is neither male nor female . . . one who perceives through enlightenment has the dharma, which is neither male nor female.[67]

However, as I also point out, these statements about the irrelevance and emptiness of gender were made in an androcentric context, which has limited their historical impact and effectiveness, just as parallel statements from Christian scriptures have not been translated into Christian institutional forms. Like many other feminists, I do not believe that sex-neutral statements, by themselves, are ever sufficient to overcome androcentrism because sex-neutral ideals do not affirm femaleness and are often covertly male. Nevertheless, because these debates in Buddhism occur in a context in which all that is at stake is the relevance of gender for humans, not symbols of ultimate reality, parallels between the Buddhist and the monotheistic situations need to be carefully drawn.

The concept of indwelling Buddha-nature (*tathagatagarbha*) states that all beings—not merely human beings, but all beings without exception—have the potential to become enlightened, to be manifest as Buddha. This teaching has always been the cornerstone of my Buddhist feminist inspiration and critique, though its feminist implications have not been noticed in traditional Buddhist thought. For this "enlightened gene," as Buddha-nature has sometimes been described in modern terms, is gender neutral and gender blind. It is not stronger or more vigorous in men, weaker and more recessive in women. The feminist implications of this teaching are clear. As I wrote:

That all sentient beings, certainly all men and women, equally have
inherent potential for enlightenment provides an extremely strong
criticism of existing Buddhist institutions. If women and men have
the same basic endowment, the same potential for enlightenment,
then their vastly different achievements, as recorded throughout Bud-
dhist history, can only be due to inadequate Buddhist institutions, to
institutions that promote, encourage, and expect men to achieve
higher levels of insight and realization.[68]

How can we account for pervasive male dominance in Buddhist
spiritual life and practice if the symbol system and conceptual
framework do not lend themselves to patriarchy? I find two in-
terlocking explanations. Conceptually, the pan-Indian concept
of karma, or cause and effect, with its corollary expectation of
rebirth, provides a logically consistent explanation for male-
dominant social and religious institutions. Traditional Buddhist
thought admitted that women are disadvantaged in patriarchy, but
their difficulties are seen as a result of their karma, accrued in past
lives. Women can, however, overcome their suffering in the future
by being reborn as men. Dissatisfying as this solution is to someone
with feminist values, it does at least admit that male dominance is
unpleasant and difficult for women and tries to offer hope in the
long run.

A feminist would, of course, suggest that what needs to be eliminated is not female rebirth in the future, but the *present* conditions
that make life difficult or intolerable for women. But this kind of
internal critique is not part of the usual repertoire of Buddhist values. Its absence is the second factor explaining long-standing Buddhist complaisance about male dominance. Though Buddhism has
a strong ethical tradition, it does not have a tradition of social activism and criticism, what could be called the prophetic voice.
Rather, Buddhists tend to regard the world or society at large as
intractable and unreformable. In my Buddhist feminist analysis
I have called for "the willingness and the courage to name oppres-

sion as *oppression*, not as normal, not as the way things have to be, not as inevitable and unchangeable, but as oppression, deriving from the self-interest and habitual patterns of both oppressors and oppressed."[69]

In the final analysis, feminist evaluation of Buddhist history, institutions, and core teachings yields the verdict of a massive and irreconcilable conflict between view and practice, between what is affirmed and how it is put into practice. Buddhist teachings directly prescribe gender equity and equality, and the religion lacks any patriarchal symbolism for ultimate reality. But the treatment of Buddhist women both in the past and the present contradicts this view. Buddhist women were rarely as well-educated as men, the nuns' order has been lost in many forms of Buddhism, and women have had little opportunity to name reality in Buddhism. No Buddhist school would argue that philosophy and practice should conflict with each other. This intolerable contradiction must be resolved by acknowledging that, in this case, the view is more authoritative and basic than the practice. Therefore, rather than altering the nonpatriarchal Buddhist worldview, the patriarchal institutions surrounding Buddhist spirituality need to be reformed and reconstructed. Such is the difficult agenda of Buddhist feminism—an agenda that would also eventually have subtle implications for the Buddhist view.

It's Too Broken to Be Fixed: The Feminist Case against Feminist Theological Transformation of Traditional Religions

The analyses and transformations of Judaism, Christianity, Islam, Hinduism, and Buddhism suggested here are not convincing to all feminist theologians. Their voices are integral to the symphony of feminist theology and enrich the thinking of everyone concerned with undoing and replacing patriarchy in religion.

The case *against* feminist transformation of major world religions has been made most cogently in the case of the biblical religions. This is simply because religious feminism is more developed in the biblical religions, and, therefore, more well-trained religious feminists have come through biblical religions, especially Christianity, than through Islam, Hinduism, Buddhism, or the East Asian religions. And those who can make this judgment most cogently and effectively are, indeed, those who once sought to work within their traditions as feminists before abandoning them. Those who have never worked "inside" the tradition in that manner, but have only rejected it and criticized it, have not generally had the same tools or brought the same passion to their post-Christian or post-Jewish feminist critiques.

Post-Christian and post-Jewish feminist theologians contend that the biblical traditions are simply too broken to be fixed, that patriarchal values and symbolism are too essential and too central to their worldviews ever to be overcome. They do not see patriarchy, in its many levels of manifestation and meaning, as accidental or secondary to the biblical outlook, or as merely an unfortunate outgrowth of outmoded cultural habits. Therefore, they contend, no woman will ever experience wholeness, healing, integrity, and autonomy while committed to a biblical religion. Continuing to claim loyalty to traditions that inevitably and invariably demean women is counterproductive at best, and harmful at worst.

Biblical and postbiblical feminist theologians disagree intensely over what the core symbol of biblical traditions actually is. Many reformists see it as *liberation*, whereas revolutionaries see it as *patriarchy* and argue that without patriarchy, biblical religions would be unrecognizable. For example, the male deity who rules and judges the world from afar, who calls his followers away from the physical world to a spiritual realm, and who tolerates no diversity or disagreement is an intensely patriarchal symbol. Jewish and Christian feminists consistently reply that this portrait is a caricature of biblical religions. Post-Christian and post-Jewish theologians respond that if it is a caricature, it must be an extremely accurate one, since so many thinkers, authorities, and laypeople, to say nothing of the radical religious right, do indeed think in such terms. They insist that God the Father is the only way to symbolize deity, and they demand that societies and families mirror that patriarchal image.

But rather than carry on this imaginary debate, we should let the revolutionaries speak for themselves. The two most eloquent such feminists thus far are Carol P. Christ and Mary Daly. Their works are especially valuable because each began as a radical reformer, publishing important books and essays in which they hoped to make sense of biblical religions and to call them away from their sexism. Eventually each became convinced that this effort would fail because patriarchy is too integral to the outlook of those religions. Each has written of her conversion process away from biblical religions to post-Christian feminist spirituality.

Mary Daly's journey, which she recounts in her post-Christian introduction to the second edition of *The Church and the Second Sex* and continues in her recent autobiography *Outercourse* (1994), began earlier.[70] One of the very first feminist accounts of Christianity, *The Church and the Second Sex* was written between 1965 and 1967 and published in 1968. In 1969, Daly was given a terminal contract by Boston College, a dismissal that generated widespread criticism of the school. Later that summer, the president of Boston College relented, informing Daly that she had been granted tenure and promotion, "without congratulations."[71] Though the book brought Daly fame, her experience in academia also radicalized her. She ceased "to care about unimaginative reform but instead began dreaming of a woman's revolution."[72]

> *I moved on to other things, including a dramatic/traumatic change of consciousness from "radical Catholic" to post-christian feminist. My*

*graduation from the Catholic church was formalized by a self-
conferred diploma, my second feminist book,* Beyond God the Father: Toward a Philosophy of Women's Liberation, *which appeared
in 1973. The journey in time/space that took place between the publi-
cation dates of the two books could not be described adequately by ter-
restrial calendar and maps.*[73]

The problem with Catholic feminism, Daly wrote, is that it appeared that a door had opened "within patriarchy." But later she
learned, through her experiences and reflections, "that *all* male-
controlled 'revolutions' are essentially movements in circles within
the same senescent patriarchal systems."[74]

Daly concludes this reflection by writing that she longs for the
arrival "of the sisters of Plato, of Aristotle, of Kant, of Nietzsche:
sisters who will not merely 'equal' them, but do something different, something immeasurably more."[75] Her later works demonstrate that "something more" in dense, difficult books that are not
readily summarized. One of them, *Beyond God the Father,* deals
with many of the topics of systematic theology—deity, evil,
Christology, morality, the church—but all from the viewpoint of
women who, having had their power of naming stolen from them
in patriarchal thought, are now naming themselves, the world, and
the deity. Such naming involves "a *castrating* of language and images that reflect and perpetuate the structures of a sexist world."[76]
Women, as the "primordial eunuchs" of patriarchy, "are rising up
to castrate not people, but *the system* that castrates—that great
'God-Father' of us all which indulges senselessly and universally in
the politics of rape." Thus, the primary event in the arrival of
"something immeasurably more" requires the "death of God the
Father in the rising woman consciousness and the consequent
breakthrough to conscious, communal participation in God the
Verb."[77] God the Verb has been Daly's contribution to the postpatriarchal naming of deity. For her, though she sometimes uses the

term *goddess*, any noun is too static for the meaning that must be communicated by the word that stands for the Be-ing that Daly celebrates and evokes in this and later works.

Carol P. Christ has documented her journey out of Christianity into post-Christian feminist spirituality especially vividly in her book *Laughter of Aphrodite: Reflections on a Journey to the Goddess*.[78] In contrast with Daly, Christ's move beyond God the Father has taken her into a remythologizing of *goddess*, a term she uses frequently in her writings. But in this chapter, I will focus on the reasons for her journey away from biblical religion. Christ's journey to the goddess began with her conviction "from the time I became a feminist that our language for God had to be changed if women were to see ourselves fully in the image of God."[79] In 1975, she experienced her first introduction to the women's spirituality movement, and very soon thereafter knew she had left the church for good.

Christ left Christianity primarily because of the effects of religious symbols on consciousness. In a reply to Rosemary Ruether's very strong criticism of the feminist spirituality movement, she writes, "The reason I do not use the biblical tradition as the basis for my feminist vision is a judgement about the effect of the *core symbolism* of biblical tradition on the vast majority of Christians and Jews."[80] Citing Daly, Christ points out that, although the theological tradition may claim that the biblical deity is beyond gender, that claim has no real impact because of the stranglehold of male language and imagery on the psyche of the average believer. "The effect of repeated symbolism on the conscious and unconscious mind and imagination"[81] is to make male domination appear to be normal and legitimate, a mirroring on earth of male authority "on high."

Like other feminist theologians, myself included, Christ did not realize how profoundly she had been left out of biblical religions until she said "God-she" or "goddess." Doing so can illustrate the power of male language and imagery on people's consciousness from another side. Christ writes,

> I must also acknowledge that for me *the symbol of Goddess is different than anything I ever found in the Christian tradition. My relationship with Yahweh was a dynamic one and filled with the biblical symbolism of chosenness, demand, judgement, rejection, and ultimate acceptance. . . . I was particularly moved by the prophets' concern for social justice and harmony with nature. For me, the biblical God was "beyond sexuality" as theological tradition asserts, but "he" retained a certain aura of masculine presence and authority. Not until I said* Goddess *did I realize that I had never felt fully included in the fullness of my being as a* woman *in masculine or neuterized imagery for divinity.*[82]

Christ also disputes the claim of Christian and Jewish feminists that the Bible's core message is one of liberation; she seeks to show that the Bible also contains core messages of intolerance and xenophobia. She writes that for every prophetic injunction to look after the needy and pursue justice, there is a condemnation of those who worship "'on every hill and under every green tree' (Amos 2:6)." Many of those thus condemned were women who were at the same time being excluded from roles of religious leadership in the Yahweh religion. In addition, Christ finds it impossible to "embrace the prophetic tradition of the Hebrew bible, which is vindictive against those who worship in other traditions." She suggests that this prophetic tradition is one of the key roots of intolerance in the West and that the intolerance is not "incidental to an otherwise liberating vision. I think it is fundamental to the particular shape that monotheism takes in both the Hebrew and the Christian scriptures."

Against Ruether and others who cite the Exodus narrative as indicative of the Bible's fundamental concern with liberation, Christ claims that this narrative is modeled on the "holy warrior ideal. Yahweh proves himself the most powerful holy warrior by drown-

ing Pharaoh's horsemen with their horses. This is not for me a liberating vision of divine power."

Finally, she takes up the New Testament models that have inspired many Christian feminist theologians. Though Jesus included women and the dispossessed in his community, Christ
writes that the New Testament "clearly portrays it as *his* community and the message to women is that they must turn to a male to
find salvation."[83] The idea that women can be saved only by men is
not good for women's sense of self, which is "Why Women Need
the Goddess,"[84] to quote the title of Christ's most influential essay.

Conclusions

Having concluded this survey of answers to the question, Are the
world's religions inevitably sexist?, how can we describe that which
divides those who answer no from those who respond yes? What
separates those who still give their energies and loyalties to one of
the mainstream religions, no matter how critical of it they may be,
from those who actively dissociate themselves from it? My commitment to the cross-cultural, historical, and comparative study of
religion makes me want to ask the question as a scholar of religion
rather than as a theologian in the first instance. But I have also contributed feminist theological commentary to two of the religions
discussed in this chapter—Judaism and Buddhism. Thus I, like
Christ and Daly, began my work in the context of biblical religion
and, like them, did not find biblical religions sufficient. However,
unlike them, I do not feel a need to *write against* these traditions on
feminist issues, though I have criticized them on issues of pluralism and diversity.

In the long run, all feminists, whether Christian or Jewish, post-
Christian, post-Jewish secular, or committed to another religious
tradition, affirm relatively similar symbols. We all agree that symbols, images, and doctrines that empower women are necessary.
Furthermore, within Christianity, virtually all feminist theologians

are involved in the task of renaming the central symbol of their tradition—the monotheistic deity. None of them is content with the
patriarchal god of the fathers. Those writing for and those opposing biblical religion affirm many of the same names and symbols
of God-she. What once seemed to be a major difference between
reformists and revolutionaries has ceased to be so obvious. But
though we all agree, in broad terms, about what needs to change in
religious symbolism, we differ about where to put our energies to
effect those changes. And, clearly, feminist discourse is by far the
richer for that pluralism and diversity. It is a mistake (almost a
throwback to male monotheism) to try to settle the question of
who is "right," the reformists or the revolutionaries.

Nevertheless, commenting more as a historian of religions than
as a theologian, I do not think that people usually stay in or leave a
religion because of its symbols. This is not because religious symbols and images are unimportant; they are. But symbols do not determine what the religious community will affirm; the religious
community determines what symbols it will affirm and either
grows into its postpatriarchal vision of itself or stagnates in patriarchy. As a historian, I do not agree that religious symbols cannot change. Therefore, people leave a religion not because its symbols cannot change, but because they are unlikely to change fast
enough.

One major disagreement between the two schools of feminist
theology concerns where feminist reform is likely to be most effective. Feminists wrestling with this decision must take into account
the fact that traditional religions will probably continue to lack, for
the foreseeable future, enough *communal use of feminist symbols* to
make the community an affirming place for women. Although it is
not difficult to fix the patriarchal symbolism of biblical religion or
the patriarchal institutions of Buddhism, it has been very difficult
to convince most religious leaders and believers to do so. Thinkers
like Daly and Christ have shown how painful this situation can be.

But Christian and Jewish feminist theologians, Western feminist converts to Buddhism, and many others make a different judgment—that their critical loyalty to their tradition is not a waste of time but will bear fruit in the long run, proving to be worth the pain.

A second major difference, perhaps related to the first one, separates the reformists and the revolutionaries. Some revolutionaries eagerly mine nonbiblical traditions for useful myths and symbols. Though there are exceptions, Christian and Jewish reformers generally do not, remaining much more narrowly within the orbit of biblical symbolism and the Western theological tradition. Rarely do they study deeply and let themselves be inspired by ancient goddess mythology or by non-Western religions.[85] This aspect of their loyalty to their faith is, in my view, the greatest weakness of much Jewish and Christian feminist theology, for the language and the symbolism of "God-she" is more easily inspired through wide acquaintance with the myriad goddesses of world religions. But I also fault the revolutionaries on this score, for though they love goddesses, they rarely know much about goddesses other than those of Western prebiblical antiquity.

Despite these differences between the major schools of feminist theology, we should recall what they have in common, for these will become the watchwords for the postpatriarchal future of religion. First, feminist theologies agree that human experience is the source of and authority for authentic religious expression. And second, adequate religious expressions, expressions worthy of surviving for centuries and millennia, must promote the full humanity of women, as they have always promoted the full humanity of men.

CHAPTER FIVE

Has It Always Been That Way ?
Rereading the Past

OUR SURVEY thus far has focused on feminist analysis of the *present* forms of religion and the status of *current* religious studies scholarship. These concerns lead inevitably to questions of origins and history, to questions about the *past*. Has it always been that way? Have men always dominated women? Was there a time when things were different, and women and men were more equal? How did male dominance come to be so common? Is the historical record on these issues accurate? And can history be a useful resource for feminist reconstructions of our own tradition? To return to the questions and categories suggested in chapter three, can we find a past that is both *accurate* and *useful*? What would such a past look like?

In recent years, both scholarly and popular feminist histories have raised the radical possibility that patriarchy is a recent invention and that even the familiar religions that now seem so patriarchal did not begin that way. Feminist investigations have completely challenged the notions of religious history that were commonplace a generation ago. In the 1950s, scholars were certain that history began in the urban cultures of ancient Egypt and Mesopotamia, in societies that were already male dominated. Religious histories were primarily concerned with the development of monotheism, but not monotheism's fostering of patriarchal attitudes and social structures. A second major area of study was the development of the early church, but women's prominent role in the earliest church was ignored. This was certainly the religious history that I was taught as a graduate student in the history of religions at the University of Chicago.

Today feminist historical scholarship has changed this story significantly. We must now consider the possibility that "it has *not* always been that way," that men have not always dominated women or taken sole leadership in crucial and formative moments in history. Feminist scholars also propose that history began well before Sumer, with women in much more dignified and positive positions in society than they subsequently occupied; that monotheism affected women's social and religious lives profoundly, though the nature of that effect is intensely debated; and that the growing patriarchalization of the early Christian church, beginning late in its first century, was the most significant development in the early church.

Feminist scholarship has had a particularly dramatic effect on *Western* culture's understanding of its historical development. Because of the unique *religious* significance of history in the theology of Western religions, claims that "it hasn't always been that way" are powerful and must be discussed at some length. In this chapter, I will survey some of the more important questions that feminist history raises, taking us from human religious beginnings to the patriarchalization of Christianity. I focus on these stories, despite their Eurocentric bias, because they have such religious significance for most people in Western societies. Many people are not aware of the profound effect these stories, in their androcentric tellings, have had on our consciousness, or how much changes when they are told differently. This focus will, however, prevent me from discussing feminist contributions to postbiblical Christian history, including the discovery of the church's large-scale persecution of women as witches[1] and from surveying historical issues in other traditions.

Although the work of feminist historians may make the historical record more accurate and may empower women who want to claim their place in history, it can also be quite threatening, having a revolutionary effect on how one understands the world and one's place in it. This is another way in which descriptive and constructive issues intertwine in religious studies.

The Prepatriarchal Hypothesis: An Introduction and Assessment

The prepatriarchal hypothesis is both a sacred history for many women—the sacred history of the feminist spirituality movement[2]—and a scholarly hypothesis, which argues that "the creation of patriarchy"[3] occurred in the relatively recent past because of certain causes and conditions. The hypothesis is often accompanied by speculation about religion and society in the prepatriarchal world, with many portraying it as a "feminist utopia."

Drawn from work in several disciplines, including prehistory, archeology, anthropology, mythology, history, and the comparative study of religions, the prepatriarchal hypothesis has generated a great deal of controversy both inside and outside the feminist community. Because the scholarship on which this hypothesis is based is quite technical and difficult, and because of the passion with which feminists argue for and against this hypothesis, critically examining this issue can feel like walking through a minefield.

What is at stake in the validity of this hypothesis? Why does it raise so much passion and controversy? Insofar as communities constitute themselves on the basis of their remembered past, contemporary social change is more likely if memories are extended further into the past. Determining that patriarchy is a relatively recent historical development means that patriarchy is not inevitable and that male dominance is not somehow written into our genes. It is no accident that new forms of biological determinism, such as sociobiology, became popular soon after the current wave of feminist thinking became established. Nor is it accidental that extreme claims for an evolutionary and genetic basis for male dominance, such as Lionel Tiger's *Men in Groups*,[4] as well as diatribes about the biological dangers of egalitarian social arrangements, such as George Gilder's *Sexual Suicide*,[5] became popular at the same time. Arguments based on biology or nature often seem stronger than claims based on history and culture. Therefore, both feminists and antifeminists have a great deal at stake in arguments about the nature of the first human societies.

Sorting through the polemics of advocates and critics of the prepatriarchal hypothesis is not simple, but I will use the following guidelines. First, I will emphasize the conclusions of prehistorians, archeologists, anthropologists, and historians who are both informed by feminist values and conversant with relevant scholarly literature. The most vehement advocates and attackers of the prepatriarchal hypothesis often treat this material lightly in their writings. Second, I will base my critique on scholarly, rather than popular, versions of the prepatriarchal hypothesis. Obviously the cogency of the prepatriarchal hypothesis should not be tested on the basis of literature produced by those who lack expertise in the relevant subjects. Finally, and most important, I will assume that casting doubt on a single aspect of the hypothesis does not invalidate the entire hypothesis. Therefore, I will evaluate the various components of the prepatriarchal hypothesis separately, rather than try to reject or justify the whole complex. The three parts I will analyze are as follows. First, is it reasonable to conclude that patriarchy arose relatively recently in human history? Second, does the thesis of a prepatriarchal "golden age" for women hold up? Third, what are the best explanations for the emergence of patriarchy in human history?

Is Patriarchy the Original Form of Society?

To best understand the prepatriarchal hypothesis, one should place equal emphasis on both words in the term. The word *hypothesis* indicates that this account of early society is a probable reconstruction from limited information, rather than an incontrovertible fact. Like all hypotheses, it is subject to continual revision and possible replacement if a better explanation is developed. The modest term *prepatriarchal* simply indicates that it is extremely unlikely that patriarchy prevailed in the earliest human societies. Patriarchy requires the kind of social stratification and social complexity that develop with high population density and urbanization—not the conditions of early human societies. What the term *prepatriarchy* does *not* attempt to describe is what the earliest forms of human society were like. Specifically, the prepatriarchal hypothesis, at least in its scholarly form, does not assert or assume a prior *matriarchy*. As futurist Riane Eisler notes, people stuck in dualistic, either-or thinking often assume that "if it isn't patriarchy, it must be matriarchy,"[6] an assumption made by Bachofen as well as by many recent popular writers.

By far the most skeptical critics of any version of the prepatriarchal hypothesis are those trained in the history of religions and the study of classical civilizations. Because the societies studied by these scholars have been patriarchal for so long and because these societies have become so dominant over so much of the globe, classicists and historians of religion often find the hypothesis of non-patriarchal social organization unbelievable. For example, the historian of religions David Kinsley rejects the prepatriarchal hypothesis because of "the few examples we have of cultures in which men do not dominate women. The tendency toward male dominance is strong in both historical cultures and in nonliterate cultures."[7]

By contrast, anthropologists and archeologists trying to reconstruct the earliest foraging and horticultural societies simply do not agree with the conclusion of universal male dominance any longer. As anthropologist Peggy Reeves Sanday says in her major study of the origins of male dominance, "Male dominance is not an inherent quality of human sex-role plans. In fact, the argument suggests that male dominance is a response to pressures that are most likely to have been present relatively late in human history."[8]

In my view, if one thinks about the requirements for human survival from an androgynous, rather than an androcentric, point of view, it is difficult to imagine that humanity could have survived if early humans had insisted on wasting female productivity and intelligence in the way that patriarchal societies have always done. Anthropologists no longer believe that the earliest human societies could have depended solely on men for their food supply, or that men alone were responsible for the refinement of tools, the development of language, or other crucial advances made by early humans.[9] All convincing reconstructions of early foraging life posit an interdependence and complementarity between women and men, rather than male dominance and patriarchy. Nothing in the material conditions of early human life would suggest that male dominance would have been adaptive or likely. Furthermore, even though sex roles are often relatively well-defined in contemporary foraging societies, male dominance is rare. The sexes are seen as complementary and of equal importance.[10] Although everyone recognizes that the ethnographic present cannot establish an archeological past, and that reconstructions of prehistory will probably always remain hypothetical, the notion of a strongly male-dominant, patriarchal foraging past seems to be an especially unlikely hypothesis.

Regarding early Neolithic horticultural (hoe-using) societies, a similar moderate reconstruction is sensible. Because women usually specialize in gathering plant foods in a foraging economy, most anthropologists and archeologists think that women probably discovered how to cultivate seeds. Therefore, their contributions to the survival of a community that depended on horticulture were immense. In fact, the period of Neolithic horticulture is probably the time least likely to have been male dominated. Even many nonfeminist scholars have suggested that during Neolithic times women enjoyed higher status and more autonomy than they typically did later. Even nonfeminist scholars also recognize that goddesses were central to Neolithic religion. As with earlier foraging Paleolithic societies, there is nothing to suggest that male dominance would have been practical or adaptive for Neolithic horticulturalists. And, as with contemporary foraging societies, contemporary or recent horticultural societies do not usually exhibit strong male dominance and patriarchy, though some do. But some of the more recent societies that have been deemed noteworthy or curious because in them women have considerable autonomy and power, such as the Iroquois and the West African kingdoms,[11] are horticultural.

Therefore, without making any claims about the nature of prepatriarchal society, it is reasonable to conclude that an accurately reconstructed early history of humanity is empowering and useful for women, simply because claims for eternal male dominance make no sense and are not supported by contemporary anthropology and archeology. "It hasn't always been that way." Foraging and early horticultural societies were probably not patriarchal. As we shall see, we may not be able to establish any adequate models for the postpatriarchal future in the prepatriarchal past. Nevertheless, it alters our perceptions and assumptions greatly to realize that it makes no sense to claim that male dominance stretches as far back into the past as we can see. At the conclusion of her book *Women in Prehistory*, which no one could fault for lack of caution in its interpretations, Margaret Ehrenberg states the case well:

> Although the social status of women has long been inferior to that of men, it must also be remembered that the foraging societies of the Paleolithic and Mesolithic spanned an immense period, many hundred times longer than the mere 12,000 years or so from the Neolithic to the present, and that many of the world's people continued to be foragers long after farming had been discovered in the Near East. So, through-

out human history, the great majority of women who have ever lived had far more status than recently, and probably had equality with men.[12]

Interpreting Prepatriarchal Evidence

That patriarchy arose in history because of certain causes and conditions seems to me to be as certain as any historical hypothesis ever can be. Nevertheless, there is no easy passage, and probably no passage at all, between establishing that patriarchy is a late development to establishing the kind of prepatriarchal feminist utopia claimed by the most ardent advocates of the prepatriarchal hypothesis. Their attempted reconstruction of prepatriarchal religion and society is, in my view, the weak link in many versions of the prepatriarchal hypothesis.

As I have previously stated, many advocates of the prepatriarchal hypothesis believe that the prepatriarchal period was a "golden age" for women. Paleolithic foraging societies, Chatal Huyuk (a town in Anatolia), Old Europe, ancient megalithic cultures, and especially Crete are the cultures most commonly discussed by advocates of this position, particularly because they worshipped numerous and powerful goddesses. Advocates of this golden age posit an era of peace, prosperity, stability, and egalitarian social arrangements that prevailed far and wide for a long period of time before being destroyed violently and relatively quickly by patriarchal and pastoral nomads, including the precursors of both the Indo-Aryans and the Semites. In this prepatriarchal world, women enjoyed autonomy, power, and respect under the aegis of the goddess, who was universally revered by all members of society and was the embodiment and source of life, death, and renewal. Gradually, as societies became more male dominant, both women and the goddess lost their power, autonomy, and dignity; this process culminated in the eclipse of the goddess by the Hebrew Bible and the thinking of classical Greece.

Such a hypothesis has always enjoyed some currency, going back at least to the nineteenth-century theories of J. J. Bachofen, discussed in chapter two. Early in the twentieth-century women's movement, the thesis was again popularized by feminist writers such as Elizabeth Gould Davis and Merlin Stone.[13] Since then, scholarship on the topic has flourished. Historian Anne Barstow examined Chatal Huyuk, one of the most famous Neolithic sites cited in contemporary discussions, in an influential and extremely balanced article.[14] The well-established archeologist Marija Gimbutas, whose interpretations of the culture of Old Europe pioneered a new chapter in prehistory, took up this reconstruction with passion and conviction.[15] Students of mythology, such as Elinor Gadon[16] and the team of Anne Baring and Jules Cashford,[17] have written engaging and complete histories of the various ancient goddesses, from Paleolithic examples to medieval veneration of the Virgin Mary. Relying on the archeological work done by Gimbutas and others, Carol P. Christ has made the prepatriarchal hypothesis central to her goddess thea-logy.[18]

The most visionary and poetic reconstruction, which sees the prepatriarchal past as part of an unfinished, but absolutely essential evolutionary transformation still awaiting completion, is Riane Eisler's *The Chalice and the Blade.*[19] Pulling together a great deal of information from prehistory, classical biblical and Greek materials, and contemporary ecological issues, Eisler contrasts the values of the chalice with those of the blade. The chalice represents a "gylanic" (that is, peaceful and egalitarian value) system prevalent in the prepatriarchal world, whereas the blade represents the androcratic values of the "dominator" societies that overthrew and partially, but never completely, destroyed the gylanic values held by prepatriarchal societies of empowered women, peaceful men, and strong goddesses. Clearly, "remembering" such a past could be empowering and useful in today's world.

Why then am I, like other *feminists*, as well as antifeminists, skeptical of this component of the prepatriarchal hypothesis? The answer is twofold. Some feminists object that such "spiritual" issues are largely irrelevant to contemporary women. They note that goddesses frequently coexist with male dominance and that the presence of goddesses does not ensure high status or autonomy for women. Many such feminists feel that economic, political, and social issues are of far higher priority and that antiquity holds few models in this regard. They may also believe that goddess worship in the *present* does little to alleviate women's real problems.

Other feminists are not especially opposed to goddess worship for contemporary women and agree that the ancient world included many powerful and impressive goddesses. But these feminists are skeptical of the scholarship that has reconstructed a *utopian* or a *female-dominated past*, based on the existence of these goddesses. Many argue that extreme caution is required when interpreting material artifacts and that one cannot easily deduce ideology or social structure from them. The ease with which Gimbutas, Gadon, or Baring and Cashford, for example, infer extremely detailed myths and rituals from limited and opaque material artifacts is a major defect, in my view, because such reconstructions are easily subject to projection and wishful thinking.

Such disclaimers about the prepatriarchal hypothesis are especially numerous among academically trained scholars of religion who are otherwise interested in or sympathetic to feminism, such as David Kinsley,[20] Katherine K. Young,[21] and Joan Townsend.[22] All three of them have published sharply worded critiques of these reconstructions of the prepatriarchal period. Young and Townsend both express the opinion that the feminist reconstruction of the prepatriarchal past, in Townsend's words, "puts forth as *historical fact* the myth of a golden age of the past to give ego reinforcement, to weld a bond among women in order to create a unified force, and to provide women with historical precedent for their aspirations."[23] In other words, this particular remembered past, however *useful* it might be, is not *accurate* and is therefore unacceptable.

Rosemary Ruether has also been a longtime critic of the vision of a feminist utopian past. As she states in her 1992 book *Gaia and God*, she finds the claims for the innocence or goodness of pre-patriarchal societies untenable because such claims link failure and greed with patriarchy and men, instead of with human beings, both female and male.[24]

Why do some scholars embrace a feminist utopian past, whereas others do not find it credible? What is the evidence supporting this view of the past? That many depictions of the female body have been found by archeologists is uncontested. It is equally certain that early mythological literature tells of many important and powerful goddesses. However, these facts do not prove that men and women were equal in the modern sense of the term, or that women lived lives with which modern women could be satisfied, or that the numerous female figures that have been discovered can easily be interpreted as mother goddesses. When interpreting these numerous female figures, it is much safer to note their presence and to hypothesize that they may well indicate appreciation of female sacredness (though even that is not certain), rather than to speculate in great detail about their theology or to try to determine if they are goddesses or priestesses. The certainty with which Eisler and Gimbutas sometimes retell the myths and restage the rituals of prepatriarchal societies does not seem justified.

Though it may never be possible to demonstrate what prepatriarchal societies were like in detail, or to interpret their symbol and myth systems with certainty, it does seem reasonable to me to conclude both that women were less dominated than in latter societies and that female sacredness was more commonly venerated. Because patriarchy had not yet evolved, it seems quite likely that women's relationships with men were more satisfactory, by feminist standards of assessment, than they later became. And it seems even more likely that female sacredness, whether human or divine, was a commonplace of religious ideology for both women and men, simply because portrayals of women engaged in religious rituals are so common and female figures are so abundantly found in settings that seem to be sacred places. These modest and, to my mind, relatively certain conclusions are both accurate and useful, while avoiding the extremes of both those who reconstruct details of a prepatriarchal feminist utopia without sufficient information and those who reject the prepatriarchal hypothesis entirely.

Three other theses central to many standard feminist reconstructions of prepatriarchal societies and religions deserve comment. Feminists often claim that these prepatriarchal societies were both egalitarian and peaceful. They also postulate that the respect accorded to women and the perception that females, whether divine or human, are sacred, both contributed to this desirable state of affairs.

Critics have questioned these conclusions about the nature of prepatriarchal societies. Joan Townsend argues that many bodies buried in supposedly peaceful Chatal Huyuk showed evidence of severe blows to the head,[25] and Katherine K. Young argues that private property, which undercuts egalitarianism, could have begun in the Neolithic age.[26] But the descriptions of the town plans, the houses themselves, and the art of Neolithic Europe, which occur in source after source, support the conclusion that Neolithic European societies were relatively peaceful and egalitarian, *especially when compared with later societies.* To say that these societies were peaceful is to say that they did not expend major resources, human or material, on organized, large-scale warfare—not that individual conflicts, resulting in severe head wounds, never occurred. It is important to recognize that feuding and private fights, which seem impossible to avoid in human society, are completely different from diverting major resources and human energy into defensive or offensive warfare. This is a critical distinction, since it is naive to attribute the human tendency to aggressive behavior to patriarchal social arrangements. Patriarchy may encourage such tendencies, but it does not create them.

On the other hand, the nonmilitary prepatriarchal societies give evidence to a critically important conclusion. *Human beings can live together and deal with their aggressions without resorting to large-scale, organized warfare as a major preoccupation and use of re-sources.* Even a nonfeminist historian, Thorkild Jacobsen, locates the beginning of warfare as a major threat to human life in the third millennium B.C.E.,[27] but not earlier, when, in his view, famine was a much more severe threat. And early private property was not sufficient to result in the great inequities of wealth or poverty char-acteristic of later societies, as is clear from descriptions of town plans and houses.

However, it may not be possible to establish that this peaceful, egalitarian lifestyle was *caused* by the relatively high status of women and the veneration of female sacredness, as is so often claimed. On the one hand, the archeological evidence supports the likelihood of relative peace and egalitarianism and argues against large-scale warfare and significant hierarchy in early foraging and horticultural societies. It also supports the view that women had relatively higher status in these societies than in later patriarchal societies.

But, on the other hand, *once large-scale warfare and significant social hierarchies became part of human society, both women and goddesses readily supported both.* This embarrassing fact argues against the conclusion that earlier societies were relatively peaceful *because* women insisted upon peace. Women's preferences for or against hierarchy or warfare do not seem to be the driving causal link in human development. It seems to me, rather, that certain technological capabilities, once unleashed, are hard to restrain from bringing hierarchy and violence in their wake. It is to this topic that we now turn our attention.

The Creation of Patriarchy

With the transition from horticulture to intensive agriculture, which began somewhere in the fertile crescent of ancient Egypt and Mesopotamia after 5000 B.C.E., male dominance first becomes clear-cut and obvious. Again this conclusion of archeologists is supported by anthropological evidence; contemporary agricultural societies are almost always male dominated, whereas foraging and horticultural societies are not.

How did this transition come about? Advocates of the most extreme forms of the prepatriarchal hypothesis claim that men from groups that were already patriarchal and violent invaded and conquered the peaceful Neolithic societies, using their superior physical strength and weapons to initiate a reign of terror and dominance.[28] Although the invasions of Indo-European and Semitic nomadic warriors are one factor in the decline of some prepatriarchal societies, this broad explanation raises obvious questions. *Where did these men come from? And why did they turn to warfare, violence, and domination when more peaceful ways of living were available?*

These questions are difficult to answer if one explains the creation of patriarchy as being due to invasions by already patriarchal outsiders. Lurking in the background of this explanation as an unstated assumption is an essentialist understanding of male and female natures. Women prefer peace; men are more prone to violence. Therefore, matrifocal societies are peaceful and egalitarian because, in them, women have more power; patriarchal societies are violent and authoritarian because men are dominant. Biological determinism is as central to this feminist hypothesis as it is to many androcentric justifications of patriarchy. And as already argued, biological explanations for male dominance, if accurate, would suggest that efforts to eradicate patriarchy are futile.

If, on the other hand, patriarchy is the result of specific conditions that came into being at some point in cultural evolution, then, when those conditions change, patriarchy can die a natural death. An explanation for the creation of patriarchy that looks into changing technologies rather than moral differences, rooted in biology, between men and women, is certainly more useful for feminists; in my view, it is also more accurate because varying cultural and historical circumstances account for so much in human life, and so few universals can be found. Therefore, I suggest looking beyond the immediate cause of the decline of many prepatriarchal societies—conquest by patriarchal outsiders—to the more basic causes that led to the development of warrior, male-dominated societies in the first place.

Patriarchy emerged because the *material conditions* of life promoted male dominance for the first time. Newer technologies—the plow, use of draft animals, complex irrigation systems—and a new emphasis on labor-intensive grain crops favored men as the primary producers, and women were reduced to the role of processing agricultural products. Labor-intensive agriculture increased the demand on women to bear children at the same time that an increased food supply permitted higher rates of fertility. Women began to have more babies, and populations increased greatly. Specialization and social stratification became possible. As the population grew, resources became scarcer, and competition for them increased, making organized, communal violence (warfare) attractive and seemingly advantageous. Specialization also made possible an increase in private property, which heightened competition for now-scarcer resources, and made warfare more attractive. All of these factors were essential in the transition from a kin-based society to the process of early state formation. And, to some extent at least, these processes seem to have occurred in many societies throughout the world.

Thus a complex web of technological, social, and material changes, rather than moral changes (such as women's decreasing public power) or religious changes (such as the decline of goddess worship), made dominance and hierarchy, including male dominance over women, possible for the first time relatively late in human history. Contrary to some feminist claims, the decline of women's public power and of goddess worship are undoubtedly *effects* rather than *causes* of patriarchy. Historian Gerda Lerner arrives at this conclusion, as do many anthropologists and archeologists.[29] Thus, we have established the first claim about patriarchy again, but on different grounds. The part of the prepatriarchal hypothesis claiming that patriarchy, as we have experienced patriarchy in most or all societies since the Bronze Age, is the product of changing cultural and historical circumstances, rather than a timeless human condition or the result of male moral depravity, seems as certain as any historical hypothesis can be.

When discussing the creation of patriarchy, it is also important to explore the role of warfare and invasion in the demise of prepatriarchal societies. Although evidence seems quite clear that Old Europe and the Mediterranean regions were, in fact, overrun by patriarchal outsiders who violently and quickly destroyed peaceful, matrifocal Neolithic villages,[30] it seems equally clear that in the ancient Near East, in Mesopotamia, among other places, *internal* developments leading toward social hierarchy, including male dominance, preceded large-scale warfare as a major threat and preoccupation.[31] Thus, ultimately, even warfare may be an *effect* of changing technologies, rather than the *cause* of the end of prepatriarchal societies. Increased population pressures and competition for scarce resources were more likely the *causes* that made warfare an attractive option in the first place—a lesson that is certainly important in contemporary times as well.

Finally, we can return to the link between symbols of sacred females and the emerging patriarchal order. It seems quite unlikely that the new emphases on warfare and male dominance occurred because patriarchal symbols and beliefs replaced woman-honoring ones. If anything, the reverse occurred. When technological changes increased male domination, religion changed to accommodate it. As we know from the cross-cultural and historical studies of religion, material or technological changes and changes in symbolism or religious and social ideology are always closely bound together. But in this particular case, it does not seem cogent to give religious symbols the role of causal agent because male dominance more likely resulted from changing technology than from new beliefs.

However, given that religious symbols and social norms always reflect and reinforce each other, advocates of the prepatriarchal hypothesis are also right when they claim that the patriarchal ideologies, symbol systems, and social systems that now predominate on this planet could never produce a return to peace and egalitarianism. Peace and egalitarianism will require postpatriarchal symbols and ideologies as well as postpatriarchal technologies. And, in my view, postpatriarchal symbols and ideologies will resemble prepatriarchal symbols of female sacredness and egalitarian gender relationships more than they will resemble patriarchal symbols and gender relationships.

Some Concluding Comments on the Prepatriarchal Hypothesis

I have not yet discussed two weaknesses endemic to the prepatriarchal hypothesis as usually presented in feminist literature. One is its obvious Eurocentric bias, and the other is its unilinear model of cultural evolution. The prepatriarchal hypothesis explains *Western* patriarchy, not other forms of male dominance. And it seems to assume that patriarchy emerged *once*, in Western antiquity. Both of these omissions need to be addressed.

Very little research has been done concerning the cultural and religious development from prepatriarchy into patriarchy in other parts of the world. Though the case has not been made very thoroughly, existing archeological and historical data could warrant extending the hypothesis to include India, because India also was invaded by Indo-Aryans. However, even though the waves of cultural contact that explain Western patriarchy could serve for India as well, they could not do so for East Asia, which has a different history. East Asian patriarchy has not been explained to any great extent. In a noteworthy exception, Robert Ellwood has argued that the mythological narratives of early Japan (late third to early fourth centuries C.E.) seem to indicate that Japan was then experiencing a change from matrifocal to patriarchal societies.[32]

Nevertheless, though the Eurocentric bias is regrettable, its consequences are not as serious as one might at first suspect. It is difficult to imagine that foraging and horticultural societies were vastly different in other parts of the world than they were in Europe and the Middle East. Therefore, bias does not necessarily invalidate the hypothesis.

The unilinear model of evolution into patriarchy is a more serious problem, for it assumes that all societies proceed, lockstep, through the same historical processes. As discussed in chapter two, this hypothesis was popular in nineteenth- and early-twentieth-century anthropology, but it has not been taken seriously for many years. The work of Peggy Reeves Sanday in *Female Power and Male Dominance*, introduced in chapter three, offers an important corrective concerning theories of the origins of male dominance. Rather than isolating single, or even multiple, chains of cause and effect leading to male dominance, she locates cultural patterns that tend to be associated with male dominance and, alternatively, with female power. Chief among her findings is that it is possible to talk of female power and male-female equality when women have economic and political decision-making powers, which they do in about 32 percent of past and contemporary societies she studied. Only 28 percent of the societies in her large sample are clearly male dominated. The remaining 40 percent are neither clearly egalitarian nor male dominated, but fall between those poles.[33]

Sanday studies many factors that affect the level of male dominance in a society. If the physical environment and climate are beneficent, then women and men tend to work together, men spend time with young children, and individuals develop what Sanday calls an "inner orientation," including a symbol system that features female creative beings. Such societies are not usually male dominant. By contrast, if the physical environment is harsher, so that providing basic necessities produces stress, or if people's livelihood centers around husbandry of large animals or migration, individuals develop an "outer orientation," in which the creative powers are viewed as male. Male dominance is likely in these societies, in part because men and women do not work together and men spend little time with children.

But these lines of explanation are not neat and unilinear. Though, in some cases, one can "establish a causal relationship between depleting resources, cultural disruption, migration, and the oppression of women," male domination of women, when it occurs, "is a complex question, for which no one answer suffices."[34] In the long run, Sanday's less than neat, nonlinear discussion of female power and male dominance is more satisfying than even the refinements of the prepatriarchal hypothesis that do no more than explain the emergence of patriarchy in Western antiquity. Her findings are useful not only to historians who want to explain the rise of patriarchy, but also to ethicists and theologians seeking to envision the postpatriarchal future of religion.

Finally, we must return to the question of whether prepatriarchal religion and society could form an accurate and usable past. As we have established, it is accurate to speak of prepatriarchal pasts. But can they be useful to contemporary people? I suggest that prepatriarchal pasts provide proof of the possibility of a postpatriarchal future, but are not a model for it. We need to recognize, with Barstow,[35] that modern women should find the forms and symbols of ancient religion only of limited utility in constructing postpatriarchal religion. Why is that? Most interpreters of ancient female forms and symbols see them as representations of fertility and maternity. But, although motherhood is an important part of many women's religious experience, it is by no means sufficient in scope to provide complete meaning for female sacredness in today's religious universe. Considering that increasing reproductive demands on women, which resulted in increased population density and competition for scarce resources, is probably one of the causes of patriarchy, feminists should be loath to enshrine physical reproduction as the primary symbol of female sacredness. Furthermore, human population growth is a grave threat to the environment, and since environmental stress is one of the root causes of male domination, feminism needs to sanctify alternative models of female impact on the world that reverse and undercut excessive physiological reproduction. Such models are in short supply in the prepatriarchal world, at least as interpreted by many of its advocates.

Another useful lesson can be learned by studying some of the less accurate versions of the prepatriarchal hypothesis that speak of utopian conditions destroyed by patriarchy. It is futile to look for the birth of human aggression, or whatever else we may see as the genesis of human misery, in the birth of patriarchy. Patriarchy adds its own special and unnecessary dimensions to human misery, to its grasping nature and the resultant suffering, but it is naive and unhelpful to locate the origins of grasping and aggression, tendencies basic to being human, in the origins of patriarchy. They will continue to challenge us even in postpatriarchal religion and society. To regard "the fall" as a historical, preventable event rather than an ahistorical mythic event, which happens when the origins of patriarchy are equated with the origin of evil and suffering, is an uncritical appropriation of one of patriarchal religions' most destructive beliefs.

From the Creation of Patriarchy to the Triumph of Male Monotheism

Between the creation of patriarchy and the eventual triumph of male monotheism as the dominant religious symbol system lie several millennia[36] during which goddesses were an integral part of all religions. Exclusively masculine God-talk, taken for granted as normal by most people in Western societies for so long, was an even later development in cultural evolution than the creation of patriarchy. In fact, most of the literary evidence and much of the iconographic material about the various and numerous goddesses of the ancient world come from this period. Furthermore, though we may presume that prepatriarchal religions and societies must have existed in the non-Western world and that they too experienced the creation of patriarchy, their goddesses and female images of the divine did not disappear as quickly or as thoroughly. Western monotheism is unique in its fear and denial of images of female divinity.

The Goddesses of Ancient Patriarchy

The long story of the goddesses' decline has often been told, especially in recent years.[37] Though it is not possible to summarize that story in these few pages, I will highlight a few important themes. First, male-dominated societies outside ancient Israel had no qualms about the existence or presence of goddesses. Although the goddesses did gradually decline in importance and strength, no nonmonotheistic religion ever tried to suppress veneration of goddesses or labeled it idolatry.

One story of the impact of patriarchy on the goddesses comes from ancient Mesopotamia, from the fourth through the second millennia B.C.E. Though the story is long and complex, records demonstrate an obvious decline in the power and importance of the regions' goddesses, especially Inanna, an utterly provocative and unconventional Sumerian goddess.[38] In early literature, Inanna is a powerful and impetuous deity whose sexuality is lyrically celebrated in some of the world's most beautiful erotic poetry. She rules heaven and earth and confers fertility to the land and authority to the king in the sacred marriage ritual. The tale of her descent to the underworld is told in many versions, but all of them affirm her central importance; unless she is brought back from the underworld, life will end. However, in later literature, such as the second millennium B.C.E. *Epic of Gilgamesh*, she is rejected as a lover by the human hero Gilgamesh and generally plays a minor, unimportant role in human and divine affairs.

But nothing so completely reflects the gradual decline of once powerful goddesses as the Babylonian creation epic, the *Enumah Elish*. The hero of the epic is the young warrior god Marduk. His struggle with the older generation of deities culminates in his hand-to-hand combat with the primordial mother goddess Tiamat. He wins the combat and makes the earth on which we live out of her mutilated carcass.

> *The lord rested, examining her dead body,*
> *To divide the abortion (and) to create ingenious things,*
> *He split her open like a mussel into two parts;*
> *Half of her he set in place and formed the sky (therewith) as a roof.*[39]

Continuing from another translation,

> *Below, he heaped a mountain over Tiamat's head, pierced her eyes to*
> *form the sources of the Euphrates and the Tigris . . . and heaped simi-*
> *lar mountains over her dugs, which he pierced to make the rivers from*

the eastern mountains that flow into the Tigris. Her tail he bent up
into the sky to make the Milky Way, and her crotch he used to support
the sky.[40]

Though the genders of the hero and the victim were ignored in my
graduate school studies of this text, it is impossible not to read this
text as a celebration of the triumph of patriarchy when it is read
against the background of the prepatriarchal hypothesis. Read in
any feminist context, the hostility and violence displayed toward
the primal mother Tiamat are frightening.

The revisions of goddess mythology and symbolism just discussed were carried on by Semitic people, one of the two ethnic
groups often cited as central in the triumph of patriarchy. The
other, the Indo-Aryans, also left their mark on goddess imagery
and mythology, this time on the mythology of classical Greece.

Feminist studies of various Greek goddesses have shown that
many of the goddesses were also worshipped in prepatriarchal
Crete and that they are present in classical Greek mythology only
in a diminished form.[41] No Greek goddess really manifests wholeness, and no Greek goddess is a female equivalent of or equal to
Zeus, the male head of the pantheon. Instead, each goddess represents a limited range of options and possibilities rather than a full,
well-rounded lifestyle. For example, the most powerful and independent goddesses, such as Athena and Artemis, are also virgins
without sexual lives. The primordial married goddess, Hera, is very
unhappy and frustrated in her marriage. Nor is Aphrodite, the
most erotic of the Greek goddesses, well married. Furthermore,
most Greek goddesses in the Homeric pantheon are not mothers
themselves, though some of them help human mothers.

Contrasting with the Homeric goddesses who live on Mount
Olympus is Demeter, goddess of the harvest and of the earth's fertility, who most successfully among the Greek goddesses retained
her prepatriarchal meanings. She is very popular with feminists because she does not conform to the limitations imposed on most

other Greek goddesses. Motherhood is central to her mythology, and the story of her relationship with her daughter Persephone is frequently retold and interpreted in feminist literature. Even more important, Demeter was the patron deity of the Eleusinian Mysteries, one of the most important religions of salvation in the pre-Christian world. It was still alive and important when the triumph of Christianity led to the demise of goddess religions in the ancient world.

The Struggle over Male Monotheism

As we have seen, the Babylonians and the Greeks did not attempt to rid religion of goddesses. Instead, their myths reflected a growing male dominance as once powerful and independent goddesses became the consorts of more recent, more powerful male gods. The story of ancient Israel is different. Historically, monotheism has been unwilling to tolerate alternative conceptions and symbols of deity. Although monotheism targeted all foreign deities, not just goddesses, in its battle to secure exclusive loyalty to its deity, the net effect is that monotheism ended goddess worship. The single most potent factor in the eventual loss of female symbolism of the divine was the eventual triumph of monotheism, whose single deity most definitely was not female.

This struggle, as it occurred in biblical times, is now being reconstructed by contemporary feminist theologians and historians. Two stories have come to the fore. One is that goddess religions coexisted with male monotheism for centuries and prospered until well into the Christian era. In addition to the Eleusinian Mysteries, dedicated to Demeter and Persephone, goddess religions were alive and well in the form of devotion to Isis at the beginning of the Christian era. When Christianity triumphed over "paganism," goddess religions ended in the Western world.[42] This fact alone, concealed by conventional accounts of Christian origins, is sobering. When we add to this story the history of the decline of nonpatriarchal forms of early Christianity, to be discussed in the next section of this chapter, it is even clearer that conventional accounts of the history of monotheism and Christianity have omitted basic information.

The second important story about the struggle between monotheism and goddesses is that male monotheism did not easily win over people's imaginations, even in ancient Israel. Furthermore, the primordial goddesses remain, even within the scope of biblical thought.[43] In Judaism, both biblical and postbiblical, the pull to feminine imagery continued after the triumph of male monotheism. Several female personifications of God's attributes gained growing popularity in later Israelite history, particularly during the period of the second temple. The most important is Lady Wisdom, who appears in the Book of Proverbs; she later evolved into Sophia, who has become quite important in some recent feminist theological reconstructions.[44] Postbiblical Judaism also continued to experience this pull, most noticeably in the mystical Jewish tradition, the Kabbalah, once a dominant form of Judaism, which clearly envisioned a deity who is both male and female.[45] Going even further, many who claim that a divine feminine is inevitable and unsuppressible cite the widespread popular veneration of the Virgin Mary in Christianity;[46] the less-known tradition of the "motherly Jesus" in medieval Christian piety also evidences this tendency.[47]

Even *during* the transition to male monotheism in ancient Israel, the appeal of goddesses was widespread, as Raphael Patai demonstrates in his book *The Hebrew Goddess.*[48] The Bible itself conveys the impression that the acceptance of male monotheism was smooth and clear in ancient Israel; only deviant people are shown objecting to this religious ideal or being attracted by "foreign" religions, including those with goddesses. However, Patai suggests that for many centuries following the initial disclosure of male monotheism to Israelites, "this religion, idealized in retrospect, remained a demand rather than a fact."[49] The world of the

Hebrew Bible and Israelite religion itself gives evidence of ongoing attraction to female counterparts of Yahweh, such as Asherah.[50] Furthermore, rather than being foreign, Patai claims that

> there can be no doubt that the goddess to whom the Hebrews clung
> with such tenacity down to the days of Josiah, and to whom they re-
> turned with such remorse following the destruction of the Jerusalem
> Temple, was, whatever prophets had to say about her, no foreign se-
> ductress, but a Hebrew goddess, the best divine mother the people had
> had to that time.[51]

Most people growing up in the West have been taught that the advent of monotheism represented an immeasurable advance in the quality of human life. Usually it has also been assumed that women too benefited from this change. However, feminist study of religion has challenged this assumption, creating one of the more intense debates within feminist religious studies. I will conclude this section of this chapter by summarizing and evaluating two scholarly works that offer opposite points of view on this question.

Ancient Near Eastern specialist Judith Ochshorn's book *The Fe-male Experience and the Nature of the Divine*[52] compares gender and concepts of the divine, the relationship between gender and power, and the relationship between gender and participation in religious practice in polytheistic and monotheistic religions. She challenges the "underlying belief that the advent of monotheism represented for women and men alike a seminal moral and spiritual advance over polytheism."[53] She finds that women are *not* better off in societies that have done away with polytheistic religious systems that include images of the divine feminine.

As a result of these comparisons, Ochshorn concludes that polytheistic religions gave at least some classes of women a significant role in public religious practice, unlike early Israelite religion. She also states that polytheistic religions did not consider the exercise of divine power to belong exclusively to either sex, since female and male divinities both engaged in the broad range of activities indispensable to the human community, and that, therefore, neither sex was deemed inferior to the other. Ochshorn also claims that in the polytheistic religions, expressions of fear of female biology and reproduction were "conspicuously absent." "In time, this androgynous outlook gave way to the radically new vision of monotheism, which encompassed an association of power and powerlessness with gender in a manner quite foreign to the polytheistic mentality."[54] She compares "the more androgynous attitudes prevalent in ancient Near Eastern polytheistic religions" to the monotheistic biblical views:

> It may be, then, that among the most radically new ideas advanced by the biblical vision of divine-human relationships was the concept of worth, autonomy, and power as inextricably linked to gender, and the polarization of feminine and masculine in apprehensions of the divine and prescriptions for the organization of the human community.[55]

In my view, Ochshorn has clearly located a significant and real change in the continuing shift of consciousness that must have accompanied the long transition from prepatriarchal religion and society to male monotheism. She has also shown a *correlation* between monotheism and male dominance on the one hand, and between polytheism and more egalitarian forms on the other. However, it is not clear that there is a *causal* relationship between the two correlations. As we have already seen, male dominance was affecting even polytheistic societies at that time, as male deities usurped goddesses' functions.[56] In my view, full-fledged patriarchy would probably have eventually emerged in any case, with or without monotheism. Though contemporary male monotheism is a major contributing cause to the *survival* of contemporary patriarchy, I do not think one can *attribute* ancient patriarchy to the development of male monotheism. In fact, I believe the causal relationship should be reversed. Male monotheism is one of the last, but most pervasive and powerful *results* of an emerging patriarchy and one of its most potent tools for sustaining its power.

The critical question that Ochshorn's work raises is whether monotheism can support social systems and ways of symbolizing deity that are androgynous and egalitarian, as Jewish and Christian feminist theologians claim. If it can, why was it historically so strongly linked with patriarchy? Why did monotheism play such a crucial role in the eclipse and demise of the goddesses, who were among the deities seen and hunted down as "idols" and "pagan" in both the Hebrew Bible and the New Testament? Perhaps these questions will never be answered completely satisfactorily. But research in nonbiblical religion is essential to the search.

Near Eastern and biblical scholar Tikva Frymer-Kensky surveys the same territory that Ochshorn does—though without reference to her work—in *In the Wake of the Goddess*, and her conclusions about monotheism's effect on women are much more sympathetic to the Hebrew Bible and to claims often made for it. She finds that the "essentially masculine God of Israel" could easily absorb all relevant functions and attributes of polytheistic male gods, but not of the female goddesses. This caused "major changes in the way the Bible—compared with ancient texts—looks at humanity, culture, nature, and society."[57] Specifically, in the Hebrew Bible, "gender had disappeared from the divine, and there are no more 'male' and 'female' functions."[58]

Also counter to Ochshorn and to other feminist assessments of the Hebrew Bible is Frymer-Kensky's argument that in the Hebrew Bible, apart from the social subordination of women, there is no essential difference in the images of men and women. She claims that "there is nothing distinctively 'female' about the way that women are portrayed in the Bible, nothing particularly feminine about either their goals or their strategies."[59] Furthermore, "this biblical idea that the desires and actions of men and women are similar is tantamount to a radically new concept of gender."[60]

The differences between male and female are only a question of geni-
talia rather than of character. This view of the essential sameness of
men and women is most appropriate to monotheism. There are no
goddesses to represent "womanhood" or a female principle in the cos-
mos; there is no conscious sense that there even exists a "feminine."[61]

Nevertheless, Frymer-Kensky does recognize that life in ancient Israel was not at all free of gender. "The Bible's gender-free concept of humanity contrasted sharply with Israelite reality."[62] A standard repertoire of male- and female-gendered tasks is found in Israelite society, but only because of long-standing tradition, she contends, not because of gender ideology.

The monotheistic deity, the "one god of Israel YHVH . . . is a predominantly male god referred to by the masculine pronoun (never by the feminine) and often conceived of in such quintessentially masculine qualities as warrior and king."[63] Nevertheless, "the monotheistic god is not sexually a male. He is not at all phallic and does not represent male virility." She explains the fact that in the Bible, "God is not imagined below the waist,"[64] is probably due to another monotheistic innovation. "To the Bible, the sexual and the divine realms have nothing to do with each other. Indeed, the Bible is concerned to maintain their separation, to demarcate the sexual and sacred experiences and to interpose space and time between them."[65]

In the concluding chapters of the book, Frymer-Kensky argues that issues of sex and gender are the unfinished agenda for the biblical worldview, which the modern world must resolve. In particular, she concedes that the lack of any biblical vocabulary for discussing sexual and erotic experience (as opposed to behavior, which the Bible legislates) created a serious vacuum. And that vacuum "was ultimately filled (in Hellenistic times) by the complex of antiwomen and anticarnal ideas that had such a large impact on the development of Western religion and civilization."[66]

As to how to complete the unfinished agenda of biblical thought, Frymer-Kensky ends by affirming that monotheism provides something religiously profound and useful. To her, monotheism cannot be improved upon and is ultimately true because it provides "the sense that ultimate reality is a unity, neither a multiplicity of counterbalancing forces that compete for our attention and allegiance, nor a complementarity of 'male' and 'female,' yin and yang."[67]

I find some aspects of this work problematic. Certainly Frymer-Kensky's claim that monotheism involved major changes in the ways that humanity, culture, nature, and society were conceptualized is correct, but it is less clear that these changes benefited women or were completely unrelated to "antiwomen and anticarnal ideas" that she herself finds detrimental.

What of the claim that in the Bible there is no essential difference in the image of men and women? Even if this is the case, I would argue that this lack of differentiation occurs not because women are truly men's equals, but because the worldview of the Hebrew Bible is quite androcentric. The loss of distinctive feminine traits could merely indicate that women have been absorbed into male standards and have become invisible.

Frymer-Kensky's distinction between a deity who is male in terms of gender but not in terms of sex is also difficult. Can we really separate gender from sex that completely, and why is it necessary to do so? It is true that the Hebrew Bible never discusses God's male sex, but that does not mean that ancient Israelites were able to ignore it successfully or completely. As Howard Eilberg-Schwartz's intriguing book *God's Phallus and Other Problems for Men and Monotheism*[68] argues, the maleness of God is just that—maleness—and a deity who is male but not female creates problems for men as well as for women.

Frymer-Kensky does point out the most significant change that monotheism caused: the separation between sexuality and the sacred. But it is difficult to find ways in which this change might have benefited women. This is perhaps the strongest point of contrast with polytheistic religions of the ancient world and elsewhere, in which divine and human sexuality are celebrated. To me, it seems inevitable that if sexuality and the sacred are widely separated, then, at least in a male-dominated society, women will be treated as inferiors and phobias about their sexuality will develop, as eventually did happen in biblical thought. This development calls into question Frymer-Kensky's claims about gender blindness in the biblical concept of humanity and strengthens Ochshorn's argument that polytheism was less afraid of women's sexuality than monotheism. Most feminists regard fear of embodiment, including denigration of sexuality, as one of the hallmarks of patriarchy, an aspect reinforced by the biblical insistence on separating sexuality and the sacred.

Works such as Frymer-Kensky's and Ochshorn's, which reread history from the earliest societies through to the period represented by the end of the Hebrew Bible, have brought to light much information about religious symbolism and philosophy that was largely unknown before feminist scholarship. This knowledge has forever changed our understanding of the triumph of male monotheism as the orthodox and normative theology of the West. Whatever one's conclusions about the prepatriarchal hypothesis or the value of polytheistic religions, one must concede that the religious concepts that accompany patriarchal societies are latecomers to the history of humanity.

At the end of this historical consideration of male monotheism, it is important to remember that these discussions are *historical*. They are about what happened in the ancient world, *not* about what the Bible means today to those who regard it with faith as a charter for their lives. Rather, as we saw in chapter four, contemporary readings of the Bible are a matter of *interpretation*, and the crucial question is whether the interpreter reads the text with the humanity of women in mind. These historical debates are interesting but in a certain sense irrelevant to contemporary uses of the Bible to promote or oppose feminism.

Patriarchy and Early Christianity

To many Christian feminists, the story of the origins of Christianity is even more important than the story of the triumph of monotheism. Clearly, for those to whom the Christian vision of life remains meaningful and fulfilling, it would be very useful to demonstrate that earliest Christianity was not male dominated. This is especially the case because Christianity has always regarded the life, times, and manners of Jesus and his immediate followers to be models for our time. Christianity holds to historical models quite seriously.

Feminist Christian history builds on the thesis, discussed in the last chapter, that Jesus was a feminist, and from that beginning point describes the gradual evolution of the orthodox patriarchal church. Significantly, feminist scholars have shown that Christianity began as a radically diverse group with many competing sects, some of which were much more sexually egalitarian than the one that eventually became dominant. They have also sought to discover how the original primitive "discipleship of equals,"[69] in the words of Elisabeth Schüssler Fiorenza, became the patriarchal entity that historically survived.

For many people, no information learned in the study of feminism and religion is more revealing or more shocking; few Christians are aware that Christianity was originally more diverse than it is today, nor do they know that some versions of early Christianity worshipped a deity with feminine names and permitted women priests. Like most "winners" throughout history, when the newly patriarchal orthodox sect became dominant, it sought to suppress all knowledge and memory of these alternative forms of Christianity; its modern heirs continue that questionable practice.

Gnostic Christianity

Among the diverse versions of early Christianity, none is more fascinating to a feminist than gnostic Christianity, now able to speak for itself since the discovery of a cache of texts in Egypt in 1945. These texts were Coptic translations of gnostic texts that had been destroyed by the orthodox church and lost for centuries. The gnostics were among the most controversial of Christian sects, and until these texts were translated and interpreted, they had been known primarily through what their detractors had said about them. Obviously, such biased information is never completely trustworthy.

The gnostic movement was not limited to Christianity, for Jewish and nonmonotheistic versions of gnostic spirituality also flourished in the Greco-Roman world. This spirituality literally stressed *gnosis*, or knowledge. But the kind of knowledge and the effects of that knowledge are especially significant. *Gnosis* is insight, intuitive knowledge of ultimate reality. Such gnosis is secret because it is the fruition of deep introspection and inner transformation, which is regarded as basic to spiritual fulfillment. In gnostic spirituality, to know oneself thoroughly and completely is to know ultimate reality, human nature, and human destiny. Therefore, complete self-knowledge brings knowledge of deity.

This proposition is clearly at odds with the version of Christianity that became dominant, which insists "that a chasm separates humanity from its creator: God is wholly other."[70] One of the earliest and perhaps most popular Christian "heresies," gnosticism had lost out to orthodoxy by 200 C.E. But before that time, many gnostic texts circulated, which, according to Elaine Pagels, a noted authority on the subject, "use Christian terminology, unmistakably related to a Jewish heritage. Many claim to offer traditions about Jesus that are secret, hidden from 'the many.' "[71]

Among the most important secret traditions hidden from "the many" are several that honor women. One gnostic text, *The Gospel of Mary*, positions Mary Magdalen as one of Jesus' spiritual heirs. In this text, the disciples, frightened and discouraged after the crucifixion, ask Mary to share the secret teachings that Jesus had given to her alone. She agrees, but Peter objects, furious that Jesus could have given teachings to Mary that he had not given to the male disciples. The others rebuke Peter, saying, " 'If the Savior made her worthy, who are you indeed to reject her? Surely the Lord knew her very well. That is why he loved her more than us.' "[72] After hearing her, the other disciples are encouraged and go out to preach. In another gnostic text, Jesus himself rebukes Peter for trying to silence Mary and later tells Mary that anyone whom the Spirit inspires to speak is ordained to do so, whether male or female.[73]

Many gnostic traditions speak of the deity as both feminine and masculine. According to Pagels, these traditions are quite diverse, though she finds three major motifs in gnostic discussions of the divine feminine. First, the divine Mother is sometimes imagined as part of an original couple that is a metaphor for the essential indescribable deity. In other gnostic writings, the trinity consists of Father, Mother, and Son, so that the Holy Spirit is the Mother. Supporting this notion, gnostic writers have Jesus claim the Spirit as his divine Mother; Jesus then goes on to contrast his earthly mother Mary with the Holy Spirit and his divine Father with his earthly father, Joseph, in that earthly parents give death but the true heavenly parents give life.[74]

Finally, continuing the tradition of biblical wisdom literature, gnostics described the divine feminine as Wisdom. This feminine Wisdom was sometimes seen as the first creator who brought forth all things; in other contexts, she is also described as that which enlightens people and makes them wise. Many of these gnostic teachings about the divine feminine claim to come from Jesus himself; others are based on commentaries on the Hebrew Bible. For example, in the first creation story (Gen. 1), the deity proposed creating humanity "in our image, after our likeness" (Gen. 1:26); since humanity was created "male and female" (Gen. 1:27), most likely the deity itself is also both masculine and feminine.[75]

These views of deity had practical implications for both theories of human nature and the social roles of women and men in gnostic religious institutions. Continuing to interpret the first creation story, some gnostics concluded that the first creation was an androgynous being who included both genders. Pagels quotes one gnostic author as saying that "'the male and female elements together constitute the finest production of Mother Wisdom.'"[76] Acting upon these views of both deity and humanity, the gnostic Christians continued to allow women to teach and to perform the sacraments after their orthodox counterparts had discontinued these practices.

Other contemporary Christians were aware of these practices, and some orthodox writers criticized them. Tertullian, a second-century orthodox church father is often quoted: "These heretical women—how audacious they are! They have no modesty; they are bold enough to teach, to engage in argument, to enact exorcisms, to undertake curses, and it may be, even to baptize!"[77] Another orthodox church father, Irenaeus, was at a loss to explain why women seemed to be unduly attracted to gnostic forms of Christianity. He could explain defections from his own congregation to the gnostic teacher Marcus only by claiming that his rival was a "diabolically clever seducer" who concocted aphrodisiacs.[78]

According to Pagels, from the year 200 C.E. onward, there is no evidence that women took prophetic, priestly, or episcopal roles in orthodox churches. She goes on to comment: "This is an extraordinary development, considering that in its earliest years the Chris-

tian movement showed a remarkable openness toward women. Jesus himself violated Jewish convention by talking openly with
women and he included them among his companions."[79] Additionally, in many societies within the Greco-Roman world, women
had relative autonomy and participated widely and equally in culture and religion. Nevertheless, writes Pagels, "despite the previous
public activity of Christian women, the majority of Christian
churches in the second century went with the majority of the middle class in opposing the move toward equality, which found its
support primarily in rich . . . circles."[80]

Earliest "Orthodox" Christianity

In the period before 200 C.E., women played a significant role in
the emerging Christian community, including those versions of
the community that later evolved into patriarchal orthodoxy, according to the most authoritative feminist retellings of this story.

In a complex and important book, *In Memory of Her: A Feminist
Theological Reconstruction of Christian Origins*, Elisabeth Schüssler
Fiorenza undertakes that task. She takes her title from a quotation
in the Gospel of Mark. In Mark's passion narrative, there are three
major characters, two well-known men, Judas and Peter, and the
nameless, who anoints Jesus. Of her, Jesus says, "And truly I say to
you, wherever the gospel is preached in the whole world, what she
has done will be retold in memory of her" (Mark 14:9). Schüssler
Fiorenza comments ironically, "The name of the betrayer is remembered, but the name of the faithful disciple is forgotten because she was a woman."[81] This vignette faithfully captures the thesis of her book:

> The inconsistencies in our New Testament sources indicate that the
> early Christian traditioning and redactional processes followed cer-
> tain androcentric interests and perspectives. Therefore the androcen-
> tric selection and transmission of early Christian traditions have

manufactured the historical marginality of women, but they are not
a reflection of the historical reality of women's leadership and partici-
pation in the early Christian movement.[82]

In Memory of Her discusses how an original discipleship of
equals became the patriarchal church. Like many others', Schüssler
Fiorenza's reconstruction of the Jesus movement stresses the inclusivity of his message and community and the central role
women played in founding and spreading the Jesus movement in
Palestine. In addition, she makes several suggestions about Jesus'
thinking. First, she suggests that Jesus understood God, at least in
part, as Sophia, or Lady Wisdom. Since, as we saw earlier in this
chapter, Sophia was a popular figure in Jewish religious imagery of
that day, Schüssler Fiorenza claims that the parable of the lost coin,
in which Jesus "images God as a woman searching for one of her
ten coins"[83] is not at all surprising. She suggests, given the importance of Sophia, that "Jesus probably understood himself as the
prophet and child of Sophia" and reminds us that "the earliest Palestinian theological remembrances and interpretations of Jesus'
life and death understand him as Sophia's messenger and later as
Sophia herself."[84]

Second, she establishes that "liberation from patriarchal structures" was, in fact, a major theme in and for the Jesus movement,
not simply a derivative or less central concern. Though her arguments are complex, her central evidence is an exegesis of Matthew
23:9: "Call no one father among you on earth for you have one
heavenly father." She points out that the father name of God is not
used by Jesus to justify patriarchal structures and relationships in
the community, but precisely to reject such claims. She concludes
that "liberation from patriarchal structures is not only explicitly
articulated by Jesus but is in fact at the heart of the proclamation
of the *basileia* (realm) of God."[85]

Schüssler Fiorenza's feminist reconstruction of Christian

origins then discusses the early pre-Pauline Christian missionary movement (30–60 c.e.), which, like the Palestinian Jesus movement, continued to be a "discipleship of equals." In the early decades of the Christian movement, traveling missionaries and house churches (worshipping in private homes rather than in public buildings) were critical to the spread of the new movement. Women, she claims, were leaders in both areas, traveling as missionaries and opening their homes to the new movement. Since most Christian communities then met in someone's home, women converts who welcomed early Christian communities into their homes were particularly important.[86]

Theologically, these early missionary churches identified the risen Lord not only with the Spirit of God, but also with God as Sophia, Lady Wisdom, thus continuing the tradition of Jesus and Judaism. Schüssler Fiorenza concludes her discussion of this pre-Pauline missionary movement by pointing out that the earliest churches, like other Greco-Roman associations, shared table fellowship, "the major integrative moment in a socially diversified Christian house community,"[87] as their major ritual and that a female image of the divine was a central part of that ritual. At their table fellowships, "Christ-Sophia" was the Spirit in which they all shared equally and without exception: "Jews, pagans, women, men, slaves, free poor, rich, those with high status and those who are 'nothing' in the eyes of the world."[88]

The final chapter before the transition from "discipleship of equals" to "a community of patriarchal submission"[89] concerns the ambiguous legacy of Paul, not the earliest Christian missionary by any means, but the one whose works survived and disproportionately influenced what came after him. Schüssler Fiorenza sees Paul's impact on women's leadership in the Christian movement as "double-edged." Paul did affirm Christian equality and freedom, and he also opened up the new option that women could remain free of the bond of marriage, living an independent Christian life instead. But, on the other hand, he subordinated *married* women to their husbands and women's behavior "in the worship assembly to the interests of Christian mission," which restricted their rights not only as "pneumatics" (those filled with the Spirit) but as "women." The legacy of these teachings was devastating:

> The post-Pauline and pseudo-Pauline tradition will draw out these restrictions in order to change the equality in Christ between women and men, slaves and free, into a relationship of subordination in the household which, on the one hand, eliminates women from the leadership of worship and, on the other, restricts their ministry to women.[90]

After this point, the story of Christian origins turns to tracing out the adoption of the post-Pauline patriarchal household codes found in Colossians, 1 Peter, and Ephesians by the newly established churches. Then this story intersects with the other story told about early Christianity in this chapter, as the newly patriarchal "orthodox" church sought to root out gnosticism and other more egalitarian forms of Christianity. Eventually, as already pointed out, this story also intersects with the story of goddess religions, as the newly empowered orthodox church closed the last pagan temples in the Roman Empire, including those dedicated to goddesses.

"What If . . . ?" A Speculative Comparison of the Histories of Western and Hindu Patriarchy

Many advocates of the prepatriarchal hypothesis emphasize the role of patriarchal Indo-Aryan conquerors in the development of patriarchy in the West. As already indicated, they are especially important in the history of Crete and Greece and in the development of a male-dominated polytheistic pantheon in Homeric and later Greek mythology and religion. As we have seen, their strategy was not to fight against the worship of goddesses to ensure the worship of their male gods; instead, in Homeric mythology, the prepatriarchal goddesses were married or mated with the Aryan male gods—

in male-dominant marriages to be sure—or they became their daughters. Although dominated by gods, goddesses did not disappear entirely. As we have just seen, only when "paganism" lost out to Christianity did the goddesses disappear (though many would contend that a covert goddess reappeared in Christianity as the Virgin Mary).

The case of India provides an intriguing comparison and contrast. Like Greece, India was invaded by Indo-Aryans who worshipped male gods. But today Hinduism, India's major religion, is the only major theistic religion in which female names and forms of deity are at least as legitimate, popular, and important as male ones, though Hinduism's social and ritual forms are decidedly patriarchal. What accounts for the difference?

The Indo-Aryan invasions into northwestern India began in approximately 1500 B.C.E. Indo-Aryan religion is well documented in texts called the Vedas, and their pantheon was decidedly male dominant. In most discussions of Vedic deities, the goddesses take up a mere paragraph, if they are even mentioned. But Hinduism, a complex, multifaceted religion that includes many distinct and diverse cultural and religious streams, includes powerful and popular goddesses from at least the so-called medieval period (600–1800 C.E.), if not earlier. As already discussed in chapter three, though Western scholarship on Hinduism was slow to acknowledge these goddesses, often presenting them as a collective poor third in relationship to the male gods Vishnu and Shiva, these perceptions were simply a result of androcentrism and did not reflect Hindu theism. Goddesses in popular Hinduism are at least as frequently worshipped and at least as important to many people as are the gods. Their icons are omnipresent in restaurants, in fruit stalls, on the dashboards of scooter rickshaws, and on people's home shrines. It is interesting for a feminist to experience a religious culture in which both women and men talk quite matter-offactly and naturally about goddesses because they are taken for granted in their religious universe.

What appears to have happened is that as the god-worshipping Indo-Aryans lived among and married the goddess-worshipping indigenous people of India, goddesses slowly and imperceptibly became mainstreamed. Most Indologists believe that some of the many Hindu gods came from the indigenous rather than the Indo-Aryan streams of Indian culture, and goddesses are probably among them. By contrast, in Greece after the Indo-Aryan conquest, *both* Indo-Aryan and indigenous Greek religion, as well as the hybrids that were developing, were wiped out by monotheism. I have often wondered what Western religions might look like today if Greek and other Mediterranean mythologies, rather than Hebrew mythologies, had been the dominant force driving the religious imagination in the West.

Of course, one could claim that the difference doesn't matter, since Hindu social and ritual forms are also patriarchal, even though their religious imagery is not. That brings up a question that cannot be answered empirically and about which opinions will vary widely. Given a patriarchal situation, are women in patriarchal religions better off with goddesses or without them? Some claim that subservient goddesses, such as the Hindu Sita (or the Christian Mary for that matter), sanctify and valorize patriarchal social norms, making them that much harder to question. But, on the other hand, deities *never* simply mirror human society, especially in polytheistic mythologies. Some goddesses in virtually every pantheon defy and reverse patriarchal stereotypes, as does Kali in the Hindu pantheon.

What is the impact of such goddesses on women? Though the evidence is just beginning to be collected, it does seem that Kali functions as a positive role model for some Hindu feminists.[91] The most intriguing question, about which little research has been done, concerns the psychological comfort provided by divine feminine role models, even subservient ones like Sita or Mary. In my view, the claim of some feminists that goddesses don't help women because they don't provide legal, political, or economic autonomy and equality is somewhat shallow. Such goddesses may still provide a great deal of psychological and spiritual comfort, which should not be overlooked. Furthermore, since male monotheism has never been completely successful in removing female imagery, it seems clear that both men and women feel better when their images of the divine include female beings. How else could we explain the immense popularity of Mary in much of the Christian world, the success of the medieval Jewish Kabbalah, and Muslim women's devotion to female saints? The major difference between Hinduism and Western religions on this point is that Hinduism offers a divine feminine that is considered legitimate and normative, not controversial or the object of repeated unsuccessful purges.

What If History Isn't Normative? Feminist History and Buddhism

Because history is a uniquely important facet of religion in the West, a disproportionate portion of this chapter has been devoted to the feminist retellings of the Western story. But all religious traditions have histories that need to be investigated from a feminist methodological stance in order for scholars to have an accurate history of those traditions. Because feminist scholarship is not as well developed in the study of non-Western religions, this scholarly effort lags behind.

Would such history be *useful* to religions that do not take history so seriously—that is, to most of the other major religions of the world? In the brief space still available in this chapter, I will sketch a few of the results of the study of Buddhist history from a feminist perspective.[92]

Buddhism is part of an Indian religious tradition that regards historical events as illusory and irrelevant, mere ephemeral repetitions of cosmic patterns. Thus the Indian religions are as strongly antihistorical as the Western traditions are historical. This difference generates some interesting dissimilarities regarding the uses of history. Since, according to Buddhism, everything is impermanent, historical events cannot be normative precedents but only fluctuations in the endless process of change. What has been is not an eternal precedent but simply a transient event. Furthermore, given this impermanence, nothing on earth lasts, not even patriarchy. Logically, instead of espousing eternally valid truths about sex and gender, as it sometimes has, Buddhism should regard patriarchy as feminism does: nothing more than the result of certain causes and conditions at a certain point in human development. The Buddhist tradition has not quite seen this point, to say the least, but the claim follows logically from the most fundamental Buddhist understandings of how things work.

To illustrate this point concretely, I offer a story that has become a mainstream treasure of Western Buddhism. One of the first women in generations to seek full ordination as a Tibetan nun, an American, was discussing her situation with an important Tibetan male hierarch. When she noted the depressing history of the nuns' order in Buddhism, he replied, "That's history. Now it's up to you."[93]

So, according to Buddhism, historical precedent is not so important. Such a possibility represents an exceedingly important alternative to the typical Western fixation on historical precedent as model, which has been religiously underscored in Western thought for centuries. This lack of reliance on history helps explain why the story of women in Buddhism may differ from that of other religions. Many new religious traditions eagerly seek women's participation and leadership in their first generations, but then decline into patriarchy. In some cases, specifically that of the powerful early nuns' order, this is also true of Buddhism. But, in other ways,

Buddhism may be the only religion in which the position of women grew stronger, not weaker, in premodern times. Tibetan Vajrayana Buddhism, the last form of Buddhism to develop historically, includes both a very strong tradition of female sacred beings who are essential to the practice of the religion, and an injunction against denigrating women. Neither of these were found in the earliest Buddhist traditions. In addition, according to historian Miranda Shaw, women were among the important leaders and teachers who first developed Vajrayana Buddhism.[94]

Tibetan Vajrayana Buddhism's formal injunction against maligning women is something unique in the major world religions, to my knowledge. This injunction is one of the vows or obligations specific to the practice of Vajrayana Buddhism and is required of anyone who wishes to do advanced meditation practices. The vow states:

> *If one disparages women who are the nature of wisdom, that is the fourteenth root downfall. This is to say, women are the symbol of wisdom and Sunyata, showing both. It is therefore a root downfall to dispraise women in every possible way, saying that women are without spiritual merit and made of unclean things, not considering their good qualities.*[95]

Two things are especially noteworthy about this injunction. The first is that its very existence indicates that people were, in fact, disparaging women. No one makes rules prohibiting what no one is doing, and Buddhist tradition records its share of misogyny. But the weight of authority is thrown *against*, rather than with, these sentiments. These obligations, called *samaya*, "vows," are taken with utmost seriousness by all Vajrayana practitioners and are widely known and disseminated.

Second, the justification for the obligation is extremely interesting. It states that women are not to be denigrated because of women's true nature—"the nature of wisdom," and "the symbol of wisdom and Sunyata, showing both." As in other religions, there is an old tradition in Buddhism of personifying wisdom as feminine, and that appears here. But this declaration goes further in stating that *physical human women* actually incarnate or embody that wisdom, as well as *shunyata*, the complex key concept in Mahayana Buddhism usually translated as "emptiness."[96] Therefore, women themselves cannot, legitimately, be scorned. The implications of such an injunction for a feminist reconstruction of Buddhism are, obviously, profound. For one thing, it becomes far easier to understand the dismissal of historical precedent with the comment, "That's history. Now it's up to you!" What normative power could historical precedent have in the face of such commands?

If historical precedents are not considered binding, does that mean the past is simply dismissed? Are there no stories from the past that people lovingly tell and retell? Such a possibility does not seem very likely, given how religions usually work. Instead, I find that *sacred biography* plays the same role in Buddhist religious life that *sacred history* plays in the Western religions, including the feminist spirituality movement. The stories that are told and retold, elaborated and embellished, are the biographies of those men, women, and children who have modeled the way by attaining enlightenment. What they did, how they practiced meditation, how they attained enlightenment, are all of intense interest to the generations that follow them.

From among the many sacred biographies of Buddhism, I will discuss two: the life stories of the historical Buddha (the best-known Buddhist biography) and some stories about female role models in Buddhism. The life story of the historical Buddha, which has been retold many times,[97] is not very positive for women, at least as commonly interpreted. The stories that stand out are the Buddha's initial refusal to permit women to renounce the world in order to lead the lifestyle that early Buddhism saw as helpful to spiritual maturity, that of homeless wandering. Persuaded by a male disciple to relent, the Buddha immediately allowed women to join the monastic community, but only if they accepted eight special rules that effectively subordinated all nuns to all monks. Seniority, otherwise so important, played no part in interactions between nuns and monks; all nuns were automatically junior to even the youngest, most recently ordained monk. In addition, the stories go on to report that the Buddha then prophesied that because women had been allowed to join his monastic community, the life of the religion would be cut in half—from a thousand years to five hundred years.[98] On the surface, one could see how some contemporary male Buddhist leaders, not interested in restoring the ordination of nuns, justify their position. As they see it, the Buddha didn't want to institute the nuns' order anyway.

This reasoning, however, is far more appropriate to Western attitudes toward history than Indian ones. Furthermore, Western scholars have concluded that, historically, these events did not occur but were later interpolated into the record by conservative monk-successors to the Buddha. Using the standards of Western historical scholarship, these conclusions make sense, but this conclusion is relatively meaningless in Buddhist terms, since the Buddhist world has never read its texts driven by concern for accurate historical reconstruction.

In my own discussion of these stories, I argued that we need to look at the stories in terms of a usable past, which fits more with a guideline of "That's history. Now it's up to you." We have to decide which part of the text to take seriously, since the text is self-contradictory in that the supposedly omniscient Buddha made an inaccurate historical prediction. (According to this story, Buddhism should have disappeared two thousand years ago.) Thus, first one needs to critically reassess the authority of the pronouncements attributed to the Buddha. I wrote in *Buddhism after Patriarchy* that "the omniscience of a Buddha, whatever it may mean, does not include eternally accurate scientific or historical statements, nor eternally valid institutional forms and rules."[99] In other words, even if the Buddha was anti-women, that doesn't mean his follow-ers should be, a point made explicit by those who formulated the injunction not to denigrate women.

But how much, and to what extent, is this story in fact negative toward women? Traditional commentators have always focused on the Buddha's initial reluctance to allow women into the monastic community and his unfulfilled prediction about how short-lived the religion would be as a result. In so doing, they have overlooked another important element in the story.

The Buddha, persuaded by the logic of the argument that women, who have the same spiritual capabilities and needs as men, would benefit equally with men from the pursuit of the most helpful and ap-propriate religious disciplines, changed his mind. . . . This is, in fact, the most useful model we could have. . . . Would that the male hier-archs who hold almost every position of importance in the Buddhist world today would focus on this theme of the story and take it to heart![100]

As feminists in other traditions have asserted, who gets the training and the permission to interpret texts makes a critical difference in the interpretations put forth.

Because Buddhism does not include belief in gods or goddesses per se, the historical Buddha has never played as central a role in Buddhism as has Jesus in Christianity. In many ways, he became much less central in Mahayana and Vajrayana Buddhism, the later forms of Buddhism, than he had been in the early period of Bud-dhist history. As others, including women, duplicated his enlight-enment, their stories also became inspirational and important. Collections of biographies from two different periods in Buddhist history have been especially inspiring and are being studied seri-ously in the contemporary Buddhist feminist movement.

Early Indian Buddhism, interestingly, not only produced the story of a Buddha reluctant to admit women to the monastic order; it also produced a collection of texts about the women who became *theri*s, female elders or enlightened disciples of the Buddha.[101] My own assessment of these stories is that the *Therigatha*, as their collected enlightenment poems are called, is the most underutilized resource in Buddhism and should be cited every time someone appeals to the stories about the Buddha and women. This source would balance the record.[102]

Biographical literature, used for inspiration and role modeling, is especially important in the Vajrayana tradition, both late North Indian and Tibetan. Therefore, it should be no surprise that Buddhist women who combine a religious practice of Vajrayana Buddhism with feminist values have sought to collect and comment upon these stories. The earliest and most extensive such collection is Tsultrim Allione's *Women of Wisdom*, a widely used, accessibly written account.[103] Allione does not tell the story of Tibet's most famous and perhaps best-loved female guru or spiritual teacher— Yeshe Tsogyel, consort of the great teacher Padmasambhava and, with him, cofounder of Tibetan Buddhism. In my own feminist reworking of the Buddhist tradition, I have relied heavily on her example, finding her story inspiring and useful.[104]

Conclusions

Throughout this chapter on rereading history, we have focused on the theme of finding a past that is both useful and accurate from a feminist perspective. As we have seen, feminist scholars have begun to establish a past that is both significantly more accurate than the androcentric story of history and at least somewhat useful to feminists. The perception that men have always dominated women in the ways that they do under patriarchy proves to be not very accurate history, which is extremely useful information for feminists working toward a postpatriarchal future for their religions.

But as we look toward the postpatriarchal future of religion, we also need to remember that the past offers no wholly adequate models. We cannot return to a Neolithic paradise of a mother goddess, first, because that world probably never existed in the utopian form claimed by certain feminists, and second, because maternity is by no means a sufficient symbol and life purpose for contemporary women. We cannot return to gnostic Christianity or the early "Jesus movement" because we live in a vastly different world socially, culturally, politically, and economically. And certainly there are no moments in Buddhist history in which Buddhism fully manifested its gender-free ideology. But, in commenting on living in a world without models, both Mary Daly and Rosemary Ruether have suggested that it is, in fact, a patriarchal method to enshrine some ideal figure from the past and then try to imitate that figure.[105] Therefore, living in a world without adequate models is not more than a feminist can bear.

CHAPTER SIX

What Next ? Postpatriarchal Religion

HAVING STUDIED FEMINIST understandings of religions in the past and the present, we are now ready to survey feminist visions for going forward. In this chapter, I will describe the major themes in this body of work, evaluate some of these visions, and present some of my own ideas on the topic.

It would be helpful first to review the themes that have dominated our discussion of feminism and religious studies thus far. The basic methodological theme is the *paradigm shift* from the androcentric model of humanity to a gender-inclusive model, which I call the androgynous model of humanity. In chapter three we explored ways in which the paradigm shift affects the disciplines within religious studies, to include the study of both women and men. We then surveyed feminist transformations of *present* religions in chapter four.

The fundamental feminist question about the world's religions is how amenable to feminist transformation they may be. In describing how feminism is changing religious thought and practice, I emphasized two themes. Since women have been largely excluded from androcentric theology and religious leadership, *women's experiences* need to be discovered, recovered, and taken seriously. When that is done, a *new naming of reality* begins to occur. Some feminists explore nonpatriarchal ways of reading major texts and discussing religious concepts, whereas others decide that such an exercise is futile and reject the traditional religions in favor of other forms of spirituality. In chapter five, we saw what results when feminist scholars of both persuasions begin to study the *past* anew, looking for an accurate and usable past, whether within the world's religions or in the prepatriarchal, prebiblical period. Nevertheless, the conclusion that there are no fully adequate models in the past is unavoidable.

Now we are poised to survey those aspects of feminist vision most likely to become the postpatriarchal future of religion. Before we begin, it is important to emphasize the overarching theme integral to all forms of postpatriarchal religion: the *transformation* of patriarchy. No feminists are content merely to inhabit the patriarchal status quo of the world's religions as equals, having recognized that such a position cannot by definition exist. There may be significant disagreements about how much a tradition needs to be transformed, about whether any continuity can exist between religious patriarchy and the transformation beyond patriarchy, or about how feminist issues should be integrated with other issues (such as class, race, or sexual orientation). But the vision of transformation beyond patriarchy forms a common thread among these perspectives.

Often feminists talk about their visions by using metaphors from women's traditional occupation of cooking. It is frequently said that religious feminism is *not* about getting our piece of the pie or our *fair share* of the pie. It is about developing a whole new recipe and a whole new method of baking, which is much more basic, threatening, and inspiring. Or, even more accurate, religious feminism is about the coexistence, flourishing, and interaction of quite a few recipes. Some of those recipes have already been tested and have provided satisfactory fare for some feminists; others are just emerging and still need further refinements. Some of the recipes result in somewhat familiar tastes; others seem exotic. The critical question is not whether or not a recipe is unfamiliar, but whether it is genuinely postpatriarchal.

I will begin by discussing a number of postpatriarchal rituals and practices now being explored by several religious communities and then continue with a discussion of some recent postpatriarchal theologies. In both cases, I will arrange the recipes from those with the most familiar taste to those with the least. The second half of this chapter will list the emergent themes and emphases in the feminist transformations of religion that, in my view, cut across denominational, religious, and ideological lines and most likely will become even more significant in the future.

Ritual Practices

I will begin by discussing ritual, or praxis (rather than theory, theology, symbol, myth, or worldview), because, time after time in the development of religious feminism, ritual development seems to lead theological development, even though those ritual developments cannot be fully understood until they have been thoroughly contemplated theologically. As recounted in chapter two, it was the pain of exclusion from leadership roles and ritual practices that first motivated many feminists to challenge the patriarchal status quo. This discontent, for example, concerning women's roles in Christianity and Judaism, first led to experimentation with new ritual forms. Then continued reflection and experiences led us to the realization that we were excluded from ritual and leadership because of certain theological concepts, especially the image of deity as exclusively male. It became clear that if patriarchal control of ritual was eliminated, the patriarchal naming of God would closely follow, which could lead to even more experimentation with praxis in other areas.

And so it goes. Wherever it starts, feminism eventually changes every part of the interwoven fabric of religion. In the complex interweaving of myth and ritual, of theory and praxis, of theology and liturgy, if you pull on one thread, it affects all the other criss-crossed threads. Or, as I sometimes say in my class in feminist theology, "It's like the hemstitch on a skirt. If you pull it, before you know what has happened, the whole thing has come undone."

My favorite example of this process took place many years ago in Eau Claire, where I live and work. At that time, in the mid-1970s, one of the local Lutheran churches was hosting its first woman pastor, and at the same time, a woman in that congregation was taking my course "Emancipating Eve and Adam." When the class discussed female God-language, my student narrated the following story. Her three-year-old daughter had come home from Sunday School to report that they had learned about the goodness of God, that he makes all the good things in the world, and that he even makes chocolate for chocolate chip cookies. The mother asked her daughter if she thought God could be a she. The daughter thoughtfully replied, "Well, if Kathy can be a minister, I guess God could be a woman."

Inclusive Language

Feminism precipitated a paradigm shift in English language applicable to all aspects of culture by making clear the utter ambiguity of supposedly gender-neutral, generic masculine language. Because *man* sometimes means "male" rather than "female," but can also mean "human" rather than "nonhuman," a woman really never knows for sure which meaning is intended. We have had too many experiences of being told we were included in the human, only to find that it wasn't really the case. No wonder early feminists asked for greater clarity—that people say what they mean and mean what they say when using gendered language. Most feminists concluded that after centuries of patriarchy and androcentrism, conventional generic masculine usage simply could not carry a message of gender inclusivity. Only gender-neutral and gender-inclusive language could perform that function.

Because of the profound and subtle links between language and consciousness, postpatriarchal religious expression is impossible without gender-inclusive language regarding both humanity and deity. Even familiar liturgies affect people quite differently when translated into generic language, making the humanity of women much clearer. For this reason, reforming current liturgies and creating new liturgies has been a major focus for the postpatriarchal practice of world religions.

Some Protestant Christians have experimented quite successfully for years with gender-inclusive liturgies. Many denominations have issued revised hymnals and liturgies, but one of the most accessible and representative of these collections is the *Inclusive-Language Lectionary*, already mentioned in chapter two, commissioned by the National Council of the Churches of Christ. The tendencies evident in this lectionary are common in Christian liturgical transformations. Language about humans is gender neutral or inclusive, rather than masculine, and language about deity clearly indicates that "the god worshipped in the church today could not be regarded as having gender, race, or color." Therefore, some names for God become less gendered. For example, "Lord" becomes "Sovereign," and "God the Father" becomes "God the Father [and Mother]."[1]

Are such postpatriarchal liturgies widely accepted? Though insufficiently feminist for some, they are bitterly resisted by others. For example, after *The Lutheran Standard* published a very well argued, not at all radical justification for using feminine pronouns and the metaphor "mother" for deity in the mid-1980s, one female reader wrote to the editor, "[The author] belongs in an insane asylum—not having her garbage printed."[2] Likewise, the "Re-Imagining Conference," sponsored by the World Council of Churches and held in Minneapolis in November 1993, generated extreme backlash, with some local congregations withholding local dues from their denominations' national offices because they had provided modest financial support to the conference. Many were especially incensed about frequent appeals to God-she as Sophia, even though, as we saw in chapter five, this figure is ancient and well known.[3]

But there are also signs of hope. An example especially meaningful to me occurred during a visit in the mid-1980s to Rhinelander, Wisconsin, the small town in the hinterlands of northern Wisconsin where I grew up. Returning to attend the wedding of a cousin several times removed, I was first surprised and pleased that the ceremony was being conducted by a woman minister, since that would have been unthinkable when I was growing up there. I was even more pleased to notice that she carefully refused to use any generic masculine language for humanity or any specifically male pronouns or metaphors for deity. When I asked about her training, she reported taking one course in feminist theology in seminary, reading *Womanspirit Rising*, and being influenced by scholarship concerning female God-language, including mine. When my students express despair over ever being able to change something as massive and unyielding as the church, I tell this story to point out how much things can change and how important it is for each of us to do our part to effect those changes.

Jewish inclusive language, sometimes using newly translated prayer books and sometimes agreed upon verbal conventions, is similar. Regarding humans, since the traditional liturgy refers most frequently to the forefathers of the faith and to the sons of Israel, inclusive language includes the foremothers—Sarah, Rachel, Leah, and Rebecca—and the daughters of the covenant in the community of the faithful. Such language is now relatively common.

Inclusive language for the divine is a much more difficult problem, both because Judaism is less prone to theological speculation than Christianity, and because in the Hebrew language, both nouns and verbs always carry gender markers—there is no way to indicate neutral or inclusive language. Usually Jewish communities are much more comfortable with gender-inclusive language for humanity than for deity, for reasons already discussed in chapter four.

But others address deity in feminine terms. For example, in 1980, Congregation Beth El of Sudbury River Valley in Massachusetts, a Reform Jewish congregation, published its translation of the prayer book. When introducing the new prayer book to the congregation, a member of the ritual committee explained that, although they had first rejected the idea of a nonsexist prayer book as "more politically fashionable than theologically sound," later, after almost completing their translation, they came to realize that "the exclusive use of male imagery to describe God was unacceptable on theological grounds!" Starting over, by unanimous decision, they used a combination of the pronouns *he*, *she*, and *you* in their new translation.[4]

Another solution has been taken by the very small synagogue in Eau Claire that I sometimes attend. Prayers said in Hebrew, which most worshippers do not understand well, are left in their original form; therefore, masculine language is always used both for deity and humanity. But all prayers are also read in English, and though the published prayer book from which people are reading uses generic masculine language, the congregation recites the prayers using nouns, and no pronouns at all, for either deity or humanity. (For example, "His protecting care over Israel" becomes "God's protecting care over Israel.") In my view, that a small nondenominational congregation, far from major Jewish population centers and able to hold services only once a month, has made these changes indicates the extent to which postpatriarchal religion is being adopted. As with the example of the woman minister in Rhinelander, discouragement concerning the slow pace of change should be tempered by remembering that significant change has occurred in thirty years.

These issues are not confined to monotheistic contexts. As

Asian religions, especially Buddhism, become more established in North America, feminists also raise the issue of inclusive language in their chants. But because these religions have experienced less feminist input than Judaism and Christianity, gender-inclusive language is much rarer. Asian male teachers often lead these communities, and the chants are often recited in Asian languages, thus blunting the gender issue. But some Buddhist organizations, including the one with which I am affiliated, have translated all the texts and chants into English, with disappointing results. Even a second attempt at retranslation, in the late 1970s, did not completely remove generic masculine language, which is especially frustrating because, in many cases, the original Tibetan is more gender inclusive than the English translations. Repeated protests, discussions, recommendations for new translations from a Tibetan female religious authority, and informal concessions from leaders have yet to result in a new translation of the chant book. The future of postpatriarchal Buddhism will necessarily include more appropriate responses to feminist insights.

"Women-Church" and Its Counterparts

For many, postpatriarchal religion requires more than inclusive-language liturgies sometimes led by women. Some versions of Christianity and Judaism do not ordain women, so the transformative sight of a woman leading traditional liturgy is unavailable. Furthermore, many situations of utmost concern to women are not addressed by traditional liturgy (or even the gender-inclusive versions) at all. The female life cycle, including menarche, menstruation, menopause, and even childbirth, is completely uncelebrated and unmarked in most traditional liturgies. Divorce, abortion, lesbian sexual orientation, the trauma of sexual violence—these common experiences of women do not even exist in the vocabulary of most conventional liturgy. Therefore, it is not surprising that the feminists who wanted to address these issues would form their own Christian or Jewish organizations in which to do so.

The Women-Church movement, briefly introduced in chapter two, is one of the most accessible Christian movements, though other similar ventures exist.[5] I will describe the Women-Church movement as an example of a postpatriarchal Christian community. The Women-Church movement grew out of Roman Catholic women's frustrations with their attempts to gain ordination within Roman Catholicism, but is limited neither to Catholics nor to women. According to Rosemary Ruether, the turning point was a conference in Chicago in 1983, called "Woman Church Speaks."

> It was the first effort to define and to collectively experience a new stance toward being feminists in exodus within the church. It defined a new theological and practical standpoint that intends to claim the authentic theological ground of being church, and no longer to be defined by the ecclesia of patriarchy nor to ask for inclusion to ministry or for the right to experience sacramental life on its terms.[6]

This stance is both postpatriarchal and Christian. Though Women-Church communities worship separately because "patriarchy is rejected as God's will,"[7] nevertheless, Women-Church makes the "claim to *be* church." Women-Church is not schismatic or sectarian. Rather, it speaks "as Church, not in exile from the Church, but rather that the Church is in exile with us, awaiting with us a wholeness that we are in the process of revealing."[8]

The historical and theological justification claimed by Women-Church is likewise both postpatriarchal and Christian. Ruether states that most religions, including Christianity, function most of the time to maintain the status quo. But "biblical religion is unique in having a theological world view that breaks with this function of religion as sacralization of the status quo."[9] Ruether bases this claim on the image and event of the Exodus, which she takes as the model for Women-Church.

Historically, Women-Church is justified by repeated betrayals of women, who, time after time, have participated in renewal movements that promised them inclusion, only to be cut out again as the movement became routinized, as the sect became the church, to use language common in the sociology of religion. Ruether includes black, Latin American, and Third World liberation theologies in this critique, discussing how they often evaluate feminism as a white, Western, middle-class movement and discourage "their" women from considering the problems they face *as women*, in addition to the problems they face related to race and poverty. She concludes that "it is clear from the history of promise and betrayal in male liberation movements that women cannot trust their liberation to male liberators." Women-Church, which does not leave women's liberation to males, "represents the first time that women collectively have claimed to be church and have claimed the tradition of the exodus community as a community of liberation from patriarchy."[10]

Women-Church, a group of feminists who meet as an intentional community to strengthen and support each other, while remaining in dialogue with conventional Christianity but not accepting its limits, is distinguished from earlier similar theological conclusions by its *praxis*. Mary Daly had used exactly the same image of the Exodus some years earlier in her famous sermon at Harvard Divinity School, described in chapter two. But Daly used the image to describe *her own exodus* from the church, her conviction "that we must go away,"[11] while Ruether insists that *the* church is Women-Church and refuses to let the patriarchal church force her either to renounce Christianity or temper her feminism. This Women-Church tactic is important, Ruether argues, because "the feminist option will be able to develop much more powerfully at the present time if it secures footholds in existing Christian churches and uses them to communicate its option to far larger groups of people."[12] Therefore, Women-Church sees itself as a developmental stage, eventually to be transcended by a community of women and men liberated from patriarchy. Then it will no longer be Women-Church, but again, simply "church," though Ruether expects this process to take more than a few years.[13]

Since Women-Church is a *community*, praxis and ritual form the core of its life. In her book *Women-Church*, Ruether suggests drawing on the varied resources of Christian, Jewish, and nonbiblical ancient Near Eastern ritual patterns to re-create the weekly, seasonal, and life cycle ceremonies that were part of the conventional church's liturgies. New rituals have also been created to help people deal religiously with crises unnoticed by the patriarchal church: rites of healing from incest, from abuse, from rape, from abortion, after divorce, for coming out as a lesbian, and for rededication of a house after burglary, to list a few.[14] I find it fascinating to see how traditional forms are being adapted to fit present needs.

In Judaism, gender-inclusive ritual communities date back to the late 1960s, whereas overtly feminist gatherings and concerns are more recent. The movement toward Jewish intentional communities, the *havurah* movement,[15] began about the same time as feminism. From the beginning, as a movement of intentional renewal within Judaism, the inclusion of women was a major concern of many *havuroth*.

For example, one of the oldest, the Upstairs Minyan of the University of Chicago Hillel Foundation (founded in 1966), of which I was a founding member and in which I participated enthusiastically in the late 1960s, very early made changes in traditional Jewish rituals that were radically inclusive of women. Almost from the beginning, women were counted in the *minyan* (the minimum congregation of ten required for communal recitation of prayers) and took on all ritual roles in the congregation. (Both practices were postpatriarchal innovations in Jewish ritual.) As Marian Nuedel pointed out, as the Upstairs Minyan became more inclusive of women, women became more and more knowledgeable in traditional Jewish skills that had formerly been reserved for men, such as chanting the Torah (Bible) readings during the weekly Sabbath services.[16] This pattern has been repeated all over the Jewish world, as Jewish women acquire Jewish educations and liturgical skills they had never been taught before. It can only intensify as more Jewish women demand postpatriarchal inclusion in their rituals.

Deliberately feminist innovations, such as women's groups and new rituals to honor the previously ignored female life cycle, have occurred more recently, for the most part. Ritual celebrations specifically for women help solve the problem of creating a meaningful ritual life for women in the context of traditional Judaism, in which sex segregation has long been maintained. Some Jewish women, especially orthodox women with traditional Jewish educations, have formed prayer groups for women only. These groups practice the traditional prayer service from which they are excluded in orthodox Jewish practice, including reading from the Torah scrolls, the central moment in the service. Women in such groups argue that since no men are present, the traditional reason for disallowing female participation in the service—men's tendency to be distracted by women—does not apply. Unfortunately, "orthodox male religious authorities have universally condemned women's prayer groups."[17] One reason for this condemnation is that the prayer groups are said to result from the influence of secular feminism, not from Judaism. Other Jewish women have been inspired by a traditionally little-used ritual for women, Rosh Hodesh (New Moon), to form women's groups to engage in "mythmaking and ritual-making."[18] Originally inspired by Arlene Agus's 1976 article, "This Month Is for You: Observing Rosh Hodesh as a Woman's Holiday,"[19] such groups are much less constrained by tradition than are orthodox women's prayer groups, and they frequently focus on using Jewish traditions as "seeds for countless new traditions to be invented."[20]

Those "seeds for countless new traditions" have been cultivated in many new rituals collected in the anthology *Lifecycles: Jewish Women on Life Passages and Personal Milestones* (1994), which its editor, Debra Orenstein, claims would have been difficult to imagine "even as recently as ten years ago."[21] Orenstein lists four major types of rituals that women have created: observances of the life cycle that formerly were celebrated only for men; traditional rituals, such as divorce or marriage, altered to be more sensitive to women; ritualizing of women's biological cycles; and sacralizing of life experiences not noticed by traditional ritual, such as aging or healing from abuse.[22] Undoubtedly, Jewish feminist rituals will become more fully developed as postpatriarchal Judaism matures.

The Feminist Spirituality Movement

Though it has a sacred history and a theology, the feminist spirituality movement, also known as Wicca, specializes in ritual—especially rituals specifically designed to meet women's spiritual needs—and is most at home *doing* religion rather than thinking about religion.

Wicca looks to many traditions, including the inspiration of ancient goddesses, Eastern religions, Native American and African religions, and pre-Christian European paganism, as sources for spiritual practices. Its most immediate and important ancestor, however, is the neo-pagan movement, an attempt to recover pre-Christian European religions. Like neo-pagans, most spiritual feminists believe that their movement represents the reemergence of the ancient pre-Christian pagan religions of Europe after centuries of suppression and persecution. Paganism, as a full-fledged, organized religion, is said to have coexisted peacefully with Christianity until "the burning times," the well-documented persecution of "witchcraft" by both Catholic and Protestant churches from the early fifteenth century until the end of the seventeenth century. According to Wiccan sacred history, "the craft" survived the burning times by going underground and was practiced in secret,

passing from initiate to initiate for generations, until finally it became possible to practice the craft more openly in the twentieth
century.[23]

Is this history accurate? Scholars disagree about how much of
the Wiccan movement actually descends from pre-Christian European religions that survived Christian persecution. That there was
a widespread movement in European Christianity between 1400
and 1700 to exterminate "witchcraft" and that the majority of this
movement's victims were women are indisputable facts. What
scholars debate is whether there was any organized pagan religion
that the church was persecuting or whether the witch hunters' portraits of this supposed religion existed mainly in their own imaginations. Also debated is whether anything survived the persecution to be passed down secretly from generation to generation, or
whether modern neo-paganism, including feminist Wicca, was
created in the imagination of nineteenth- and twentieth-century
authors.[24]

For many women and some men, feminist spirituality is a vibrant and vital ritual form. One can read about its rituals in many
books, the most influential of which are written by Zsuzsanna Budapest, the first practitioner and popularizer of the movement, and
Starhawk, one of its best-known, highly respected spokeswomen.[25]

Ritual work can be done alone or collectively, to celebrate a wide
variety of occasions and for a great variety of purposes. A common
understanding of ritual underlies the various forms. The feminist
spirituality movement, more than mainstream religions, understands both *that* ritual works and *how* it works. Because ritual
works by changing the consciousness of its performer, effective ritual forms are carefully cultivated by Wiccan ritualists. Altars, ritual
implements, and robes enhance the change in consciousness
effected by ritual. Collective ritual is almost never done in large impersonal groups, but in a small group, sometimes called a coven,
that has worked together for some time, deliberately cultivating

members' trust in one another. Collective rituals are also performed in a circle, with all members facing one another as active
participants, rather than with one speaker positioned in front of a
largely passive congregation sitting in rows and looking at one another's backs. All practitioners of Wicca would agree that the sense
of involvement and trust makes ritual more likely to succeed and
consciousness more likely to change. Whether ritual also works because the goddess responds to it would be much more hotly
debated.

Magic, exorcism, spell casting, and hexing are all part of contemporary Wicca. Though spiritual feminists disagree over exactly
what these terms mean and how these processes work, they are part
of the recognized common vocabulary of the feminist spirituality
movement.[26] Starhawk, Budapest, and many others have given in-
structions for a number of spells in their books. The list of occasions for spell casting is fascinating, both similar to and different
from ritual occasions in other feminist traditions—for health, for
love, to influence others, to stop harassment at school or work, to
improve psychic powers, to raise a storm, to still the winds, to pun-
ish a rapist, to free political prisoners, for money, to get a job.[27]

Wiccan ritual, like other feminist ritual work, ritualizes and celebrates life experiences that have been ignored or denigrated by patriarchal religion. A "croning" ritual, done for women who turn
sixty, is a good example, since it honors older women in a culture
that discards them. The significance of menstruation has also been
reclaimed and is consistently celebrated. Wiccan women often try
to spend time doing special things and nurturing themselves emotionally during their menstrual periods. Women's bodies altogether are celebrated in the rituals of feminist spirituality. One of
the most beautiful of these rituals is Budapest's self-blessing ritual,
published in *Womanspirit Rising*.

The feminist spirituality movement also celebrates a yearly cycle
of holidays. Some groups celebrate a lunar cycle, meeting on full

moon days and sometimes on new moon and dark moon days as well. These lunar holidays are sometimes called esbats. The sabats, or solar holidays—solstices, equinoxes, and the four days that fall halfway between the solstices and equinoxes—are even more popular. These eight holidays celebrate the life of the goddess, who is reborn at the winter solstice, and also the life of the god, in covens that celebrate a masculine principle.[28]

Though ritual implements placed on the altar and some of the liturgy changes from holiday to holiday,[29] most Wiccan collective rituals share a relatively similar form, though variety and inventiveness are encouraged. First, the space must be prepared and an altar set up. Though meeting outdoors is preferred, a living room is often the only viable option. When everyone has arrived and is seated in a circle, the ritual formally opens with casting the circle by invoking the four directions. Each participant rises and turns toward each direction in turn, her arms upraised, as all recite an invocation. Once this has happened, the boundary between ordinary and sacred time has been crossed, and people should not leave the circle.

The most common ritual that occurs while the circle is intact is called "raising energy" or "the cone of power." Before a ritual begins, participants agree on the purposes for which the cone of power is being raised, such as political goals, personal healing, or earth healing. Ritual participants raise energy by standing in a circle, chanting and sometimes drumming and dancing. "As the chanting reaches a dramatic pitch, the participants will raise their hands, until, at a signal from the leader or by common consensus, they will fling their arms wide and 'send the power' to its appointed goal."[30]

After releasing the power, the participants fall to the ground or the floor, "grounding the energy," considered to be an essential element of the ritual. Then the circle must be formally opened, again by invocations to the four directions. The formal ritual ends with a benediction. The following benediction, popularized by Starhawk, gives a good flavor of Wiccan ritual:

> By the earth that is Her body,
> And by the air that is Her breath,
> And by the fire of Her bright spirit,
> And by the living waters of Her womb,
> The circle is open, but unbroken,
> May the peace of the Goddess go in your heart,
> Merry meet and merry part, and merry meet again.[31]

Frequently, participants in ritual then linger to socialize, share food and drink, and talk with one another.

Feminism and Lay Buddhism in the West

Though ritual is part of Buddhist religious practice, it is not central to it. What does take center stage is the discipline of formal meditation, done under the guidance of a meditation instructor. And, though Buddhism has perpetuated its share of patriarchal religious practice, the most important division in traditional Buddhist societies is not between women and men, but between monastics, both monks and nuns (if present), and laypeople. Monastics and laypeople traditionally formed a symbiotic community in which the monastics devoted themselves to meditation practice and other spiritual disciplines; meanwhile, laypeople lived householder lifestyles and earned merit by providing economically for the monastics, but were not expected to have either the time for or interest in serious meditation practice.

For many Buddhists, restoring the ordination of nuns or upgrading their training and status is the most important issue on the feminist agenda.[32] But although I support that goal, I do not believe it to be the most important one. Rather, the most innovative and radical trend in the Buddhist world today is the way Western Buddhists are combining serious practice of Buddhist meditation with lay life. Therefore, it is critical, as I have argued on a number of occasions, that this practicing lay Buddhism also be *feminist* Buddhism. Because of what I have called the "auspicious coincidence of Buddhism and feminism in the West,"[33] this could happen, to the benefit of Buddhism worldwide.

This auspicious coincidence involves the arrival of large numbers of Asian Buddhist teachers in the West at precisely the same time that feminism began to transform women's visions of their lives and possibilities. Therefore, women began serious meditation practice alongside the Western men, rather than handling all the domestic and child-care work to free men for meditation practice, as would surely have happened in prefeminist times. As a result, the greatest difference between Asian and Western Buddhism, as several people have observed, is the obvious and frequent presence of women in meditation halls, a place where they are rarely seen in many forms of Asian Buddhism.

The structural changes that meditating laywomen bring to Buddhism occur largely outside the meditation hall, rather than inside it. The practice of meditation itself is utterly without reference to gender; since it is not a patriarchal practice, it cannot be made into a feminist one. Aside from translating the short chants into gender-inclusive English and bringing more female icons into the shrine room, feminism will not change the most basic forms of Buddhist meditation—the formless, silent practice of using one's breathing as the reference point for developing mindfulness and awareness. However, meditation is also time consuming and demanding. Serious Buddhist practice requires far more than an hour a week. Long retreats involving many hours of meditation practice are common and required throughout one's life. These time demands explain why meditation practice was traditionally reserved for monastics, who had no other occupation.

When laypeople take on these disciplines, a great deal must change in the lives *outside* the meditation hall, and these changes follow feminist directions. Both work and domestic arrangements need to be radically altered to make it possible for both women and men to engage in serious meditation practice. Workaholism, for men or for women, is definitely not a Buddhist virtue. This means that the man and, increasingly in contemporary times, the woman whose work life is out of balance with the rest of life is not idealized in any way. Rather, one of the priorities for Buddhists is to find work situations that do not demand an undue and inappropriate amount of one's life. This is clearly a feminist issue in a world in which the time demands on working people continue to increase unreasonably for those fortunate enough to be employed.

Not only must work be limited appropriately; so must reproduction. If Buddhists are to have enough time to engage in serious meditation practice, they do not have enough time to raise large families. Furthermore, as I have argued extensively in another context, reproduction is not a religious obligation in Buddhism, as it is in most other religions.[34] Since excessive reproductive demands have been one of women's greatest burdens throughout history, this is clearly an important feminist issue. Finally, if women engage in serious meditation practice, they must, and generally do, demand two things. One is child care during intensive periods of meditation; the other is sharing of parenting responsibilities. In contemporary American Buddhism, many innovations are arising to meet both these demands. As a result, for the first time in Buddhist history, child care is being discussed as a form of meditation in action—the mindful, aware, and calm way of living one's everyday life, which is the purpose and the result of all the time spent in formal meditation practice.[35]

Transformative Feminist Namings of Reality

For Jews and Christians, as well as for many radical post-Christians and post-Jews, feminist transformations of the naming of reality will continue to involve deity. Many of the feminist ways of naming deity that have a strong continuity with Judaism or Christianity have already been discussed in chapter four; these will undoubtedly continue to be important to the feminist transformation of religion. But in this chapter, I will concentrate on feminist namings of ultimate reality that are even more innovative. Much of this new language openly and directly invokes the goddess, but there will also continue to be a feminist theological tradition that talks of God, though in radically new ways.

The Ecological Feminists

Because the environmental crisis so threatens human survival, ecological theology—attempting to name a deity who is ecologically responsible and promotes ecological consciousness—will be among the most important of the new feminist namings. From its beginnings, feminist theory has explored a link between exploitation of the earth and exploitation of women. In patriarchal consciousness, women are often associated with nature, and both are viewed as "other," existing for the pleasure and utility of men, needing to be tamed and controlled by men and made pleasing and useful. In feminist theology, from the beginning, these aspects of patriarchal thinking have been linked with the patriarchal naming of deity as a male ruler and warrior, who transcends the physical world and calls people away from it. Rosemary Ruether's 1972 essay, "Motherearth and the Megamachine: Theology of Liberation in Feminine, Somatic, and Ecological Perspective," raised many of these issues in a preliminary way. For another example, part of Carol P. Christ's growing disillusionment with Christianity stemmed from her deep commitment to the religious significance of the earth and the need for religious values to encourage care for it, combined with her skepticism about Christianity's ability to support such religious values and visions.

In the early 1990s, two of the theologians whose namings of deity we considered extensively in chapter four, Rosemary Ruether and Sallie McFague, published ecological theologies.[36] Both McFague's book *The Body of God: An Ecological Theology* and Ruether's book *Gaia and God: An Ecofeminist Theology of Earth Healing* are primarily concerned with ways in which religion could more effectively address planetary environmental disaster and the distinct possibility that humans will destroy most life on earth. In some ways these two theologies are very similar, in other ways, quite different. Reading them together will clearly show just how varied and rich the feminist transformation of religion is.

As in their previous works, McFague is less explicitly feminist than Ruether, but her theology is clearly feminist. She routinely uses the feminine pronoun, as well as the masculine, for deity and draws upon feminist literature to support her claims. This is one important model for the feminist transformation of religious studies; ideally, it will eventually not be necessary to label one's work as "feminist" because all religious studies and theology will have been transformed by feminism.

McFague's central concern is to name deity in such a way that humans would understand their place in the scheme of life, prompting them to take better care of the earth. Her suggestion is conveyed by her title; the entire book is a contemplation of the universe as God's body. Her book invites us "to do something Christians have seldom done: think about God and bodies" and "*to think and act as if bodies mattered.*"[37] Her resources for this project are feminism and the ancient organic model of the universe (which stresses the interrelatedness of all things) as reinterpreted by contemporary science, especially in the common scientific creation story (which posits that everything issued from a condensed bit of matter millions of years ago).[38]

Using these resources, McFague invites us to consider several important reconceptualizations. First, we need to realize that, as humans, we *are* bodies, rather than thinking that we *have* bodies.[39]

Second, we need to realize that we are at home here on earth. "We are not aliens or tourists on earth, as some religious traditions with otherworldly leanings would have us believe." Since we are not tourists, we need to stop thinking of earth as a hotel with an endless supply of hot and cold running water and towels that we can simply dump in the middle of the floor when we've used them. Knowing that earth is our home, it is important to learn and pay attention to the house rules.[40] Third, knowing the immensity of time and space, we must first move away from the traditional conceit of anthropocentrism and then recenter ourselves as the creatures who are, more than any other beings, "the guardians and caretakers of our tiny planet."[41]

Justifying her model of the world as the body of God, McFague contends that Christianity is, in fact, "the religion of the incarnation, *par excellence.*"[42] (This claim would be disputed by some who have studied Hinduism.) Inviting us to take incarnationalism seriously, she asks, "Were we to imagine 'the Word made flesh' as not limited to Jesus of Nazareth but as the body of the universe, all bodies, might we not have a homey but awesome metaphor for both divine nearness *and* divine glory?"[43] This model, she suggests, would lead us to experience the world "not as the work of an external deity, but as a sacrament of the living God. We would see creation as bodies alive with the breath of God."[44]

When the world is considered to be God's body, what should be the relationship between deity and the world? McFague suggests that a *panentheist* concept of deity can best answer this question. In panentheism, everything that exists is within deity; deity is in all things, but is not identical with the universe.[45] When seeking images to express that relationship, McFague argues that traditional images of a transcendent deity and a deity incarnate only in one person will no longer be adequate. She also argues that traditional images of deity as monarch are inappropriate. Nevertheless, to remain within the Western paradigm, language about deity needs to remain at least to some extent personal and to convey some sense of deity's agency within the world.

McFague's solution is to image deity primarily as spirit, which is, among other things, life breath. "We are suggesting, then, that we think of God metaphorically as the spirit that is the breath, the life of the universe, a universe that comes from God and could be seen as the body of God."[46] And how does the world come from deity? "A metaphor to express this source of all life is not the Architect who constructs a world, but the Mother who encloses reality in her womb, bodying it forth, generating all life from her being."[47] Certainly, as anyone with even the most passing acquaintance with traditional Christian metaphors would recognize, this is a profoundly transformed image of deity.

Rosemary Ruether's book shares McFague's concern for the earth as well as her use of modern science as theological resource and her reliance upon the sacramental tradition and invocation of the "cosmic Christ" as resources within Christian tradition that might encourage more earth-centered and ecologically responsible theology. Yet her book is different in many ways. As she often does, Ruether presents a great deal of historical perspective on the theological constructs and images that have led to the current ecological crisis, as well as those that could lead us into a more ecologically responsible theology.

In *Gaia and God*, Ruether's main goal is to discuss how humans must change to become ecologically responsible, not to present a radically changed concept of deity as agent for human ecological behavior. Much of the book concerns practical questions, such as the appropriateness of eating meat, alternatives to fossil fuels, and forming base communities that can support one another in ecological lifestyles. But, in her concluding chapters, she suggests that two Christian traditions can be helpful in constructing an ecofeminist theology: the covenantal tradition and the sacramental tradition. She interprets them as two "voices of divinity from nature." The covenant tradition, she says, speaks in masculine tones from mountaintops. It is the voice of law and commandment, which, when it speaks authentically, speaks on behalf of the powerless. On the other hand, "there is another voice, one that speaks from the intimate heart of matter. It has long been silenced by the masculine voice, but today is again finding her own voice. This is the voice of Gaia. Her voice does not translate into laws or commandments, but beckons us into communion." And, Ruether concludes, "We need both these holy voices."[48]

In heeding both these voices, Ruether claims that an ecological spirituality must be based on three premises: "the transience of selves, the living interdependency of all things, and the value of the personal in communion."[49] Though these certainly are not the truths that Christianity traditionally teaches, they are central premises in most feminist thought. Ruether's most basic recommendation is not directly theological, but it certainly is fundamental to feminist vision.

> It is the male rather than the female life-style that needs, however, the deeper transformation. Males need to overcome the illusion of autonomous individualism, with its extension into egocentric power over others, starting with the women with whom they relate. Men need to integrate themselves into life-sustaining relations with women as lovers, parents, and co-workers. They need to do regularly what they have hardly ever done, even in preagricultural societies: feed, clothe, wash, and hug children from infancy, cook food, and clean up wastes.
>
> Only when men are fully integrated into the culture of daily sustenance of life can men and women together begin to reshape the larger systems.[50]

Post-Christian Conceptions of the Divine

The post-Christian thinkers I will survey here all agree that it is no longer possible to use the term *God* in feminist discourse. And most or all of them also see little hope that monotheistic religions can change themselves sufficiently or quickly enough to meet the urgent need for postpatriarchal religion and culture.

In her post-Christian book *Beyond God the Father*, Mary Daly still attempted to use the word *God* and to breathe some new life into it. Though this book signaled her break with the Catholic Church, its topics and issues are still reflections upon and reactions to Christian doctrine. In the book, after demonstrating the inadequacy and idolatry of popular concepts of God, Daly asks, "Why speak of God?" Like secular feminists, she entertains the possibility that the women's movement should just "go about its business of generating a new consciousness, without worrying about God." But she rejects that possibility because that would involve overlooking a basic question of human existence. Daly continues, "It is reasonable to take the position that sustained effort toward self-transcendence requires keeping alive in one's consciousness the question of ultimate transcendence, that is, of God."[51]

Her attempt to transform the word *God* in *Beyond God the Father* is justly famous. Not only is it unnecessary to anthropomorphize deity in any way; it is dangerous. Furthermore, she is no more interested in God the Mother than in God the Father. Instead:

> Why indeed must "God" be a noun? Why not a verb—the most active and dynamic of all? Hasn't the naming of "God" as a noun been an act of murdering that dynamic verb? And isn't the Verb infinitely more personal than a mere static noun? The anthropomorphic symbols for God may be intended to convey personality, but they fail to convey that God is Be-ing. Women now who are experiencing the shock of nonbeing and the surge of self-affirmation against this are inclined to perceive transcendence as the Verb in which we participate—live, move, and have our being.

> *This Verb—the Verb of Verbs—is intransitive. It need not be con-*
> *ceived as having an object that limits its dynamism.*[52]

In her next book, *Gyn/Ecology*, Daly partially retracted that position. Her concern with being as ultimate reality continues. But
the word *God* must be discarded.

> *There is no way to remove male/masculine imagery from God. Thus,*
> *when writing/speaking "anthropomorphically" of ultimate reality, of*
> *the divine spark of being, I now choose to write/speak gynemorphi-*
> *cally. I do this because God represents the necrophilia of patriarchy,*
> *whereas Goddess affirms the life-loving be-ing of women and*
> *nature.*[53]

As in *Beyond God the Father*, however, her emphasis is not on imagery for ultimate reality. Labeling, she writes, "stops us from Spinning. Thus Goddess images are truthful and encouraging, but
reified/objectified images of 'the Goddess' can be mere substitutes
for 'God,' failing to convey that Be-ing is a Verb, and that She is
many verbs."[54]

Daly's characterizations of patriarchy are among the starkest of
any feminist thinker. In *Gyn/Ecology*, she wrote, "*Patriarchy itself is*
the prevailing religion of the entire planet, and its essential message
is necrophilia." The world's major religions, she contends, are
merely subsects of patriarchy.[55] That patriarchy is necrophilic is evident from its death wish, expressed as its militarism and approval
of aggression. But patriarchal necrophilia also represents the male
need to live off of female energy in a manner that victimizes
women into a state of living death, and it is expressed in men's attraction to women who are willing to be reduced to such a state of
living death.[56] As an example of "patriarchal necrophilia" contrasted with "female biophilia," Daly points out that cosmic energy
can be symbolized as the Tree of Life, "which is the Goddess." "This
Cosmic Tree, the living Source of radiant energy/being, is the deep
Background of the christian cross, the dead wood rack to which a

dying body is fastened with nails."[57] But female energy is essentially biophilic, which means that the female body/spirit is the primary target of the "unceasing war against life itself" that is the mainstay of patriarchy.[58]

One of the major criticisms of Daly is that she seems to collapse men and patriarchy, so that men cannot avoid being patriarchal and necrophilic, whereas women are essentially biophilic and have only to remember their true nature and reject alliances with men. When discussing the fact that her work is labeled "anti-male," she derides women who are intimidated by the label. Under the sub-heading "Naming the Enemy," she writes:

> *The courage to be logical—and the courage to name—would require that we admit to ourselves that males and males only are the origina-tors, controllers, and legitimators of patriarchy. Patriarchy is the homeland of males; it is the Father Land; and men are its agents. . . .*
>
> *The fact is that we live in a profoundly anti-female society, a mi-sogynistic "civilization" in which men collectively victimize women, . . . Within this society it is men who rape, who sap women's energy, who deny women economic and political power.*[59]

Although all of Daly's points may be true, I believe that a distinc-tion needs to be made between men and patriarchy. If men not only *are*, but also *must be*, necrophilic patriarchs, by virtue of their male bodies, there can be no hope for any human future. Daly does not seem to address this issue.

But Daly balances her condemnation of men with an ecstatic celebration of women's discovery of their own worth and power, a naming more joyful than many of the writings discussed in this book. When explaining the title *Gyn/Ecology*, she writes that the term represents:

> *the process of knowing, of "loose" women who chose to be subjects and not mere objects of enquiry. . . . it is about dis-covering, de-veloping the complex web of living/loving relationships of our own kind. It is*

about women living, loving, creating our Selves, our cosmos. It is dis-
possessing our Selves, enspiriting our Selves, hearing the call of the
wild, naming our wisdom, spinning and weaving world tapestries.[60]

Carol P. Christ was the first of the current feminist theologians
to conclude that clearly naming deity as female is a critical feminist
issue, making the suggestion first at the 1971 Alverno College conference of women theologians mentioned in chapter two,[61] though
she did not publish on this issue until some years later. She is the
best-known member of a group of feminist theologians, including
Naomi Goldenberg and myself, who by the middle and late 1970s
were arguing that deity *must* be named as female for a feminist
transformation of religion and culture to occur. I will focus on
Christ's work to survey this very basic, important position in the
feminist transformation of religion. Christ's decisive rejection of
the claim that the traditional deity of biblical male monotheism
could function to promote women's liberation has already been
discussed in chapter four.

Her arguments explaining "Why Women Need the Goddess," to
quote the title of a 1977 essay,[62] are very well known. Unlike Daly,
Christ's radical post-Christian stance centers on the issue of female
names for ultimate reality and how those namings affect the people
who use them. If I have read Christ correctly, she sees the first function of goddesses as *psychological*, not political or economic. Quoting anthropologist Clifford Geertz on the function of religious
symbols to " 'produce powerful, pervasive, and long-lasting
moods and motivations,' "[63] she claims that worship of a male deity
keeps women in a state of psychological dependence on men and
male authority, while at the same time creating the impression that
female power is not legitimate. That women and men may not be
aware of these messages does not lessen their impact.

To correct these impoverishing "moods and motivations,"
Christ advocates goddess symbolism. In her classic essay, she fo-

cuses on four of its positive effects. "The simplest and most basic meaning of the symbol of Goddess is the acknowledgment of female power as beneficent and independent."[64] "A second important implication of the Goddess symbol for women is the affirmation of the female body and life cycle,"[65] especially the sacredness of uniquely female body processes. The third implication of goddess symbolism is the positive valuation of female will, especially in ritual practice of feminist witchcraft. Finally, Christ suggests that goddess symbolism is important in coming to value women's relationships with each other.[66]

Some feminists, both religious and secular, are highly critical of a position like Christ's, condemning as naive and romantic the claim that worshipping a goddess will solve women's problems.[67] Such critics usually point out the well-known fact that, historically, goddesses and patriarchy have often coexisted. Furthermore, they seem to feel that women need economic, legal, and social justice far more than they need the goddess; therefore, spiritual quests like Christ's are narcissistic and irrelevant.

In my view, this polarization of psychological empowerment on the one hand, and economic, political, or legal empowerment on the other hand, is unwise. Goddess religion surely could be useful for feminists working for social change, for the psychological empowerment that comes with saying "goddess" is one source for regenerating the energy needed to continue working for economic, political, or social justice issues. And without ongoing psychological and spiritual renewal, social activists usually burn out or become embittered and ineffective.

Part of my reason for siding so emphatically with Christ on this issue comes from my own experience. When I was a preschool child, a copy of the familiar picture of a very feminine guardian angel hovering over two children crossing a dangerous bridge hung in our home. I remember looking at it and comforting myself.

"God is male; I wonder where that leaves me," I mused. "And so is Jesus. But the angels are women," I thought, and took heart. Years later in confirmation class, the minister was discussing the position of Christian women, which is to be married and subservient. He proved this by appealing to the maleness of God and Jesus. I put up my hand and said, "But the angels are women." He corrected me. Artists mistakenly portrayed them as feminine, but the angels were also male. That whole series of events was so traumatic that I buried all memories of them until 1973. I was participating in a panel discussion on women's ordination. One panel member used the feminine pronoun for deity once. When we took questions, the first insistent hand was a woman's. She stood stiffly, clearly enraged. "How *dare* you refer to our lord and savior as a *female*," she demanded, her voice filled with scorn and self-loathing. Suddenly the memories flooded back, and a radical conversion occurred. From that moment, I have always insisted that we *must* be able to call God "She" if the women's movement is to succeed.

In addition, as I have discussed, even in patriarchal contexts, goddesses function to provide women with a sense of psychological strength and well-being that is impossible for women to experience when all language and images about deity are male. Even in patriarchal contexts, goddesses also function to acquaint men with the reality and attractiveness of powerful females, something that is evident in Hinduism. For example, I clearly remember listening to a male tour guide in South India retelling the story of the virgin goddess who had subdued and killed her would-be rapist. He clearly was identifying with the goddess rather than with the male rapist.

Christ is clearly correct in her insistence that women (and men) need the goddess—or at least need to live in a world in which such imagery is available and is not scorned, whether by feminists or by traditionalists.

Goddess and God in Feminist Spirituality

In its rather informal theology, the feminist spirituality movement picks up both Christ's insistence that female symbolism for the divine is crucial and the ecological theologians' concern for the religious significance of nature and the earth. To survey the theology of the feminist spirituality movement is rather difficult because the movement is decentralized, and individuals are encouraged to experiment to find what works for them. Furthermore, it is important to remember that ritual is more important to the feminist spirituality movement than any particular belief.

Many people first read of the Wiccan goddess in Starhawk's poetic language. Dealing also with the issue of belief, she says that her relationship with the goddess is similar to her relationship with rocks. She doesn't believe in rocks; she encounters them in her life. Similarly, "in the Craft, we do not *believe* in the Goddess—we connect with Her; through the moon, the stars, the ocean, the earth, through trees, animals, through other human beings, through ourselves. She is here. She is within us all. She is the full circle: earth, fire, water, and essence—body, mind, spirit, emotions, change."[68]

These words contain a number of basic themes commonly found in the theology of the feminist spirituality movement. The goddess is immanent, rather than transcendent; she is experienced as nature, as other human beings, and as ourselves. The goddess encompasses all things. "The nature of the Goddess is never single. Wherever She appears, She embodies both poles of a duality—life in death, death in life."[69] She is also plural and multiform, rather than monotheistic, even though most speak of her in the singular as *the* goddess. Furthermore, Starhawk asserts that the goddess is a manifest reality independent of human symbols as well as a psychological construct. "She exists *and* we create her."[70] Finally, she can be found both in the world and in ourselves. "Finally we learn the Mystery—that unless we find the Goddess within ourselves we will never find Her without. She is both internal and external; as solid as a rock, as changeable as our own internal image of Her. She is manifest within each of us—so where else should we look?"[71]

This deceptively simple theology is actually quite profound. Clearly, the feminist spirituality movement has not merely re-created the deity of male monotheism as "God in a skirt,"[72] but has recast many of the traditional notions of deity.

This theology is drawn from many sources. Many of the goddess traditions, like goddess rituals, come from the neo-pagan move-ment, especially neo-pagan mythology of the young male deity and the great mother. Many also rely heavily on the goddesses of Neo-lithic Europe, the ancient Near East, and Greece. Asian and African goddesses are also used, though less frequently. Another contro-versial source of theology and ritual is Native American religion.[73]

However, even more than in Jewish or Christian feminism, women's experience is the final arbiter and judge of theological truth. As Carol P. Christ wrote:

> Though nourished by ancient symbols of Goddesses from around the world, women's imagination is by no means subject to the authority of the past. Instead modern women joyfully discover what is useful to us in the past and reject what is not. . . . Using feminism as a principle of selection, we reject those aspects of ancient mythology that picture Goddesses as legitimizers of the power of men.[74]

Finally, unlike the traditional religions, feminist spirituality is not afraid to invite contemporary people to be creative with reli-gious symbols. In Monique Wittig's often quoted words:

> There was a time when you were not a slave, remember that. You walked alone full of laughter, you bathed bare-bellied. You say you have lost all recollection of it, remember. . . . You say there are no words to describe this time, you say it did not exist. But remember. Make an effort to remember. Or, failing that, invent.[75]

Christ affirms that principle. "What we cannot remember, we invent joyfully, recognizing that modern women can create symbols that express our quest for authenticity and power."[76]

How does feminist spirituality deal, if at all, with men and the male deity? These questions are commonly asked. Many spiritual feminists do not see total separation from men as either ideal or possible, but at present, many ritual circles do exclude men because many women feel that they need space and time away from men to be able to explore and express their spirituality freely. Carol P. Christ speculates that as women become more self-confident in their ritual practice, they will be willing to include men more readily. She also claims that most practitioners of feminist spirituality would be uncomfortable with a "*purportedly universal* religion that excluded men or gave them only a subordinate role."[77] Starhawk suggests that very few men actually want to be part of such a thoroughly feminist movement, even though men are not relegated to second-class spiritual status in the craft. But they must interact with strong, empowered women who will not defer to them simply because they are men, as would be the case in many traditional religious settings.[78]

Although some versions of feminist spirituality do not include male gods, both Starhawk and Zsuzsanna Budapest include sections on the male deity in their manuals for practicing feminist Wicca. Starhawk describes the horned god of witchcraft as "radically different from any other image of masculinity in our culture."

> *He is gentle, tender, and comforting, but He is also the Hunter. He is the Dying God—but his death is always in the service of the life force. He is untamed sexuality—but sexuality as a deep, holy, connecting power. He is the power of feeling, and the image of what men could be if they were liberated from the constraints of patriarchal culture.*[79]

Like the goddess, the horned god is manifest in all people, women as well as men. Like the goddess, he unifies all opposites and is complexly connected with both life, as hunter, and death, as dying god, who is reborn each year at the winter solstice. Like the goddess, he embodies love and sexuality, uniting with her each year at the summer solstice. But, unlike the male deity of traditional monotheism, the horned god is not primarily a father. Budapest sees the male deity as "manhood without violence or competition." Like Starhawk, she stresses the playful, joyous character of the horned god and emphasizes how helpful such an image could be for both men and women.[80]

Carol P. Christ, however, is not completely satisfied with these images. She sees developing the image of the male deity as part of the still unfinished agenda of feminist theology and speculates that more satisfying images will be found when large numbers of men become deeply committed to feminism and to feminist spirituality.[81]

Delving Deep into Goddess Imagery: Cross-Cultural Resources

One of the problems with much discussion of the goddess is that it is based on rather superficial knowledge of any specific culture in which goddesses are worshipped. I have long argued that feminist theology needs to become genuinely cross-cultural in its discourse and become more *widely* informed about religion. But using goddess imagery from cultures other than one's own cannot be an exercise in mindless syncretism or shopping in the great spiritual supermarket. Rather, as I will discuss more fully at the end of this chapter, it should be based on deep, years-long immersion in and knowledge of the culture whose images one is utilizing.

Such apprenticeship could include familiarity with the scholarly literature about the goddesses one is worshipping, studying the language and artwork of the culture from which one is borrowing, traveling to the place or living among the people from whom one is learning, studying with living teachers, if possible, and engaging in the spiritual disciplines utilized by native practitioners of the religion. Otherwise one's appropriations of ancient or contemporary religious symbols may well be superficial projections, which will not further one's spiritual development. They may also be deeply offensive to those from whose religion one is borrowing. This is especially the case at the present time, when many aboriginal peoples are offended by the superficial appropriation of their religions by New Age movements, including some feminist spirituality movements.[82]

The work of Christine Downing presents a marvelous example of how to go about both the task of fulfilling an appropriate apprenticeship and the task of bringing insight into goddesses of another time and place to contemporary women. Deeply immersed in the world of classical Greek mythology, she serves as a guide to the depths of that world for those who seek to think about the goddess but do not have the scholarly tools to enter the world of classical Greek mythology.

Since Downing's methodology is the most fascinating and instructive component of her work, I will focus on it. Her work models the feminist ideal of engaged scholarship—accurate and competent, but also deeply attentive to the idiosyncratic personal experiences that inform all scholarly conclusions. Her scholarship involves thorough knowledge of classical Greek mythology and modern Western psychology, especially Freud and Jung; her autobiographical examples, involving deeply contemplative attention to dreams and life experience, always serve the purpose of further illuminating the material being explored rather than being mere self-display. When these two elements—scholarly knowledge and personal experience—spark each other, the result is provocative insight, though not "theology" in the classic sense.

Downing's quest is not to think about deity or ultimate reality, but rather about the classical stories of the deities and what they may teach us about ourselves if we attend to those stories. Her methods have produced insights on a wide range of topics of concern to women: menopause, sisterhood, same-sex love, gender, and mythological images of women and men.[83] The deities of classical Greek mythology both retain their identities in Greek myth and become "myth-mirrors" through which one can read one's own experiences and longings. Since I think that religious mythology and symbolism are always universally relevant human resources for thinking, as well as culture-specific solutions to existential issues, and that both dimensions of religious symbolism and mythology should be taken equally seriously, I find Downing's work illuminating and exemplary.

In my slide show "Hindu Female Deities as a Resource in the Contemporary Rediscovery of the Goddess," which I first presented in 1977,[84] I suggest ways in which feminists might be inspired by Hindu goddesses. In my view, my methodology for feminist use of cross-cultural resources is the aspect of my work most relevant to others. Convinced that women and men indeed need the goddess, and knowing Hindu and Buddhist tradition, with their rich goddess traditions, quite well, I see myself as a translator of symbolic meanings. Although I insist on portraying Hindu materials accurately, I focus on what contemporary Western seekers might learn from these images and symbols, rather than on what they mean in the Hindu context. I do not suggest that Jews and Christians begin to worship Hindu goddesses, but that specific symbols, images, and myths already well developed in the Hindu context might be inspiring to Christians and Jews as they attempt to reimagine their monotheistic deity. I look deeply into the Hindu tradition for insights about the meanings of goddess symbolism and suggest how those symbols might appear when translated into contemporary Western religious discourse. For example, attempts to reimagine the monotheistic deity as mother might be inspired by Hindu images of the life-giving rivers and religious teachers as mothers, and by the feet of the dancing goddess as the source of all energy and life. I point out that the motherhood of Hindu goddesses does not primarily denote physiological maternity, important information for monotheists reimagining their deity.

In my slide show, which I have now given for twenty years, I focus on six major suggestions relevant for reimagining deity. First, I show that Hindus do not merely replace a sole god with a sole goddess, but understand deity in an entirely different way, as indissolubly female and male. Then, I discuss five symbols that are well articulated in the Hindu tradition and surely will be essential to Western feminists. The goddess is the "coincidence of opposites," bringing both life and death. She is powerful, able to protect and defend her devotees. She is female and mother, both literally and symbolically, thus valorizing the female body. But she is not limited to maternity; goddesses also patronize the arts, business, and all other important life endeavors. Finally, she is the sexual partner of the male deity, thereby introducing sexuality directly into the symbolism of the divine.

Recently, I have returned to this kind of task, exploring Buddhism rather than Hinduism and looking into different problems. I believe that later Buddhist theories of the different meanings and levels of Buddhahood have important clues about how to think of the relationship between the goddess as external and as internal, about the relationship between abstract and anthropomorphic modes of discourse, and about the relationship between the goddess and humans.[85]

I recommend the method outlined above because, unlike some feminist theologians, I believe the unaided invention of spiritual disciplines and rituals, or religious symbols and images, that have any depth and numinosity is very difficult. They are the products of generations of inspiration, insight, and refinement, and I think our own spiritual lives will be poorer for ignoring them. It is counterproductive to bypass such rich resources and to attempt to reinvent the wheel, for we may well be unable to invent a symbol that is clearly present in another culture. I am not claiming that the feminist principle of selectivity for resources that empower women should not be used, but I am suggesting that drinking deeply at the well of cross-cultural learning is indispensable.

Buddhism after Patriarchy

Since Buddhism is not a theistic religion, and since its Mahayana forms already include female mythical Buddhas and bodhisattvas, postpatriarchal Buddhism faces different issues than do the Western religions I have focused on for most of this chapter. In fact, I have often commented that the kind of goddess so important to the feminist spirituality movement is well developed in Tibetan Vajrayana Buddhism.

Instead, I believe that the most crucial feminist issue for Buddhism is recognizing and empowering female gurus and lineage holders. Buddhism, especially the Vajrayana and Zen traditions, holds that the inner meaning of its teachings is not captured in books and cannot be memorized, but instead is passed orally from generation to generation. Those entrusted to pass on the teachings are called "lineage holders"; they receive this trust from their own teachers, who received it from still earlier teachers, going back, at least mythically, to the Buddha. These lineage holders are responsible for keeping the religion up to date, teaching the timeless dharma in contemporary language, crossing cultural boundaries when necessary, and changing outmoded forms. Traditionally, Tibetan Buddhism has had some female lineage holders, but they are not as numerous or as influential as the male lineage holders. In East Asian forms of Buddhism, there are very few female lineage holders, though that is changing in the Western Zen world, as many women receive "dharma transmission."

Given the centrality of gurus, the key *feminist* issue in Buddhism is the presence of significant numbers of female gurus. They are important, first, as role models. In addition, gurus are necessary for the spiritual seeker, especially in Vajrayana Buddhism, because

the guru shows the student how to uncover her innate enlightenment, which is said to be very difficult to do without proper spiritual guidance. (The important concept of innate enlightenment
was discussed in chapter four.) Because of their essential role in
Vajrayana Buddhism, I believe that gurus could be seen as the func-
tional equivalent of deities in this nontheistic religion. For Buddhist women to be deprived of female gurus is as disempowering
to them as for monotheistic women to be deprived of God-she.

This issue of female gurus connects with the other threads we
have been tracing for feminist Buddhism. In chapter four, I
pointed out that the concept of indwelling Buddhahood present in
all sentient beings, male and female, provides an extremely strong
critique of the traditional male dominance of Buddhist religious
institutions. Earlier in this chapter, I noted that the coincidence of
Buddhism and feminism in the West has made for a radical change
in the way Buddhism is practiced, in that women are practicing
Buddhist spiritual disciplines in about equal numbers with men.
The implications of this event are enormous:

> *The androgynization of Buddhist patterns of everyday life and prac-
> tice will produce the one thing that Buddhism has always lacked—
> large numbers of thoroughly trained, well-practiced and articulate fe-
> male Buddhist teachers* . . . who are not male identified.
>
> *The great challenge for Buddhism is to welcome such women
> rather than ostracizing them. . . . Ideally, such feminist [women],
> when they are spiritually developed, should be recognized as gurus
> and entrusted with major responsibilities for the fuller articulation of
> post-patriarchal Buddhism.*[86]

I predict that such teachers will pay much more attention to community as essential to spiritual life, understand everyday life as
spiritual practice with renewed appreciation, and transform both
the form and the goals of spiritual discipline to promote "basic
psychological grounding, deep sanity, and peace with ourselves."[87]

The rise of feminist Buddhist gurus would also present a challenge to feminist theory, since this feminist transformation would not seek to abolish religious hierarchy and spiritual authority.[88] One of the greatest unresolved, indeed uninvestigated, problems in feminist thinking is the issue of leadership in feminist circles. To date feminists have not dealt well with the simple fact that not everyone is an equally good theologian or ritual leader.

Common Themes in the Variety of Feminist Religions

What important themes are common to the widely divergent feminist positions that we have discussed? Identifying common themes across diverse traditions is perhaps the most accurate way of predicting the ideas and practices that postpatriarchal religion will embrace.

Affirming Finitude and Embodiment

Almost universally, feminists involved in the postpatriarchal transformation of religion claim that affirming our limits and our embodied condition are essential. They usually assert that conventional male-created religions long for transcendence and immortality, define perfection as changelessness, are anti-body and anti-nature, and, in short, promote dualistic and otherworldly thinking. Early in the feminist movement, Rosemary Ruether identified this mind-set as the prevailing orientation of early Christianity, which was inherited from Hellenistic thought and has held sway for two millennia. Ruether also pointed out the devastating effects of this otherworldly dualism: Women are identified with the despised body that constantly changes and finally gives evidence of its finitude by dying, and the entire natural world of change and decay is also rejected in favor of a spiritual, otherworldly ideal. Compounding the negative effects on women, the world of nature is symbolically and conceptually assimilated with the body and the female.

Buddhism too has otherworldly, anti-body tendencies, though

their strength varies widely among the different Buddhist schools. I have claimed that to interpret Buddhism as seeking freedom from the world would be relatively accurate for some sects and periods of Buddhism. But Buddhism also can be interpreted as seeking freedom *within* the world, which better describes Mahayana and Vajrayana forms of Buddhism.[89] Nevertheless, even these forms of Buddhism place great emphasis on the difficulties of dying and the horrors of possible negative rebirth in the future, and use these concepts to motivate people into spiritual practice.

Feminists reject both the Western and the Buddhist forms of otherworldly dualisms as dangerous religious ideas that have very negative consequences for humanity and the earth. Across the boundaries of Buddhism, Christianity, and feminist spirituality, feminists claim that it is important to accept finitude and death as natural processes. They also assert that it is important to live in and with our bodies, celebrating and enjoying them, rather than regarding them as less worthy than mind or spirit. We need only remember Sallie McFague's recommendation to think theologically and to act as if bodies mattered.

In some ways, it not surprising that Buddhist feminism would come to these conclusions. After all, Buddhism does not promote a desire for transcendence, so it presents no obstacles to understanding, appreciating, and accepting finitude. Buddhism has also always affirmed that the very nature of existence is impermanence, ceaseless change, and eventual death, and that the human task is to try to come to terms with them, since we cannot overcome or defy them. In fact, my early experiences with Buddhist meditation led me to deeper appreciation of finitude than anything I had previously encountered, and I began to critique aspects of feminist theology that did not fully realize that finitude and impermanence really are utterly basic, that even feminism will not cure some of life's hurts.[90] But, as a feminist, I disagree with Buddhism's overwhelming emphasis on living well mainly in order to be prepared for dying and the next rebirth. Feminist Buddhism, though not denying the possibility of rebirth, will emphasize that we know for sure that we are living *now* and that it is important to live this life well, wisely, and joyfully. Surely it is the only sensible way to prepare for death.[91]

The strength of the affirmation of finitude in Christian and post-Christian feminism is more striking, since affirmation of finitude and embodiment are rare in conventional Christianity, perhaps even more rare than female imagery of deity. In particular I am impressed that Carol P. Christ and Rosemary Ruether, who often disagree with each other quite sharply on many issues, have written very similar statements about the importance of affirming finitude.

In *Gaia and God*, Ruether wrote that classical Christian thinking made a fundamental error in attributing human finitude and death to human sin. For her, ethical thinking must "begin by a clear separation of the questions of finitude from those of sin. Finitude is not our fault nor is escape from it within our capacities." She also concludes that because of its "misnaming of death as sin," the Christian ethic has contributed to violence. The quest to escape from mortal life "has served to promote, more than to avoid, this cycle of violence."[92]

> The evaluation of mortal life as evil and the fruit of sin has lent itself to an earth-fleeing ethic and spirituality, which has undoubtedly contributed centrally to the neglect of the earth, to the denial of our commonality with plants and animals, and to the despising of the work of sustaining the day-to-day processes of finite but renewable life. By evaluating such finite but renewable life as sin and death, by comparison with "immortal" life, we have reversed the realities of life and death. Death as deliverance from mortality is preferred to the only real life available to us.[93]

In a similar vein, Carol P. Christ suggests that the only possible basis for genuine reverence for life is understanding and appreciating finitude and change as integral to it. In classical Christianity, she writes, "we are made to feel guilty for being human and told to long for a salvation that will release us from bondage to the finite." She goes on to say that "to understand death as punishment, I believe, is to misunderstand the nature of life. Death is implicit in life. The cycles of nature include birth, fruition, and decay. We all die so that others may live. This is neither punishment nor sacrifice. It is simply the way things are."[94] Recognizing that, it seems foolish and "destructive of the reality we do know to focus on an imagined reality superior to the finite, embodied reality we do know." Finally, the connection between finitude and reverence for life is clear:

> If we experience our connection to the finite and changing earth deeply, then we must find the thought of its destruction or mutilation intolerable. When we know this finite changing earth as our true home and accept our own inevitable death, then we must know as well that spirituality is the celebration of our immersion in all that is and is changing.[95]

The theme of embodiment, closely related to acceptance of finitude, has been a central concern of some feminist religious thinkers. Since embodiment is very specific, resulting in bodies that belong to a specific race, class, or culture, this concern easily links with the emphasis on diversity and the feminist insistence that *how* one is embodied, as well as the utterly basic fact *that* one is embodied, will largely shape one's thinking. A useful exploration of these concerns is Naomi Goldenberg's *Returning Words to Flesh: Feminism, Psychoanalysis, and the Resurrection of the Body.*[96]

Affirming Relationship and Community

In the feminist transformation of religion, relationship and community are seen as central to human existence, just as finitude and embodiment are central to life. Most feminist religious thinkers claim that *to be* means "to be in relationship," and they both celebrate that fact and seek ways to enhance the quality of relational, communal existence. Equally strongly, they reject what is seen as the male or patriarchal preference for autonomy, independence, alienation, and control. Just as rebellion against finitude is blamed for environmental degradation and disregard of the earth, so insufficient attention to the primacy of relationship is seen as a cause for the alienated quality of modern life and the acceptance of violence, aggression, and warfare as normal by large segments of modern society.

Some feminists link these gender preferences with biology, somewhat in the manner of Mary Daly (already discussed in this chapter), who sees women as naturally biophilic and men as naturally necrophilic. Even those who would not regard these tendencies as biologically based would agree that we live in a society that is intensely masculine, that favors and rewards men's values of autonomy and control over women's values of relationship and community. Furthermore, there is a strong feminist consensus that society as a whole needs to be transformed, so that it promotes nurturing and caring over competition and combativeness. This thesis has not been stated better than by Charlene Spretnak:

> If a person is born with a mind that does not readily perceive "connectedness" with other people and is raised in a culture that does not encourage such perceptions, he will probably go through life seeing only separations, struggling with the frustrations of this worldview ("Hell is other people."—Jean-Paul Sartre) and accepting its corollaries as truth ("War is the nature of man."—G. Gordon Liddy lecturing to college students after his prison term).[97]

As Spretnak points out, statistical averages show that men's minds, on average, tend to correlate with patriarchal values. "When it comes to grasping oneness and at-large bonding . . . , most men are simply not playing with a full deck." The solution Spretnak recommends is the cultivation of the authentic female mind. "Unless women's voices are heard, we will all be pulled into their death wish. Very soon."[98]

Much of the development of this theme in the feminist transformation of religion originated in feminist psychology and ethics, especially in response to Carol Gilligan's enormously influential 1982 book, *In a Different Voice*. One of four major sections in the 1989 anthology *Weaving the Visions*, the sequel to *Womanspirit Rising*, is devoted to "Self in Relation"; the inclusion of this theme is probably the most notable difference between the two books. In addition, several major books have explored self and community provocatively and in depth. Catherine Keller's 1986 book, *From a Broken Web: Separation, Sexism, and Self*, explores the thesis that "separation and sexism have functioned together as the most fundamental self-shaping institutions of our culture." Acknowledging that people in our culture are afraid of merger, of loss of autonomy, she challenges us to consider that "in such a fear of self-loss lurks a profound fear of women."[99] And claiming that friendship is "the ultimate political act," Mary Hunt has explored friendship as a long-neglected topic that provides a rich paradigm for "healthy relating and the goal of human community."[100] Her book *Fierce Tenderness: A Feminist Theology of Friendship* takes up many important issues concerning the primacy of friendship in human life.

The theme of affirming community and relationship has been central to the ways in which Jewish, Buddhist, Christian, and post-Christian feminist theologians envision the future of their religions. We have already seen some practical dimensions of this transformation in this chapter. Both the Women-Church movement and the feminist spirituality movement pay attention to group dynamics and process, and both groups foster intentional communities.

Judith Plaskow devotes considerable attention to the importance and transformation of community in her book on Jewish feminist theology, *Standing Again at Sinai*. She begins by noting, ironically, that Judaism and feminism both define community as central to being human and focus on community more than on individual selves. Nevertheless, Judaism has traditionally dealt with women as the "other" within the people Israel. Thus, the first proposition of a Jewish feminist theology must be to change the definition of who is genuinely included in the community, as well as the praxis that translates the theology into action. But the inclusion Plaskow envisions does not obliterate distinction and difference within the community. Plaskow wants difference to be acknowledged in such a way that it does not lead to inequality. This, Plaskow says, runs counter to Jewish tradition, which has always conceptualized "difference in terms of hierarchical separation."[101] She suggests replacing the traditional notion of "chosenness" with "the far less dramatic *distinctness*." Using distinctness as the category through which to conceptualize community, Plaskow suggests that distinct elements within larger groups be "understood not in terms of hierarchical differentiation but in terms of part and whole." This understanding brings two important conclusions:

> *While distinction is necessary, inevitable, a cause for celebration, the boundaries of distinction need not be rigidly guarded by graded separations. Boundaries can also be places where people touch. . . .*
>
> *Second, if the different groups and subgroups that make up a community or nation are parts of a greater whole, there is no whole without out all the pieces.*[102]

Unlike Judaism, Buddhism has not reflected much on itself as a communal religion. In fact, superficially, Buddhism could correctly be labeled a highly individualistic religion because of the extent to which it prizes individual spiritual growth and transformation and the extent to which some Buddhists glorify solitude and loneliness. There are, however, major aspects of Buddhism that beg to be reenvisioned through a feminist affirmation of community and relationship, and I am convinced that this will constitute a major change in postpatriarchal Buddhism. Part of the reenvisioning comes through understanding that interdependence, one of the most basic concepts in the Buddhist worldview, means that individuals seeking spiritual enlightenment do so in the matrix of their community and their relationships, not alone—even during their solitary retreats in caves and hermitages.

Another major part of the reenvisioning comes through looking into the Three Refuges from a feminist perspective. They include the Buddha as example and inspiration, the dharma as trustworthy teachings, and the sangha as the community that provides companionship and feedback. These three elements are so basic to Buddhism that the ceremony for becoming a Buddhist, everywhere in the Buddhist world, involves "going for refuge" to these three jewels. That a religion which posits the community as one of the basic refuges in a non-theistic world does not take community building or fostering relationships seriously can only be the result of lack of women's input into the dharma, the basic Buddhist teachings.[103]

The Unfinished Agenda: Widening the Canon

A blatant contradiction exists at the heart of much feminist scholarship and theology. Feminists generally have rejected the notion that the past provides adequate models for human society and in so doing have renounced the binding authority of the traditional textual canons. In fact, some have explicitly called for the creation of a new canon, as Rosemary Ruether did in her 1985 anthology of texts, *Womanguides: Readings toward a Feminist Theology.*[104] *But most of the feminists who look for insight and inspiration in a wider canon do so only within the context of Western culture.* For a movement that was born through recognition of gender difference and that has expanded its understanding of diversity to include race, class, and sexual orientation, to have such a narrowly Western focus within its own ranks is inexplicable to me. The irony is compounded by the fact that the same feminists who frequently complain that Asian studies are still very male dominated (which is true) do not themselves study Asia seriously. If feminists don't become involved in Asian studies, how will feminist Asian studies ever emerge, or the feminist study of any major or minor religion in the world?

Feminists frequently discuss the problem of sources for reenvisioning religions, since the familiar patriarchal canon is clearly inadequate. As is clear from this survey of feminist theology, three resources are most commonly included in the feminist canon: Western prebiblical religions, neglected or heterodox texts and images from the biblical traditions; and, most especially, women's contemporary experiences. I have long suggested that this canon overlooks one of the most vital and provocative resources of all— the varied and vibrant religious alternatives found in the world's religions.

Having spent my entire career happily involved in cross-cultural studies of religion and many rewarding years engaged in Buddhist-Christian dialogue, I am well aware of how much there is to be gained by using the "comparative mirror."[105] In fact, I would argue that everyone who uses the comparative mirror becomes a better scholar and a better theologian, and that "to know one religion is, indeed, to know none," as Max Müller, the founder of comparative studies in religion, argued so long ago.[106]

Nothing so stimulates one's imagination about the possibilities of religion than thorough study of or continued dialogue with a completely different perspective. It is unlikely that any single theologian or mythmaker working by herself in her familiar cultural and theological setting could develop the alternative symbols, worldviews, myths, and rituals that she can discover by learning about other traditions.

The worlds we see in the comparative mirror not only provide interesting pieces of information, but also material that is "good to think with." That is to say, after a thorough and sufficient study of other religions, one can use them in one's own world construction. This is a controversial suggestion, since most theologians and philosophers privilege Western sources, whereas most Asian studies scholars are hostile to theological or philosophical thinking and discourage such scholarship.

Privileging Western sources makes no sense for a feminist theologian, since she does not give them the authority that the Western tradition claims for them. Sometimes feminists justify their continuing reliance on Western sources by citing cultural familiarity or historical continuity. Others claim that people of Western cultures should stick to Western materials and let people from Asia, Africa, and other parts of the world explicate symbols and philosophies from their own traditions.

But these arguments make little sense in the modern world, in which all cultures communicate with one another. The argument that the various great civilizations of the world do not and should not influence one another does not make sense. It is no more difficult or unnatural for a Western scholar to become highly familiar with India or China than it is for her to study ancient Israel, Mesopotamia, or Greece. Furthermore, whether a symbol or an idea comes from India or China rather than ancient Greece or Israel, or even contemporary experience, has nothing to do with that symbol's usefulness.

However, questions of appropriation and apprenticeship do need to be addressed. As noted earlier in this chapter, cross-cultural appropriation by some religions, including segments of the feminist spirituality movement, has become a sensitive issue. Members of some religious groups, especially Native Americans, are extremely critical of the way in which outsiders "borrow" or appropriate their religions without either training or permission. What turns this borrowing into an unacceptable appropriation is precisely the lack of apprenticeship.

The single greatest challenge to using the comparative mirror is the apprenticeship required. To use the comparative mirror adequately, one has to learn a great deal of unfamiliar terminology (perhaps even another language) and empathize one's way into rather different worldviews. Though the process takes years, it is no different from the process by which a feminist theologian first learns the Western sources, which is why it makes no sense to claim it is more appropriate to use sources from ancient Israel or Greece than from India or China. But I have observed that people who are quite interested in feminist theology often do not want to expend the effort required to look deeply into the comparative mirror. I have seen this at all levels. Many feminist scholars and theologians do not attend sessions of the Women and Religion Section of the American Academy of Religion that focus on non-Western religions. Undergraduates in a course on feminist theology, even participants in a seminar on the goddess, simply tune out or complain when they are required to read non-Western materials. All have given me the same explanation—"too many foreign words."

But, given the power of the comparative mirror of another religion or culture to fuel insight and understanding, the apprenticeship is well worth the time and effort. Therefore, I would encourage all who care about the feminist transformation of religion and religious studies to add serious, in-depth training in the use of the comparative mirror to their repertoire of scholarly skills. Then other perspectives as yet undreamed of may also grow and flourish, adding to the diversity of feminist religious thought. Nor would the emergence of new perspectives be alarming, for just as feminists have renounced the ideal of "one true faith," so too we have renounced the ideal of a changeless eternal faith. We expect continually to be surprised and challenged.

Notes

Chapter 1: Defining Feminism, Religion, and the Study of Religion

1.   William E. Paden, *Religious Worlds: The Comparative Study of Religion* (Boston: Beacon Press, 1988), p. 38.

2.   *New Webster's Dictionary of the English Language* (n.p.: Delair Publishing Co., 1981).

3.   Simone de Beauvoir, *The Second Sex* (New York: Bantam Books, 1961), p. xv.

4.   Gerda Lerner, *The Creation of Patriarchy* (New York: Oxford University Press, 1986).

5.   For further discussion of the topic, see my forthcoming article "Helping the Iron Bird Fly: Buddhist Women and Issues of Authority in the Late 1990s," in *Contemporary American Buddhism*, ed. Charles Prebish (Berkeley: University of California Press, 1997).

Chapter 2: Feminism's Impact on Religion and Religious Studies: A Brief History

1.   From the title of the book by Eleanor Flexner, *Century of Struggle: The Women's Rights Movement in the United States*, rev. ed. (Cambridge, Mass.: Belknap Press of Harvard University Press, 1975).

2.   Ralph Manheim, trans., *Myth, Religion, and Mother Right: Selected Writings of J. J. Bachofen* (Princeton: Princeton University Press, 1967), p. 109.

3. Ibid., p. 171.

4. Barbara MacHaffie, *Her Story: Women in Christian Tradition* (Philadelphia: Fortress Press, 1986), pp. 93–95.

5. For example, see Anne M. Boylan, "Evangelical Womanhood in Nineteenth-Century America: The Role of Women in Sunday Schools," in *Unspoken Worlds: Women's Religious Lives*, ed. Nancy Auer Falk and Rita M. Gross (Belmont, Calif.: Wadsworth Press, 1989), pp. 166–78.

6. MacHaffie, *Her Story*, pp. 107–12.

7. Ibid., pp. 123–25. See also Susan Setta, "When Christ Is a Woman: Theology and Practice in the Shaker Tradition," in Gross and Falk, *Unspoken Worlds*, pp. 221–32.

8. Ibid., p. 125.

9. Ibid., p. 127.

10. Flexner, *Century of Struggle*, pp. 45–48.

11. Elise Boulding, *The Underside of History: A View of Women through Time* (Boulder, Colo.: Westview Press, 1976), pp. 678–79; MacHaffie, *Her Story*, pp. 101–2; and Miriam Schneir, ed., *Feminism: The Essential Historical Writings* (New York: Vintage Books, 1972), pp. 76–82.

12. Schneir, *Feminism*, pp. 76–82.

13. Elizabeth Cady Stanton and the Revising Committee, *The Woman's Bible* (Seattle: 1895, 1898; reprint, Coalition Task Force on Women and Religion, 1974), p. 14. See also MacHaffie, *Her Story*, pp. 113–16.

14. Ibid.

15. Boulding, *Underside of History*, p. 758.

16. One of the most famous and widely quoted of such role reversals was by Nelle Morton, "Preaching the Word," in *Sexist Religion and Women in the Church: No More Silence*, ed. Alice Hageman (New York: Association Press, 1974), pp. 29–31.

17. Cynthia Eller, *Living in the Lap of the Goddess: The Feminist Spirituality Movement in America* (New York: Crossroad, 1993), p. 47.

18. Rosemary Ruether, "Christianity and Women in the Modern World," in *Today's Woman in World Religions*, ed. Arvind Sharma (Albany: State University of New York Press, 1993), p. 279.

19. For an excellent survey and bibliography concerning women's

ordination, see Barbara Brown Zikmund, "Women and Ordination," in *In Our Own Voices: Four Centuries of American Women's Religious Writing*, ed. Rosemary Ruether and Catherine Keller (San Francisco: Harper and Row, 1995), pp. 291–340.

20. MacHaffie, *Her Story*; Ruether, "Christianity and Women in the Modern World."

21. Rosemary Radford Ruether, *Women-Church: Theology and Practice of Feminist Liturgical Communities* (San Francisco: Harper and Row, 1986), pp. 3–4.

22. Judith Plaskow and Joan Arnold Romero, ed., *Women and Religions*, rev. ed. (Missoula, Mont.: Scholars Press, 1974); Rita M. Gross, ed., *Beyond Androcentrism: New Essays on Women and Religion* (Missoula, Mont.: Scholars Press, 1977).

23. Important works by each include Beverly Wildung Harrison, *Making the Connections: Essays in Feminist Social Ethics* (Boston: Beacon Press, 1985); Nelle Morton, *The Journey Is Home* (Boston: Beacon Press, 1985); and Letty M. Russell, *Human Liberation in a Feminist Perspective—A Theology* (Philadelphia: Westminster Press, 1974).

24. Christine Downing, "Dear Chris . . . Love, Christine," in *A Time to Weep, a Time to Sing: Faith Journeys of Women Scholars of Religion*, ed. Mary Jo Meadow (Minneapolis: Winston Press, 1985), p. 60.

25. Valerie Saiving, "The Human Situation: A Feminine View," in *Womanspirit Rising: A Feminist Reader in Religion*, ed. Carol P. Christ and Judith Plaskow (San Francisco: Harper and Row, 1979), pp. 25–42.

26. For a classic form of the statement, see Rosemary Ruether, "Misogynism and Virginal Feminism in the Fathers of the Church," in *Religion and Sexism: Images of Woman in the Jewish and Christian Traditions*, ed. Rosemary Ruether (New York: Simon and Schuster, 1974), pp. 150–83.

27. Editorial Policy Statement, vol. 1 of *The Annual Review of Women in World Religions* (Albany: State University of New York Press, 1991).

28. Christ and Plaskow, *Womanspirit Rising*, p. 15.

29. Rosemary Ruether, "A Religion for Women," *Christianity and Crisis*, 10 December, 1979, pp. 307–10; Rosemary Ruether, "Goddesses and Witches: Liberation and Countercultural Feminism," *Christian Century*,

10–17 September 1980, pp. 842–47; Carol P. Christ, *Laughter of Aphrodite: Reflections on a Journey to the Goddess* (San Francisco: Harper and Row, 1987), pp. 57–72.

30.   Ruether and Keller, *In Our Own Voices*, p. 446.

31.   Ibid., p. 448.

32.   Ursula King, *Feminist Theology from the Third World: A Reader* (Maryknoll, N.Y.: Orbis, 1994), p. 13; Ruether and Keller, *In Our Own Voices*, pp. 430–31.

33.   King, *Feminist Theology from the Third World*, p. 394.

34.   Riffat Hassan, "Muslim Women and Post-Patriarchal Islam," in *After Patriarchy: Feminist Transformations of the World Religions*, ed. Paula Cooey, William Eakin, and Jay McDaniel (Maryknoll, N.Y.: Orbis Books, 1991).

35.   Lina Gupta, "Kali the Savior," in Cooey, Eakin, and McDaniel, *After Patriarchy*; Vashuda Narayan, in *Feminist Transformations of the World Religions*, ed. Arvind Sharma (forthcoming).

36.   These generalizations are gleaned from reading Arvind Sharma's *Today's Woman in World Religions* (see note 18), an excellent, up-to-date source of information on these movements.

37.   Nancy Auer Falk, "Shakti Ascending: Hindu Women, Politics, and Religious Leadership during the Nineteenth and Twentieth Centuries," in *Religion in Modern India*, ed. Robert Baird (New Delhi: Motilal Barnasidas, 1995).

38.   Katherine K. Young, "Women in Hinduism," in Sharma, *Today's Woman in World Religions*, p. 128.

39.   Ibid., pp. 128–31.

40.   Jane I. Smith, "Women in Islam," in Sharma, *Today's Woman in World Religions*, p. 306.

41.   Ibid., p. 322.

42.   Miriam Levering, "Women, the State, and Religion Today in the People's Republic of China," in Sharma, *Today's Woman in World Religions*, p. 175.

43.   Ibid., pp. 174–91.

44.   Ibid., p. 172.

45.   Ibid., pp. 203–24.

46. Barbara Reed, "Women and Chinese Religion in Contemporary Taiwan," in Sharma, *Today's Woman in World Religions*, pp. 226–37.

47. Ibid., pp. 237–41.

48. Kumiko Uchino, "The Status Elevation Process of Soto Sect Nuns in Modern Japan," in *Speaking of Faith: Global Perspectives on Women, Religion, and Social Change*, ed. Diana L. Eck and Devaki Jain (Philadelphia: New Society Publishers, 1987), pp. 159–73.

49. At the Sun Dance, those who have vowed to do so have skewers placed beneath the skin; the skewers are also tied to the sacred tree at the center of the circle. As the participants dance, they pull backward from the tree until the skewers break loose. For men, the skewers are placed in the upper chest. When women first began to participate in the Sun Dance, they did not pierce, but recently some women, commanded to do so by a vision, have had skewers placed beneath the skin of their upper arms.

50. Paula Gunn Allen, *The Sacred Hoop: Recovering the Feminine in American Indian Traditions* (Boston: Beacon Press, 1986), pp. 5–6.

51. Inés Talamantez, "Images of the Feminine in Apache Religious Tradition," in Cooey, Eakin, and McDaniel, *After Patriarchy*, p. 131.

Chapter 3: Where Have All the Women Been? The Challenge of Feminist Study of Religion

1. Rita M. Gross, "Menstruation and Childbirth as Ritual and Religious Experience," in Falk and Gross, *Unspoken Worlds*; Rita M. Gross, "Tribal Religions: Aboriginal Australia," in *Women in World Religions*, ed. Arvind Sharma (Albany: State University of New York Press, 1987).

2. Diane Bell, *Daughters of the Dreaming* (North Sydney, Australia: McPhee Gribble/George Allen and Unwin, 1983).

3. Eleanor McLaughlin, "The Christian Past: Does It Hold a Future for Women?" in Christ and Plaskow, *Womanspirit Rising*, p. 96.

4. An early account of such rituals is found in Falk and Gross, *Unspoken Worlds*, pp. 59–92.

5. See Peggy Reeves Sanday, *Female Power and Male Dominance: On the Origins of Sexual Inequality* (Cambridge, UK: Cambridge University Press, 1981), pp. 28–33.

6.   Falk and Gross, *Unspoken Worlds*, pp. 212–20.

7.   See chapters 6–8 and 10–12 of Falk and Gross, *Unspoken Worlds*, for examples.

8.   Ibid., pp. 106–7.

9.   Ibid., p. 133.

10.   Ibid., p. xv.

11.   For example, see chapters 10–12 of Falk and Gross, *Unspoken Worlds*.

12.   Rita M. Gross, *Buddhism after Patriarchy: A Feminist History, Analysis, and Reconstruction of Buddhism* (Albany: State University of New York Press, 1993).

13.   McLaughlin, "The Christian Past," pp. 94–95.

14.   Ibid., p. 95.

15.   For example, following McLaughlin's suggestion, many scholars have investigated the many woman mystics who were so important to medieval Christianity.

16.   Gross, *Buddhism After Patriarchy*, p. 118.

17.   For one example, see Elizabeth A. Johnson, *She Who Is: The Mystery of God in Feminist Theological Discourse* (New York: Crossroads, 1991), pp. 76–103. Virginia Ramey Mollenkott has systematically collected and studied these images in *The Divine Feminine: The Biblical Imagery of God as Female* (New York: Crossroad, 1984).

18.   Caroline Walker Bynum, *Jesus as Mother: Studies in the Spirituality of the High Middle Ages* (Berkeley: University of California Press, 1982).

19.   These arguments will be presented in more detail in a forthcoming article by Rita M. Gross, "Toward a New Model of the Hindu Pantheon" in *Religion*.

20.   An important early article was Phyllis Trible, "Eve and Adam: Genesis 2–3 Reread," in Christ and Plaskow, *Womanspirit Rising*, pp. 74–83. See also Phyllis Trible, *God and the Rhetoric of Sexuality* (Philadelphia: Fortress Press, 1978) and Elisabeth Schüssler Fiorenza, *Bread Not Stone: The Challenge of Feminist Biblical Interpretation* (Boston: Beacon Press, 1984).

21.   Frances Dahlberg, *Woman the Gatherer* (New Haven: Yale University Press, 1981) and Sally Slocum, "Woman the Hunter: Male Bias in

Anthropology," in *Toward an Anthropology of Women,* ed. Ranya Reiter (New York and London: Monthly Review Press, 1975), pp. 36–50.

22. Shirley Strum, *Almost Human: A Journey into the World of Baboons* (New York: Random House, 1987).

23. Nancy Jay, *Throughout Your Generations Forever: Sacrifice, Religion, and Paternity* (Chicago: University of Chicago Press, 1992).

24. Unfortunately, this thesis represents almost the sum total of thinking about women and religions of even someone so great as the late Mircea Eliade. His widely read book *Rites and Symbols of Initiation: The Mysteries of Birth and Rebirth* (New York: Harper and Row, 1958) uses this thesis to focus on differences between men's and women's patterns and experiences of initiation. For an early feminist discussion of this hypothesis, see Sherry B. Ortner, "Is Female to Male as Nature Is to Culture?" in *Woman, Culture, and Society,* ed. Michelle Zimbalist Rosaldo and Louis Lamphere (Stanford: Stanford University Press, 1974).

25. For example, see chapters 11 and 12 of Falk and Gross, *Unspoken Worlds.*

26. See Karen McCarthy Brown, *Mama Lola: A Vodou Priestess in Brooklyn* (Stanford/Berkeley: University of California Press, 1991); Bell, *Daughters of the Dreaming*; Erika Friedl, *Women of Deh Koh: Lives in an Iranian Village* (Washington, D.C.: Smithsonian Institution Press, 1989); and Kathleen M. Erndl, *Victory to the Mother: The Hindu Goddess of Northwest India in Myth, Ritual, and Symbol* (Oxford, UK: Oxford University Press, 1993). See also Susan Starr Sered, *Religions Dominated by Women* (Oxford, UK: Oxford University Press, 1993).

27. Gross, *Buddhism after Patriarchy.*

28. George Buhler, trans., *The Laws of Manu* (New York: Dover Publications, 1969), especially pp. 195–98.

29. See especially Susan Wadley, "Hindu Women's Family and Household Rites in a North Indian Village," and James M. Freeman, "The Ladies of Lord Krishna: Rituals of Middle-Aged Women in Eastern India," in Falk and Gross, *Unspoken Worlds,* pp. 572–92.

30. Raphael Patai, *The Hebrew Goddess* (New York: Avon Books, 1978), and Mollenkott, *The Divine Feminine.*

31. Many popular books on goddesses, often of questionable schol-

arly accuracy, have appeared. Among the most popular and influential of such books is Merlin Stone, *When God Was a Woman* (New York: Harcourt Brace and Jovanovich, 1978). More recent and more usable surveys on Western goddesses are Elinor Gadon, *The Once and Future Goddess,* and Anne Baring and Jules Cashford, *The Myth of the Goddess: Evolution of an Image* (New York: Viking, 1991). Two reliable cross-cultural surveys of goddesses in major religions, both ancient and modern, are David Kinsley, *The Goddesses' Mirror: Visions of the Divine from East and West* (Albany: State University of New York Press, 1989) and Troy Wilson Organ, *The Book of the Goddess* (New York: Crossroad, 1983). For a survey of Hindu goddesses, see David Kinsley, *Hindu Goddesses: Visions of the Divine Feminine in Hindu Religious Tradition* (Berkeley: University of California Press, 1986).

32. Christine Downing, *The Goddess: Mythological Images of the Feminine* (New York: Crossroad, 1981).

33. Falk and Gross, *Unspoken Worlds,* pp. 102–11, 125–33.

34. Sharma, *Women in World Religions,* p. 16.

35. For a survey of such movements, see Catherine Wessinger, ed., *Women's Leadership in Marginal Religions: Explorations outside the Mainstream* (Champaign, Ill.: University of Illinois Press, 1993).

36. Falk and Gross, *Unspoken Worlds,* p. xi.

37. Sanday, *Female Power and Male Dominance,* p. 232.

38. Ibid., p. 165.

39. Ibid., p. 6.

40. Ibid., p. 171.

41. Ibid., p. 9.

42. Ibid., pp. 210–11.

43. Gross, *Buddhism after Patriarchy,* pp. 312–15.

44. Ibid., pp. 314–15.

45. Katherine K. Young, "Hinduism," in Sharma, *Today's Woman in World Religions,* pp. 119–25.

46. Mary Daly, *Gyn/Ecology: The Metaethics of Radical Feminism* (Boston: Beacon Press, 1978), pp. 109–292.

47. Gross and Falk, *Unspoken Worlds,* pp. 125–33, 145–54.

Chapter 4: No Girls Allowed?
Are the World's Religions Inevitably Sexist?

1. Carol P. Christ, "The New Feminist Theology: A Review of the Literature," *Religious Studies Review* III:4 (October 1977): pp. 203–12.

2. Christ and Plaskow, *Womanspirit Rising*, p. 9.

3. Plaskow and Christ, *Weaving the Visions: New Patterns in Feminist Spirituality* (San Francisco: Harper and Row, 1989), p. 7.

4. Ibid.

5. Rosemary Ruether, *Sexism and God-Talk: Toward a Feminist Theology* (Boston: Beacon Press, 1983), p. 12.

6. Ibid., pp. 18–19.

7. Plaskow and Christ, *Weaving the Visions*, p. 3.

8. Daly, *Beyond God the Father* (Boston: Beacon Press, 1973), p. 8.

9. See Leonard Grob, Riffat Hassan, and Haim Gordon, *Women's and Men's Liberation: Testimonies of Spirit* (New York: Greenwood Press, 1991).

10. Ibid., p. 24.

11. For a short version of Trible's exegesis, see Trible, "Eve and Adam." See also Trible's "Depatriarchalizing in Biblical Interpretation," *Journal of the American Academy of Religion* (March 1973), pp. 251–58, and *God and the Rhetoric of Sexuality* (Philadelphia: Fortress Press), 1978.

12. Leonard Swidler, "Jesus Was a Feminist," *Catholic World* (January 1971), pp. 177–83.

13. Ruether, *Sexism and God-Talk*, p. 135.

14. See MacHaffie, *Her Story*, p. 26, for a list.

15. Ibid., pp. 18–21.

16. Hassan, "Muslim Women," pp. 54–57.

17. Ibid., p. 51.

18. Ibid., pp. 44–54.

19. Elisabeth Schüssler Fiorenza, *But She Said: Feminist Practices of Biblical Interpretation* (Boston: Beacon Press, 1992), p. 156.

20. Schüssler Fiorenza, *Bread Not Stone*, p. 14.

21. Ibid., p. 159.

22.   Ibid., pp. 15–22. Also, *But She Said*, pp. 57–76.

23.   Rita M. Gross, "Steps toward Feminine Imagery of Deity in Jewish Theology," in *On Being a Jewish Feminist: A Reader*, ed. Susannah Heschel (New York: Schocken Books, 1983), p. 236.

24.   Rita M. Gross, "Female God Language in a Jewish Context," in Christ and Plaskow, *Womanspirit Rising*, pp. 170–71.

25.   Gross, "Steps toward Feminine Imagery of Deity in Jewish Theology."

26.   Ruether, *Sexism and God-Talk*, pp. 68–69.

27.   Ibid., p. 46.

28.   Ibid., pp. 70–71.

29.   Anne Carr, *Transforming Grace: Christian Tradition and Women's Experience* (San Francisco: Harper and Row, 1988), p. 147.

30.   Ibid., p. 148.

31.   Ibid., pp. 150–53.

32.   Ibid., p. 153.

33.   Ibid., pp. 156–57.

34.   Sallie McFague, *Metaphorical Theology: Models of God in Religious Language* (Philadelphia: Fortress Press, 1982).

35.   Ibid., p. 167.

36.   Ibid., p. 145.

37.   Sallie McFague, *Models of God: Theology for an Ecological, Nuclear Age* (Philadelphia: Fortress Press, 1987), p. ix.

38.   Ibid., pp. xi–xiii.

39.   Ibid., pp. 101–23.

40.   Elizabeth Johnson, *She Who Is: The Mystery of God in Feminist Theological Discourse* (New York: Crossroad, 1993).

41.   Ibid., p. 75.

42.   Ibid., p. 196.

43.   Ibid., p. 243.

44.   Rita M. Gross, "Female God-Language," in Christ and Plaskow, *Womanspirit Rising*, p. 173.

45.   Chung Hyun Kyung, *Struggle to Be the Sun Again: Introducing Asian Women's Theology* (Maryknoll, N.Y.: Orbis Books, 1990), p. 48. It is interesting to hear an Asian Christian woman confirm what I had claimed

for years about the impact the rich heritage of non-Western female God-talk could have on monotheistic religious imaginations.

46. Ibid., pp. 48, 50.

47. Ibid., p. 48.

48. Ibid., p. 64. For an account of traditional Korean shamanism, see Youngsook Kim Harvey, "Possession Sickness and Women Shamans in Korea," in Falk and Gross, *Unspoken Worlds*, pp. 37–44.

49. Judith Plaskow, *Standing Again at Sinai* (San Francisco: Harper and Row, 1990), p. 150.

50. Ibid., pp. 152–54.

51. Ibid., pp. 165, 167.

52. Ibid., p. 161.

53. Ibid., pp. 160, 163, 165.

54. Ibid., pp. 155–69.

55. For a beautifully written, highly accessible scholarly account of Kali, see David Kinsley, *The Sword and the Flute: Kali and Krishna; Dark Visions of the Terrible and the Sublime in Hindu Mythology* (Berkeley: University of California Press, 1975). For a collection of Hindu devotional poems to Kali, see Ramprasad Sen, *Grace and Mercy in Her Wild Hair: Selected Poems to the Mother Goddess*, trans. Leonard Nathan and Clinton Seely (Boulder, Colo.: Great Eastern Books, 1982). For an accurate scholarly account of Hindu goddesses in general, see David Kinsley, *Hindu Goddesses: Visions of the Divine Feminine in Hindu Religious Tradition* (Berkeley: University of California Press, 1986).

56. Gupta, "Kali the Savior," p. 16.

57. Ibid., p. 17.

58. Ibid., p. 29.

59. Ibid., p. 24.

60. Ibid., p. 31.

61. See Rita M. Gross, "Some Buddhist Perspectives on the Goddess," in *Women and Goddess Traditions*, ed. Karen King (Minneapolis: Fortress Press, forthcoming).

62. For a fuller discussion of these "deities," see Gross, *Buddhism after Patriarchy*, pp. 75–77, 102–14, 196–206; and Gross, "Some Buddhist Perspectives on the Goddess."

63.   See Rita M. Gross, "I Will Never Forget to Visualize That Vajra-yogini Is My Body and Mind," *Journal of Feminist Studies in Religion* III:1 (1987): pp. 77–89.

64.   See Gross, *Buddhism after Patriarchy*, pp. 105–8, 196–206.

65.   The statement was made by Nagarjuna, one of the most important Buddhist thinkers of all time, in his *Mulamadyamikakarikas (Fundamentals of the Middle Way)*, XXIV:18–19. For a translation and commentary, see Frederick J. Streng, *Emptiness: A Study in Religious Meaning* (Nashville: Abingdon Press, 1967).

66.   The most important texts are the *Vimalakirtinirdasa Sutra* and the *Srimaladevisimhanada Sutra*. The most convenient work in which to study the relevant excerpts is Diana Y. Paul, *Women in Buddhism: Images of the Feminine in Mahayana Tradition* (Berkeley: Asian Humanities Press, 1979), chapters 6 and 8.

67.   From Paul's translation in *Women in Buddhism*, p. 236.

68.   Ibid., p. 188.

69.   Ibid., p. 145.

70.   Mary Daly, *The Church and the Second Sex, with a New Feminist Postchristian Introduction by the Author* (San Francisco: Harper and Row, 1975).

71.   Ibid., p. 12.

72.   Ibid., p. 14.

73.   Ibid., p. 5.

74.   Ibid., pp. 9–10.

75.   Ibid., p. 51.

76.   Daly, *Beyond God the Father*, p. 9.

77.   Ibid., pp. 10–12.

78.   Christ, *Laughter of Aphrodite*.

79.   Ibid., p. 105.

80.   Ibid., p. 59.

81.   Ibid., p. 60.

82.   Ibid., p. 67.

83.   Ibid., pp. 61–63.

84.   Ibid., pp. 117–32.

85.   A notable exception is Diana L. Eck's book *Encountering God: A*

Spiritual Journey from Bozeman to Benares (Boston: Beacon Press, 1993), in which Eck writes of how her study of Hinduism has enriched her Christian faith.

Chapter 5: Has It Always Been That Way? Rereading the Past

1. For a survey of this material, including bibliography, see Mac-Haffie, *Her Story.*

2. Eller, *Living in the Lap of the Goddess*, pp. 150–84.

3. The phrase is taken from the book title: Lerner, *The Creation of Patriarchy.*

4. Lionel Tiger, *Men in Groups* (New York: Random House, 1969).

5. George Gilder, *Sexual Suicide* (New York: Quadrangle, 1973).

6. Riane Eisler, *The Chalice and the Blade: Our History, Our Future* (San Francisco: Harper and Row, 1987), pp. 24–28.

7. David Kinsley, *The Goddesses' Mirror: Visions of the Divine Feminine from East and West* (Albany: State University of New York Press, 1989), p. xviii.

8. Sanday, *Female Power and Male Dominance*, p. 4.

9. Margaret Ehrenberg, *Women in Prehistory* (Norman, Okla.: University of Oklahoma Press, 1989), pp. 10–66; M. Kay Martin and Barbara Voorhies, *Female of the Species* (New York: Columbia University Press, 1975), pp. 144–211.

10. Martin and Voorhies, *Female of the Species*, p. 190.

11. For example, see Sanday, *Female Power and Male Dominance*, pp. 113–20, 135–43.

12. Ehrenberg, *Women in Prehistory*, p. 173.

13. Elizabeth Gould Davis, *The First Sex* (Baltimore: Penguin Books, 1972), and Merlin Stone, *When God Was a Woman* (New York: Harcourt, Brace and Jovanovich, 1978). Unfortunately, neither of these writers had academic training in any of the disciplines that have contributed to the prepatriarchal hypothesis.

14. Anne Barstow, "The Prehistoric Goddess," in *The Book of the Goddess: Past and Present*, ed. Carl Olson (New York: Crossroads, 1983), pp. 7–28.

15. Marija Gimbutas, *The Language of the Goddess: Unearthing the*

Hidden Symbols of Western Civilization (San Francisco: Harper and Row, 1989) and *The Civilization of the Goddess: The World of Old Europe* (San Francisco: Harper and Row, 1991).

16.   Elinor Gadon, *The Once and Future Goddess: A Symbol for Our Time* (San Francisco: Harper and Row, 1989).

17.   Baring and Cashford, *The Myth of the Goddess.*

18.   Christ, *Laughter of Aphrodite.*

19.   Eisler, *The Chalice and the Blade*, p. 24.

20.   Kinsley, *The Goddesses' Mirror*, pp. xi–xix.

21.   Katherine K. Young, "Goddesses, Feminists, and Scholars," in *The Annual Review of Women in World Religions* (1991): pp. 105–79.

22.   Joan B. Townsend, "The Goddess: Fact, Fallacy, and Revitalization Movement," in *Goddesses in Religions and Modern Debate*, ed. Larry W. Hurtado (Atlanta, Ga.: Scholars Press, 1990), pp. 180–203.

23.   Townsend, "The Goddess," p. 197.

24.   Rosemary Ruether, *Gaia and God* (San Francisco: Harper and Row, 1992), pp. 143–65.

25.   Townsend, "The Goddess," p. 194.

26.   Young, "Goddesses, Feminists, and Scholars," p. 146.

27.   Thorkild Jacobsen, *Treasures of Darkness: A History of Mesopotamian Religion* (New Haven: Yale University Press, 1976), pp. 77–84.

28.   For overviews of various accounts of the patriarchal invasion, see Eller, *Living in the Lap of the Goddess*, pp. 150–70, and Ruether, *Gaia and God*, pp. 143–72. For one of the most widely read accounts, see Eisler, *The Chalice and the Blade*, pp. 42–58.

29.   Lerner, *The Creation of Patriarchy*, pp. 15–53; Ehrenberg, *Women in Prehistory*, pp. 99–107.

30.   Eisler, *The Chalice and the Blade*, pp. 42–58.

31.   Hans J. Nissen, *The Early History of the Ancient Near East: 9000–2000 B.C.* (Chicago: University of Chicago Press, 1988), stipulates that the process of urbanization and population density leads to heightened warfare, rather than the other way around.

32.   Robert Ellwood, "Patriarchal Revolution in Ancient Japan: Episodes from the *Nihonshoki* Sujun Chronicle," *Journal of Feminist Studies in Religion* II:2 (fall 1986): pp. 23–37.

33.   Sanday, *Female Power and Male Dominance,* p. 165.

34.   Ibid., p. 8.

35.   Barstow, "The Prehistoric Goddess," p. 14.

36.   Exact dates are hard to give because patriarchy did not emerge all at once in all the world, or even in the Western world, nor did goddess worship decline all at once.

37.   For several excellent surveys of this material, see Gadon, *The Once and Future Goddess,* and Baring and Cashford, *The Myth of the Goddess.*

38.   Inanna's story is chronicled in all the standard sources already cited. For an especially fine discussion, see Diane Wolkstein and Samuel Noah Kramer, *Inanna: Queen of Heaven and Earth* (New York: Harper and Row, 1983).

39.   Alexander Heidel, *The Babylonian Genesis* (Chicago: University of Chicago Press, 1951), p. 42.

40.   Jacobsen, *Treasures of Darkness,* p. 179.

41.   See Downing, *The Goddess;* Gadon, *The Once and Future Goddess;* and Baring and Cashford, *The Myth of the Goddess.*

42.   This event happened at different times in different parts of Europe as Christianity slowly spread. By about 1000 C.E., this process was largely complete.

43.   For example, see already cited works by Gadon, Baring and Cashford, and Kinsley.

44.   For information about Lady Wisdom, see Tikva Frymer-Kensky, *In the Wake of the Goddesses: Women, Culture, and the Biblical Transformation of Pagan Myth* (New York: Free Press, 1992), pp. 168–83, and Joan Chamberlain Engelsman, *The Feminine Dimension of the Divine* (Philadelphia: Westminster Press, 1979). For use of Lady Wisdom in theological reconstructions of Christianity, see Johnson, *She Who Is.*

45.   See the works of Gershom Scholem, especially *On the Kabbalah and Its Symbolism* (New York: Schocken Books, 1965).

46.   For important discussions of whether, and to what extent, it makes sense to regard the Christian Mary as a goddess, see Kinsley, *The Goddesses' Mirror,* pp. 215–60; Gadon, *The Once and Future Goddess,* pp. 189–223; and Baring and Cashford, *The Myth of the Goddess,* pp. 547–608.

47.   Bynum, *Jesus as Mother.*

48.   Patai, *The Hebrew Goddess.*

49.   Ibid., p. 4.

50.   The role of Asherah (wooden objects symbolizing a tree) in Isra-elite religious practice is a complex scholarly issue. Two highly recommended discussions are Mark S. Smith, *The Early History of God: Yahweh and the Other Deities in Ancient Israel* (San Francisco: Harper and Row, 1990), pp. 80–114, and Frymer-Kensky, *In the Wake of the Goddesses*, pp. 153–61. For scholarly feminist discussions of this same material, as well as the entire problem of feminine imagery of the divine in the Hebrew Bible, see Gadon, *The Once and Future Goddess*, pp. 167–88, and Baring and Cashford, *The Myth of the Goddess*, pp. 446–85.

51.   Patai, *The Hebrew Goddess*, p. 13.

52.   Judith Ochshorn, *The Female Experience and the Nature of the Divine* (Bloomington, Ind.: Indiana University Press, 1981).

53.   Ibid., p. 13.

54.   Ibid., p. 15.

55.   Ibid., p. 242.

56.   Frymer-Kensky, *In the Wake of the Goddesses*, pp. 2–13.

57.   Ibid., p. 5.

58.   Ibid., p. 6.

59.   Ibid., p. 140.

60.   Ibid., p. 121.

61.   Ibid., p. 142.

62.   Ibid., p. 143.

63.   Ibid., p. 188.

64.   Ibid., p. 188.

65.   Ibid., p. 189.

66.   Ibid., p. 198.

67.   Ibid., p. 220.

68.   Howard Eilberg-Schwartz, *God's Phallus and Other Problems for Men and Monotheism* (Boston: Beacon Press, 1994).

69.   Elisabeth Schüssler Fiorenza, *In Memory of Her: A Feminist Theological Reconstruction of Christian Origins* (New York: Crossroad, 1984), p. xviii.

70.   Elaine Pagels, *The Gnostic Gospels* (New York: Vintage, 1981), p. xix.

71.   Ibid., p. xviii.

72.   Ibid., pp. 77–78.

73.   Ibid.

74.   Ibid., p. 62.

75.   Ibid., pp. 67–68.

76.   Ibid., p. 68.

77.   Ibid., pp. 71–72.

78.   Ibid., p. 71.

79.   Ibid., p. 73.

80.   Ibid., p. 75.

81.   Schüssler Fiorenza, *In Memory of Her*, p. xiii.

82.   Ibid., p. 52.

83.   Ibid., p. 131.

84.   Ibid., p. 134.

85.   Ibid., pp. 150–51.

86.   Ibid., pp. 175–84.

87.   Ibid., p. 198.

88.   Ibid., pp. 198–99.

89.   Ibid., p. 250.

90.   Ibid., p. 236.

91.   For example, see Gupta, "Kali the Savior," summarized in chapter four.

92.   For a much more complete discussion of Buddhist history, see Gross, *Buddhism after Patriarchy*, pp. 17–121.

93.   Ibid., p. 121.

94.   Miranda Shaw, *Passionate Enlightenment: Women in Tantric Buddhism* (Princeton: Princeton University Press, 1994).

95.   Janis Dean Willis, *The Diamond Light: An Introduction to Tibetan Buddhist Meditations* (New York: Simon and Schuster, 1972), p. 103.

96.   For discussion of the concept of emptiness and its profeminist usages, even in traditional Buddhism, see Gross, *Buddhism after Patriarchy*, pp. 55–77.

97.   For a standard textbook account, see Richard H. Robinson and

Willard L. Johnson, *The Buddhist Religion: A Historical Introduction*, 3rd ed. (Belmont, Calif.: Wadsworth, 1982), pp. 5–37.

98.   For a full discussion of these stories, with references to the major secondary literature on the period, see Gross, *Buddhism after Patriarchy*, pp. 29–55.

99.   Ibid., p. 39.

100.   Ibid.

101.   The most accessible version combines the two major English translations into one volume. Mrs. C. A. F. Rhys Davids and K. R. Norman, trans., *Poems of Early Buddhist Nuns* (London: Pali Text Society, 1989). See also Susan Murcott, *The First Buddhist Women: Translations and Commentary on the Therigatha* (Berkeley, Calif.: Parallax Press, 1991).

102.   Gross, *Buddhism after Patriarchy*, pp. 40–54.

103.   Tsultrim Allione, *Women of Wisdom* (London: Routledge and Kegan Paul, 1984).

104.   Gross, *Buddhism after Patriarchy*, pp. 93–99, and Gross, "Yeshe Tsogyel: Enlightened Consort, Great Teacher, Female Role Model," in *Feminine Ground: Essays on Women and Tibet*, ed. Janice Dean Willis (Ithaca, N.Y.: Snow Lion, 1987), pp. 11–32.

105.   Daly, *Beyond God the Father*, pp. 74–75, and Ruether, *Sexism and God-Talk*, p. 122.

Chapter 6: What Next? Postpatriarchal Religion

1.   *An Inclusive Language Lectionary: Readings for Year A, Revised Edition* (Atlanta, New York, Philadelphia: John Knox Pilgrim & Westminster Press, 1986), pp. 12–13.

2.   *The Lutheran Standard*, 7 October 1983, p. 16. For the article that generated the comments, see Kris Koestner, "It's Amazing," *The Lutheran Standard*, 5 August 1983, pp. 8–9.

3.   Editorial, "Report on the Re-Imagining Conference," *Journal of Feminist Studies in Religion* XI:1 (spring 1995): pp. 136–37.

4.   Personal communication from the ritual committee. For the translation, see *Vetaher Libenu* (Sudbury, Mass.: Congregation Beth El of the Sudbury River Valley, 1980).

5.   See the bibliography of Rosemary Radford Ruether, *Women-*

Church: Theology and Practice of Feminist Liturgical Communities (San Francisco: Harper and Row, 1985). See also Charlotte Caron, *To Make and Make Again: Feminist Ritual Thealogy* (New York: Crossroad, 1993).

6.   Ruether, *Women-Church*, p. 67.

7.   Ibid., p. 56.

8.   Ibid., p. 69.

9.   Ibid., p. 41.

10.   Ibid., pp. 56–57.

11.   Quoted in Ursula King, *Women and Spirituality: Voices of Protest and Promise* (New Amsterdam, N.Y.: 1989), p. 170.

12.   Ruether, *Women-Church*, p. 39.

13.   Ibid., pp. 61–62.

14.   Ibid., p. xi.

15.   For a discussion of the movement, see Arthur Waskow, *These Holy Sparks: The Rebirth of the Jewish People* (San Francisco: Harper and Row, 1983).

16.   See Marian Henriquez Nuedel, "Innovation and Tradition in a Midwestern Jewish Congregation," in Falk and Gross, *Unspoken Worlds.*

17.   Ruether and Keller, *In Our Own Voices*, p. 122.

18.   Penina V. Adelman, "A Drink from Miriam's Cup: The Invention of Tradition among Jewish Women," *Journal of Feminist Studies in Religion* X:2 (fall 1994): pp. 151–66. See also Penina V. Adelman, *Miriam's Well: Rituals for Jewish Women around the Year* (Fresh Meadows, N.Y.: Biblio Press, 1986).

19.   Arlene Agus, "This Month Is for You," in *The Jewish Woman: New Perspectives*, ed. Elizabeth Koltun (New York: Schocken Books, 1976), pp. 84–93.

20.   Adelman, "A Drink from Miriam's Cup," p. 161.

21.   Debra Orenstein, ed., *Lifecycles: Jewish Women on Life Passages and Personal Milestones*, vol. 1 (Woodstock, Vt.: Jewish Lights Publishing, 1994).

22.   Ibid., p. xviii.

23.   Ibid., pp. 170–77. See also Rosemary Ruether, *New Woman, New Earth: Sexist Ideologies and Human Liberation* (New York: Seabury, 1975), pp. 92–105.

24.   See Eller, *Living in the Lap of the Goddess*, pp. 38–61, 170–76, and Ruether, *New Woman, New Earth*, pp. 89–114.

25.   See especially Zsuzsanna Budapest, *The Holy Book of Women's Mysteries* (Berkeley: Wingbow Press, 1989), and Starhawk, *The Spiral Dance: A Rebirth of the Ancient Religion of the Great Goddess* (San Francisco: Harper and Row, 1979).

26.   Eller, *Living in the Lap of the Goddess*, pp. 115–29.

27.   Budapest, *The Holy Book of Women's Mysteries*, pp. 25–37.

28.   Ibid., pp. 115–37; Starhawk, *The Spiral Dance*, pp. 165–84; Eller, *Living in the Lap of the Goddess*, 87–89.

29.   See Budapest, *The Holy Book of Women's Mysteries*, pp. 115–33, for examples.

30.   Eller, *Living in the Lap of the Goddess*, p. 97.

31.   Ibid., p. 99.

32.   See Karma Lekshe Tsomo, ed., *Sakyadhita: Daughters of the Buddha* (Ithaca, N.Y.: Snow Lion, 1988) for an example of that point of view as well as an excellent overview of Buddhist nuns.

33.   See Gross, *Buddhism after Patriarchy*, pp. 215–21, for a full explanation of the term.

34.   Rita M. Gross, "Buddhist Resources for Issues of Population, Consumption, and the Environment," in *Population, Consumption, and the Environment: Religious and Secular Responses*, ed. Harold Coward (Albany: State University of New York Press, 1994), pp. 155–73.

35.   Gross, *Buddhism after Patriarchy*, pp. 226–40.

36.   Ruether, *Gaia and God*; Sallie McFague, *The Body of God: An Ecological Theology* (Minneapolis: Fortress Press, 1993).

37.   Ibid., pp. vii–viii.

38.   Ibid., p. x.

39.   Ibid., p. 16.

40.   Ibid., pp. 56–57.

41.   Ibid., pp. 105–9.

42.   Ibid., p. 14.

43.   Ibid., p. 131.

44.   Ibid., p. 132.

45.   Ibid., p. 149.

46. Ibid., p. 144.
47. Ibid., p. 182.
48. Ruether, *Gaia and God*, pp. 254–55.
49. Ibid., p. 251.
50. Ibid., p. 266.
51. Daly, *Beyond God the Father*, p. 28.
52. Ibid., pp. 33–34.
53. Daly, *Gyn/Ecology*, p. xi.
54. Ibid., p. xii.
55. Ibid., p. 39.
56. Ibid., pp. 59–60.
57. Ibid., p. 79.
58. Ibid., p. 355.
59. Ibid., pp. 28–29.
60. Ibid., pp. 10–11.
61. Ibid., p. 105.
62. Christ, *Laughter of Aphrodite*, pp. 117–32.
63. Ibid., p. 118.
64. Ibid., p. 121.
65. Ibid., p. 123.
66. Ibid., pp. 126–31.
67. For example, see Ruether, *Gaia and God*, pp. 149–55.
68. Starhawk, *The Spiral Dance*, pp. 77–78.
69. Ibid., p. 80.
70. Ibid., p. 81.
71. Ibid., p. 84. See also Eller, *Living in the Lap of the Goddess*, pp. 130–49, for an overview of the theology of the feminist spirituality movement.
72. The phrase is Eller's.
73. Eller, *Living in the Lap of the Goddess*, pp. 67–82.
74. Christ, *Laughter of Aphrodite*, p. 154.
75. Monique Wittig, *Les Guérillères*, trans. David Le Vay (Boston: Beacon Press, 1969), p. 89.
76. Ibid.
77. Ibid., p. 70.

78. Starhawk, *The Spiral Dance*, p. 101.

79. Ibid., p. 94.

80. Budapest, *The Holy Book of Women's Mysteries*, pp. 161–62.

81. Christ, *Laughter of Aphrodite*, p. 71.

82. Eller, *Living in the Lap of the Goddess*, pp. 74–81. See also Andy Smith, "For All Those Who Were Indian in a Former Life," *Ms.* November–December 1991, pp. 44–45.

83. Christine Downing, *The Goddess: Mythological Images of the Feminine* (1981), *Journey through Menopause: A Personal Rite of Passage* (1987), *Psyche's Sisters: Reimagining the Meaning of Sisterhood* (1990), *Myths and Mysteries of Same-Sex Love* (1991), *Women's Mysteries: Toward a Poetics of Gender* (1992), and *Gods in Our Midst: Mythological Images of the Masculine, a Woman's View* (1993). All are published by Crossroad Continuum of New York.

84. I first presented this paper and slide show at the same American Academy of Religion meeting at which Carol P. Christ first presented her paper "Why Women Need the Goddess." Carol and I had deliberately avoided talking with each other as we prepared our papers because we didn't want to influence each other. We were shocked at the similarity of our insights and suggestions. "Hindu Female Deities as a Resource for the Contemporary Rediscovery of the Goddess" was first published in *Journal of the American Academy of Religion* XLVI:3 (1978): 269–92. More popular versions are published as "Hindu Female Deities as a Resource for the Contemporary Rediscovery of the Goddess," in *The Book of the Goddess: Past and Present*, ed. Carl Olsen (New York: Crossroad, 1983) and "Steps toward Feminine Imagery of Deity in Jewish Theology," in Heschel, *On Being a Jewish Feminist*.

85. Gross, "Some Buddhist Perspectives on the Goddess."

86. Gross, *Buddhism after Patriarchy*, p. 252.

87. Ibid., p. 288.

88. For fuller discussion, see Gross, "Helping the Iron Bird Fly."

89. Gross, *Buddhism after Patriarchy*, pp. 146–51.

90. Gross, "Suffering, Feminist Theory, and Images of Goddess," *Anima: An Experiential Journal* XIII: 1 (fall 1986): pp. 39–46.

91. Gross, *Buddhism after Patriarchy*, pp. 280–88.

92. Ruether, *Gaia and God*, p. 141.

93. Ibid., pp. 139–40.

94. Christ, *Laughter of Aphrodite*, p. 217.

95. Ibid., pp. 226–27.

96. Naomi Goldenberg, *Returning Words to Flesh: Feminism, Psychoanalysis, and the Resurrection of the Body* (Boston: Beacon Press, 1990).

97. Charlene Spretnak, introduction to *The Politics of Women's Spirituality: Essays on the Rise of Spiritual Power within the Feminist Movement* (New York: Anchor Books, 1982), p. xiii.

98. Ibid., pp. 571–73.

99. Catherine Keller, *From a Broken Web: Separation, Sexism, and Self* (Boston: Beacon Press, 1986), pp. 2–3.

100. Mary Hunt, *Fierce Tenderness: A Feminist Theology of Friendship* (New York: Crossroad, 1991), pp. 2–10.

101. Judith Plaskow, "Transforming the Nature of Community," in Cooey, Eakin, and McDaniel, *After Patriarchy*, p. 97.

102. Ibid., pp. 102–3.

103. For more detail, see Gross, *Buddhism after Patriarchy*, pp. 258–69.

104. Rosemary Radford Ruether, *Womanguides: Readings toward a Feminist Theology* (Boston: Beacon Press, 1985).

105. William E. Paden, *Religious Worlds: The Comparative Study of Religion* (Boston: Beacon Press, 1988), p. 164. This book is highly recommended as an overview of the merits of the comparative study of religion.

106. Ibid., p. 38.

Index

273

Rediscovery of the Goddess,"
233–34
Gupta, Lina, 58, 133–34

Harrell, Steven, *Gender and Religion*
(with C. W. Bynum and R. Richman), 85
Harrison, Beverly, 47
Harvard Divinity School, 207
Hassan, Riffat, 57–58, 118–19;
Women's and Men's Liberation
(with L. Grob and H. Gordon),
57
Havurah movement, 208
Hera, 171
"Heterosexism," coining of term,
55–56
Heyward, Carter, *Touching Our
Strength*, 56
Hinduism, 68, 70, 83, 84–85, 99–
100; deity in, 8, 10–11; feminist
theological transformations in,
133–34, 136, 140, 141; goddesses
in, 133–34, 189, 233–34; model of
pantheon in, 76–78; practice of
suttee in, 60, 102, 103; sexism in,
106; speculative comparison of
histories of Western and Hindu
patriarchy, 187–90; view of
women in, 91–93; women's
movement and, 57, 58, 60
Hunt, Mary, *Fierce Tenderness*, 242
Hutchinson, Anne, 36

Inanna, 170
Inclusive-Language Lectionary, An,
43, 202
India, 135, 246, 247; goddesses in,

86–87, 188–90; women's move-
ment in, 59–60
Indigenous traditions, impact of
feminism on religion in, 63–64
In God's Image, 55
Iran, 90
Irenaeus, 183
Isasi-Díaz, Ada María, *Hispanic
Women* (with Y. Tarango), 55
Isis, 172
Islam, 9, 52, 70, 83, 91; and feminist
search of scriptures, 113, 118–19;
feminist transformations of, 111,
140, 141; sexism in, 106, 118–19;
view of women in, 91–93;
women's movement and, 57–58,
60–61
Israel, 169, 176, 177, 246, 247

Japan, 62–63, 135, 166
Jay, Nancy, 78
Johnson, Elizabeth, *She Who Is*,
127–29
*Journal of Feminist Studies in Reli-
gion, The*, 49, 54
Judaism, 9, 29, 38, 51, 91, 130–32;
community and relationship in,
242–43; early developments in
feminist, 39, 40–44; and feminism and religious diversity, 58;
and feminist search of scriptures, 113, 116–18; feminist transformations of, 111, 140–46;
gender-inclusive ritual communities in, 208–10; God-talk in,
121–32; and inclusive language,
203–4; ritual practices in, 200;
sexism in, 106; view of women
in, 89–90, 91, 93; and Women-

Library of Congress Cataloging-in-Publication Data

Gross, Rita M.
    Feminism and religion : an introduction / Rita M. Gross.
        p.   cm.
    Includes bibliographical references and index.
    ISBN 978-0-8070-6785-7 (pbk.)
        1. Women and religion.   2. Feminism—Religious aspects.
    3. Religion—Study and teaching.   I. Title.
    BL458.G76   1996
    200'.82—dc20
                                                96-11472